Violence Between Intimate Partners

Patterns, Causes, and Effects

Edited by

Albert P. Cardarelli
University of Massachusetts Boston

Allyn and Bacon
Boston • London • Toronto • Sydney • Tokyo • Singapore

Editor in Chief, Social Sciences: Karen Hanson
Editorial Assistant: Jennifer Jacobson
Marketing Manager: Karon Bowers
Editorial Production Service: MARBERN HOUSE
Manufacturing Buyer: Megan Cochran
Cover Administrator: Suzanne Harbison

Library of Congress Cataloging-in-Publication Data
Violence between intimate partners : patterns, causes, and effects /
   edited by Albert P. Cardarelli.
      p. cm.
   Includes bibliographical references and index.
   ISBN 0–02–319213–5 (alk. paper)
    1. Conjugal violence. 2. Wife abuse. 3. Dating violence.
  4. Gays—Abuse or. 5. Abusive men. 6. Abusive women.
  I. Cardarelli, Albert P.
  HV6626.V55   1996
  362.82´92—dc20   96–6862
                              CIP

Printed in the United States of America

10 9 8 7 6 5 4 3 2   01 00 99 98 97

Contents

Preface

Despite three decades of research, activism, and intervention services associated with family and intimate violence in the United States, much remains to be accomplished. Historically, the widespread prevalence of gender inequality meant that the cultural construction of intimate violence was defined in male terms and viewed largely as a private matter. Thus, few instances of family and intimate violence came to the attention of authorities. The "discovery" of child and spousal abuse by researchers and policymakers in the last three decades is evidence of the success of this construction. Even as the lines between public and private spheres of life become less clear, the tenacity of privacy as a cherished right in American society makes it difficult to convince a large part of the populace that violence that takes place within intimate relationships is not only a public issue but also a criminal issue with serious consequences for the social fabric of society.

In this context, it is especially important for researchers, activists, and policymakers not to lose sight of the fact that family and intimate violence are a part of a wider spectrum that includes the terrorist bombings in Oklahoma, the drive-by shootings in urban settings, the police handling of Rodney King, and the murder of Nicole Brown Simpson. Intimate violence, the subject of the present volume, is viewed as behavior falling along the continuum of interpersonal violence that includes acts of violence between strangers at one end of the continuum and intimate partners at the other end.

Furthermore, all intimate relationships carry the risk of violence and abuse regardless of the marital status or sexual preference of the partners. This perspective recognizes the varieties of intimate partnerships that exist in any culture, from traditional married couples to those involving same-sex partners. The chapters of this book demonstrate that the severity and consequences of intimate violence are influenced by the degree of intimacy and symmetry of power that characterize intimate relationships. This approach is critical in understanding the causes and effects of violence that take place between partners as they move through life in varied stages of intimacy: from dating and courtship to engagement, marriage, and separation.

Current explanations for the onset and persistence of intimate violence are also addressed by the authors. All agree that the subject of intimate violence is in much need of theory building if it is to progress beyond the unidimensional explanations that now dominate the literature. There is, for example, little evidence about the differences in the nature and extent of abuse and violence between intimate couples in varied stages of intimacy and commitment. Issues of escalation and desisting of violent behavior and the reasons for both remain largely unexplored. Furthermore, because there is increasing evidence that violence and abuse exist among dating and same-sex couples, approaching intimate violence in terms of traditional spousal couples will tell us little about how violence is incorporated into everyday systems of social action, and will likely lead to narrowly constructed preventive strategies with few lasting effects.

To move beyond the largely reactive posture in dealing with violence and abuse between intimate partners it is essential to understand those factors at both the societal and interpersonal levels that lead to this destructive behavior. Focusing exclusively on either batterers or victims will result in individually oriented perspectives that emphasize psychological defects or deficiencies. In addition, by ignoring the large numbers of intimate partners who are not violent or abusive to one another, little will be learned about the strategies that these couples employ to avoid such behavior. Understanding the ways in which such behavior is avoided or resisted is critical if society is to establish prevention strategies for those individuals who have yet to accept violence as an appropriate method for resolving interpersonal conflict.

The chapters in the present volume provide a convincing argument that intimate violence is firmly rooted in many of the fundamental activities in which partners engage during the course of their relationships. For this reason, it is essential for researchers and activists to pursue an understanding of the connections between the varied forms of violence and abuse that exist within all dimensions of intimacy. Only in this way will we understand how family and intimate violence fit in the mosaic of violence that continues to disrupt the social fabric of society.

Acknowledgments

There have been many individuals who have helped to shape the present volume. I am especially thankful to each of the contributors for their advice and patience throughout the preparation of the manuscript. Many thanks to Karen Hanson, Editor in Chief, who did everything necessary to bring the project to completion. I would also like to thank the copy editor, Joan Poole, for her insightful comments and suggestions for improving the overall quality of the manuscript. Thanks also to Marjorie L. Payne of Marbern House, who oversaw the editorial process.

Special thanks to Angela Browne of The Better Homes Foundation and Stephen Hicks, Professor of Law at Suffolk Law School, for their critical comments and suggestions for improving several sections of the manuscript.

Major thanks to Kathy Rowan of the McCormack Institute for her valued efforts in preparing the final copy of the manuscript. Thanks also to Megan Early, Ruth Finn, Pat Mullen and Madeleine Pidgeon for their assistance throughout the project's history.

All of the above individuals, as well as my colleagues at the Institute helped bring the manuscript to fruition. For their support and advice I am most grateful.

About the Authors

ANGELA BROWNE is the author of *When Battered Women Kill*, (Macmillan/Free Press) and co-author of *No Safe Haven: Male Violence Against Women at Home, At Work, And in the Community* (American Psychological Association). She authored both the American Medical Association's policy statement on "Violence Against Women" and the American Psychological Association's review and policy statement on "Violence Against Women by Male Partners." She also coauthored the AMA's review on the "Mental Health Consequences of Interpersonal and Family Violence."

ALBERT P. CARDARELLI is Senior Fellow, John W. McCormack Institute of Public Affairs at the University of Massachusetts-Boston. His areas of research and publication include community policing, legal theory, family and community violence. He is the co-author of *Child Sexual Abuse: The Initial Effects* (with B. Gomes-Schwartz and J. Horowitz). His latest research interests focus on community-policing models being implemented by law enforcement authorities.

SUSAN CARINGELLA-MACDONALD is an Associate Professor in the Department of Sociology at Western Michigan University. Her areas of research and publication focus around rape, sexual assault, violence against women, feminism and legal reform. She is presently finishing a book manuscript on *Feminism, Backlash and Rape*.

KATHLEEN F. FERRARO is an Associate Professor and the Associate Director of Women's Studies at Arizona State University, Tempe. She has published on the topic of battered women and serves as a legal expert for women charged with crimes related to their battering. Her current interests are in bridging domestic violence discourse with transformative feminist thought and practice.

MARSALI HANSEN, PH.D. is a licensed psychologist and the curriculum development specialist for the Pennsylvania CASSP Training Institute. Her duties include the development of a competency based core curriculum for children's mental health workers throughout the state of Pennsylvania. She also maintains a part-time private practice with a special focus on children and families. Dr. Hansen consults with community, state, and national organizations, and has published and presented widely on the topic of therapists' perceptions of spouse abuse.

DR. MICHELE HARWAY is the author or editor of several books including *Sex Discrimination in Career Counseling and Education* (with Helen Astin). *Handbook of Longitudinal Research* (with Sarnoff Mednick and Karen Finello), *Battering and Family Therapy: A Feminist Perspective* (with Marsali Hansen), and *Spouse Abuse: Assessing and Treating Battered Women, Batterers and their Children* (Professional Resource Press, with Marsali Hansen). Her edited book *Treating the Changing Family: Handling Normative and Unusual Events* is forthcoming from John Wiley & Sons. Dr. Harway is also a Fellow of the American Psychological Society.

JAMES M. MAKEPEACE is Professor and past Chair of the Sociology Department of College of St. Benedict and St. John's University in Minnesota. His area of research focuses on violence in courtship relationships. He has authored numerous articles in professional journals, is author/editor of a new book entitled *Family Violence*, and has appeared on numerous television and radio programs, including Oprah, Donahue, and Today.

SUSAN L. MILLER is an Associate Professor in the Sociology Department at Northern Illinois University. Her research interests include gender, deterrence, and social control, inequalities, victimology, and criminal justice policy. Her latest research explores issues of gendered justice and community policing.

JAMES PTACEK'S area of research focuses on the problem of violence against women. He has pursued this work in a variety of roles: as a researcher; a college teacher; a counselor with men who batter; and a trainer on institutional responses to woman battering both in the United States and in Sweden. He currently holds positions in both the Department of Sociology at Tufts University and the Women's Studies Program at Brandeis University.

ANGELA MOORE is currently completing her Ph.D. in Criminology at the University of Maryland. She is a research analyst in the Office of Research and Evaluation, National Institute of Justice, Department of Justice. Her research interests include domestic violence, policing, spousal homicide, and child victimization.

CLAIRE M. RENZETTI is Professor and Chair of Sociology at St. Joseph's University, Philadelphia. She is co-author of eight books, including *Violent Betrayal: Partner Abuse in Lesbian Relationships* (Sage Publications). She has also authored numerous book chapters as well as articles for scholarly and professional journals. Currently, she is editor of *Violence Against Women: An International, Interdisciplinary Journal* and co-editor of the Sage Violence Against Women Book Series.

CRIS SULLIVAN is Associate Professor of Community Psychology at Michigan State University. She is co-Principal Investigator on an eight-year study funded by the National Institute of Mental Health to evaluate the impact of a community-based advocacy intervention with abused women. Dr. Sullivan is also co-Principal Investigator on a Centers for Disease Control study examining the effects of a similar community-based project with children who have experienced and/or witnessed domestic violence.

CHARLES F. WELLFORD is Director of the University of Maryland Center for Applied Policy Studies and Professor of Criminology and Criminal Justice at the University of Maryland. He is also Director of the Office of Academic Computing Sciences in the College of Behavioral and Social Sciences and Director of the Maryland Justice Analysis Center, and serves on numerous state and federal advisory boards and commissions. Dr. Wellford is the current President-elect of the American Society of Criminology.

Violence and Intimacy: An Overview

ALBERT P. CARDARELLI

University of Massachusetts Boston

"Remember all men would be tyrants if they could. . . .
put it out of the power of the vicious and the lawless
to use us with cruelty and indignity with impunity."
—*ABIGAIL ADAMS TO JOHN ADAMS (MARCH, 1776)*

"I swear I won't call no copper if I'm beat up by my
poppa, ain't nobody's bizness if I do."
—*BILLIE HOLIDAY*[*]

The growing body of theory and research into family violence has resulted in increased specialization among academicians, policymakers, and funding agencies. Research on abuse and violence between family members and intimates includes the areas of child abuse (physical and sexual); elder, sibling, and spousal abuse; dating and courtship violence; and gay and lesbian violence. This specialization is reflected in the growing number of journals devoted to these areas of interest and concern.[1]

The revelations and contents of these subareas have expanded our knowledge and understanding of the varied patterns of violent relationships and behaviors included under the umbrella of "family" violence. Still, there remains a critical need for understanding the connections between these patterns as well as the relationships between

---

[*](Ain't Nobody's Bizness—Lyrics by P. Grainger and E. Robbins. Used by permission.)

[1]Some of the more recent journals specifically concerned with family and intimate violence include *Child Abuse and Neglect, Child Maltreatment, Journal of Child Sexual Abuse, Journal of Elder Abuse and Neglect, Journal of Family Violence, Journal of Interpersonal Violence, Violence and Victims,* and *Violence Against Women.*

1

the dynamics of interpersonal violence in group contexts, which are largely public in nature, and violence that takes place within private, intimate settings. In both settings then, it is important to understand not only the power dimensions between the participants, but whether a mutual or cooperative interchange of favors and privileges exists and whether there are variations in both the severity and persistence of violence according to the degree of mutual dependence established. Previous research has shown, for example, that when women are isolated from social networks of support or when mutual intimacy is either lacking or nonexistent, there is a greater chance that they will be victims of intimate violence and little likelihood that the violence will become public (Gelles, 1987). Thus, even with evidence of the continued transfer of private violence to the public realm, there will continue to be large numbers of violent incidents in intimate relationships in which women are socially isolated and economically dependent and the sanctions of the state hold little deterrent power.

To establish a framework for understanding the dynamics underlying intimate violence, the present volume focuses on those dyadic relationships that involve some degree of consensual intimacy, regardless of the marital status or sexual preference of the partners. For purposes of the present volume, intimacy is viewed as the level of mutual responsiveness, both psychologically and physically, between partners who enter relationships with at least a modicum of consensual agreement (Erikson, 1963; Orlosky, 1976; Acitelli and Duck, 1987; Prager, 1989). By focusing on intimacy and power as the organizing principles for understanding violence and abuse, we hope that the present volume will be better able (1) to discern the differences in the nature and extent of violence among intimate couples in varied stages of intimacy and commitment and (2) to determine the effects and reactions of individuals and groups to these events (Prager, 1989, 1991; Zietlow and Sillars, 1988; Pilkington and Richardson, 1988; Gryl, Stith, and Bird, 1991). The consequences of assault, for example, may vary in terms of emotional trauma depending on whether the assault occurs within a casual dating phase, during the first few months of marriage, or over time in a formal or committed relationship. In addition, violence and abuse that take place between those who are dating (most of whom presumably are still residing with parents or roommates of the same sex) are more likely to be recognized by external sources. In contrast, the high level of privacy associated with marriage or cohabitation is likely to keep the violence hidden. Even when spousal violence reaches the public realm, however, it is generally viewed as less serious than the violence that takes place between acquaintances and strangers. Historically, the greater the level of intimacy associated with partnerships in which violence was observed, the less likely the institutional response was to characterize the behavior as criminal. As briefly noted in the preface, the labeling of intimate violence as "domestic" not only creates the perception that it falls within the private realm of the family, but, further, that it is better treated outside the jurisdiction of the criminal justice system. Similarly, because the public associates domestic activities with the traditional family structure less attention is given to both dating and same-sex partner violence.

Intimacy, Power, and Violence

It is the overall view of the writers of the present volume that issues of intimacy and power within personal relationships are critical to understanding (1) the patterns of conflict resolution and (2) whether the resolution will involve violence and abusive behavior on the part of one or both partners. Furthermore, because of the high levels of emotional energy concentrated within intimate relationships, there will inevitably be incidents involving tension and conflict (Skolnick, 1991). Since intimacy is a critical experience that enables one to engage with others, the ways in which individuals respond to tension and conflict can have important consequences for the stability of the relationships (Baxter and Dindia, 1990; Prager, 1991). In those relationships in which there is both a need for and need on the part of one partner to maintain a dominant position over the other, any challenge to the asymmetry will involve some degree of conflict (Ball-Rokeach, 1980; Coleman and Straus, 1990). Whether this conflict will lead to violence depends on the range of solutions and resources available to the partners (Prager, 1991).

In reference to marriage, for example, Weiss (1979: 226) argues that the psychological well-being of spousal partners depends to a great extent on the level of mutual support within the marriage. He writes

> Our primary sources of sympathy and support are our spouses. We are consequently both bruised and bereft when our spouses turn from allies to critics. . . . With marital support so important, a spouse's slight can easily be felt to be a grievous injury, and what might appear to an outsider to be an unimportant misunderstanding can rise to feelings of intolerable misuse.

While Weiss's interest is directed to the interactive patterns of married couples, the writers of the present volume propose the thesis that such insights are applicable to any intimate relationship regardless of sexual preference (Kurdek and Schmitt, 1986; Kurdek, 1991; McWhirter and Mattison, 1984). Thus, in the early stages of courtship, there is the desire among many persons to merge with the other partner, to achieve a partnership based upon emotion and love—one that will overcome the separateness that many experience because of their socialization and upbringing. This idealization of the other can, however, blind individuals to a growing dependency and a declining reciprocity in the sharing of emotions and power essential to self-development (Whitbourne and Weinstock, 1979; Levitz-Jones and Orlofsky, 1985; Prager, 1991). Underlying all relationships is a level of reciprocity that is continually challenged by the failures and deficiencies of either party. When one partner fails to meet the expected response of the other, tension and criticism are potential outcomes. All intimate relationships carry the risk that one partner will use the personal faults or failures of the other as a foil of defense when appropriate resolutions to conflicting situations are unavailable. Renzetti (chapter 4) notes, for example, that some gay and lesbian partners threaten to make their partner's homosexuality a public matter "out-ing" if their demands are not met. The resolution of conflict will thus be affected not only by the degree of symmetry relative to the distribution of power between the part-ners, but also by the level of reciprocity that exists between both in the areas of emo-tional dependency and commitment (Prager, 1991). The ability of the partners to respond with positive remedies will affect the outcome of the interactive event. Partners who overreact to disappointment in their expectations may be especially prone to perpetrate abuse and violence (see Ptacek and Ferraro chapters 6 and 7 for critical overviews of the reactions of violent men; Dutton, 1992). In these instances, duties of loyalty and good faith, essential to the health of any partnership, are likely to be nonexistent or one-sided at best. In relationships characterized by asymmetry and emotional dependency on the part of the subordinate partner, it may be more dif-ficult for the dependent partner to leave the relationship at the early signs of abuse and violence. Browne (chapter 3) and Ferraro (chapter 7) both point to the difficulties and barriers encountered by many women in their efforts to leave an abusive rela-tionship, including economic insecurity, emotional dependency, fear of retaliation, and the hope that such violence will pass.

In focusing on intimate violence, the essays that follow provide an interpretative perspective on the violent interactions that take place between intimate partners regardless of their marital status or sexual preference. Taken together, the essays demonstrate a continuum of intimacy for partners along which patterns of violence emerge and persist, the meanings and effects of which vary for both victims and abusers depending on the investment made in the relationship. How the parties react to violent and abusive behavior when it takes place as well as over time involves a complex set of variables, including age, marital status, economic independence, and the existence of external support services. Thus, women who are repeatedly battered develop survival strategies based on their perceptions of the severity and dangerous-ness of their partners' violence (see chapters 6 and 7).

It is hoped that such analyses will improve our understanding of the causal expla-nations regarding the pathways of intimate violence, as well as the effects on individ-ual actors and the institutional structures that intersect with them. Equally important, such analyses will enable us to develop intervention programs for batterers that are based on sound theoretical reasoning (Tifft, 1993). Even within intimate relationships, collective structures affect the individual's capacity for individuality and self-devel-opment and, as these structures begin to take on new meanings, they will constrain or expand this capacity through coercive social control, benign neglect, or authorita-tive discourse and direction.

The Discovery and Criminalization of Intimate Violence

As we near the end of the twentieth century, an ever-growing body of research con-tinues to demonstrate the inordinate levels of violence among intimate partners throughout all levels of American society (Straus and Gelles, 1990; Ohlin and Tonry,

1989; Bart and Moran, 1993; Koss et al., 1994; Dutton, 1995; Renzetti, 1992; Viano, 1992). In fact, as Miller and Wellford (chapter 1) note in their discussion of interpersonal violence, one of the leading causes of injury to women in the United States is a direct result of the violent acts committed by their partners or ex-partners (citing Bernstein, 1993).

While the incidence of violence among intimate partners is no longer a surprise to researchers, policymakers, and activists, it is important to recall that only twenty-five years ago, little data on family violence existed (Lynch, 1985). Most research before that time was concerned with child abuse (Kempe et al., 1962; Helfer and Kempe, 1968; Gil, 1969, 1970; Paulson and Blake, 1967; Silver, 1968; Zalba, 1966; De Francis, 1963). Few articles dealt specifically with violence between intimate partners (Parnas, 1967; Goode, 1969; Charny, 1969; Bard, 1971).

Yet, women, as Abigail Adams noted in her letter of 1776, have always known how violent men can be to their partners. Raising the issue to its rightful importance within the public realm has until recently been almost impossible, given the subordination of women in a culture that has been historically patriarchal in terms of the moral imperatives underlying its institutional structures. Nowhere has this been more evident than in the family, in which society's mythic ideal of self-fulfillment emphasized reason and rationality as character traits not essential to the role of women in the family. In her analysis of the role of women in American life, (Kerber, 1991) argues that the language of individualism, essential to success in the public realm, has historically been a male-centered discourse that has served the self-interest of men while assuming continued deference from women. For the past two centuries, women were supposed to be mothers, who were not only responsible for raising morally sound and successful children but for creating a home that would provide a sanctuary from the world at large (Skolnick, 1991). With the advent of industrial society during the Nineteenth century, work shifted to outside the home. This, coupled with the cultural demands imposed on women as nurturers essential to the stability of family life, guaranteed a limited role for women in public life (Pease and Pease, 1990; Ryan, 1990; Lasch, 1977; Kerber, 1991; Skolnick, 1991; Morgan, 1966; Nye, 1960).

The subordination and exclusion of women from public life has been further supported by the emphasis given to privacy in American life (Hixson, 1987; Pleck, 1987; Schneider, 1994; Skolnick, 1991); a view accurately voiced by Billie Holiday's expression "ain't nobody's bizness if I do." As American society moved beyond the colonial era, privacy, at least for middle-class families, took on a sacred quality, one that continues to be seen by many writers as an essential barrier to the ever-growing power of the state over the family (Lasch, 1977; Cohen, 1985; Donzelot, 1979; Davis, 1988; Polsky, 1991).

In addition to these cultural and economic influences, several Supreme Court decisions during the 1960s and 1970s lent further support to the value of privacy, especially as it relates to the family. In *Griswold* v. *Connecticut* (1965), the Court posited a "right to privacy" as the constitutional foundation for the protection of relations connected with the home and the family. In *Griswold,* the Court justified its decision that the state of Connecticut's birth control statute prohibiting contraception was unconstitutional by extending privacy rights to married couples within families. Not long after, the Court in *Eisenstadt* v. *Baird* (1973) conferred this privacy right, regarding contraception, to the individuals who make up the family unit. At the same time, the decision by the Court in *Roe* v. *Wade* (1973), regarding the (limited) right to abort unwanted pregnancies, was further evidence of the Court's willingness to support the privacy of individuals in terms of highly personal beliefs and behaviors. These Court cases not only reflect the changes taking place in family units, but they add weight to the view that the privacy of family life should be protected from state interference (Lasch, 1977; Donzelot, 1979). Although the right to privacy has been the cornerstone of those advocating the right to abortion and birth control (and, more recently, the thrust of criticism against the restrictive policies of the military regarding homosexuality), it is not without its critics.

Schneider, for example, argues that ". . . concepts of privacy permit, encourage, and reinforce violence against women . . ." (1994: 36). To overcome the oppression associated with marital privacy, Schneider argues that ". . . a more affirmative concept of privacy, one that encompasses liberty, equality, freedom of bodily integrity, autonomy and self-determination, is important to women who have been battered" (Schneider, 1994: 37). Historically, male battering of women within the private sphere of family life was generally untouched by law and, when it did become public, was largely treated with a "hands-off" perspective by law enforcement and criminal justice agencies. In this respect, an ethic of privacy reinforces the viewpoint that what takes place within the confines of the family is personal and separate from the political realm where sanctions are applied by the state (Schneider, 1994).

While this belief in personal privacy—no matter the context—has been in the process of dissolution for several decades, it remains a powerful theme in American life. Billie Holiday's soulful lyrics about the right to exclude outsiders when it comes to intimate violence have begun to sound discordant to the American ear. Recent and highly visible incidents of violence and abuse involving national heroes O. J. Simpson and Greg Louganis have raised questions about the state's responsibility for personal behavior that violates the freedom and liberty of individual victims (Hixson, 1987; Pleck, 1987; Schneider, 1994).

Although Holiday's lament still prevails among many women who are abused by their intimate partners, the discovery of and public debate about the prevalence of assault in many intimate relationships cause other people to question the protection of personal violence as a private act that should remain within the realm of privacy. This is not to deny the significant tolerance of violence and abuse within the parameters of family and intimate relationships, but rather to point to the consequences of shifts in American cultural beliefs about the state's role in personal affairs. After the "discovery" of child abuse in the 1960s, every state moved to establish mandatory reporting laws regarding child abuse (Pfohl, 1977). In a similar fashion, researchers and women's advocates began in the 1970s to document the high levels of spousal violence in the United States.

Until the mid-1970s, women received little, if any, legal protection from the assaults of their marital partners. In most states, assaults against wives were considered misdemeanors even when the severity of the violence would be determinative of a felony charge if directed against an acquaintance or stranger. Also, police, for the most part, were not given the power to arrest a suspect on a misdemeanor charge unless they had actually witnessed the action. Furthermore, in most states, a wife was unable to file for a restraining order unless she was also filing for divorce (Browne, 1987; Browne and Williams, 1989). During the past two decades, major changes in the law and public policy have redefined violence against wives and other intimate partners as an appropriate area for legal intervention (Koss et al., 1994). Nearly every state today has legislation dealing with violence between partners, and a growing number of courts now admit expert testimony concerning the battered-woman syndrome in establishing a claim of self-defense for women accused of killing their partners (Pleck, 1987; and Caringella-MacDonald, chapter 8 of this volume).

Much of the success in transforming family violence, especially wife abuse, from a largely unimportant public matter to one viewed as a serious social problem can be attributed to the demands by women activists that the state respond to the problem (Pleck, 1987; Walker, 1990). Prior to the public awareness of the high incidence of wife abuse within the United States, there was little written about the problem within the major scholarly journals that dealt with issues of violence and victimization. Throughout the 1970s, the prestigious journals in sociology, for example, *American Journal of Sociology* and the *American Sociological Review,* did not contain a single article on the topic of family violence. Even the journal *Criminology,* the official publication of the American Society of Criminology, published only one article in the 1970s dealing with family violence and only five throughout the 1980s. The neglect of family violence as an appropriate scholarly topic is also evident in some of the more popular texts on social problems published in the 1970s.

In contrast, from 1974 on, the women's movement consistently demonstrated and tried to ameliorate the high levels of private violence through the creation of shelters, educational and media campaigns, and the implementation of major changes in legal remedies for abusers (see Caringella-MacDonald, chapter 8 of this volume for an analysis of these changes). The phenomenal growth of shelters from less than 20 in 1975 to more than 1,200 in 1995 is witness to the power of the public response and advocacy by women on the part of women and children victimized by abuse and violence. Furthermore, the growing presence of shelters for women and children has provided a focal point for activists to force changes in the ways in which the police and the courts both acknowledge and respond to spousal violence. The fact that there is still a significant need for additional shelter facilities is further testimony to the widespread incidence of intimate violence in American society.

Additional support for policy changes in law enforcement grew out of early research in Minneapolis by Sherman and Berk (1984), which suggested that men who were arrested and given temporary incarceration for misdemeanor domestic violence cases offended significantly less than those men who went through mediation and those who were separated from their partners. Although recent research has raised issues about the effectiveness of arrest (*The Journal of Criminal Law and Criminology,*

Spring, 1992, entire issue; Buzawa and Buzawa, 1990, 1996; Dunford et al., 1990), the Minneapolis experiment proved to be a significant impetus for police departments to change their policies regarding domestic abuse (Cohn and Sherman, 1987). The national publicity from the *Thurman* v. *City of Torrington* (1984) decision—in which the police department was held liable for not protecting a woman from imminent and serious harm—further influenced policy change, as did the *Attorney General's Task Force on Family Violence Final Report* (1984), which recommended that men who assault their wives be vigorously prosecuted for these offenses.

In this respect, there is a clear connection between viewing intimate and family violence as private and off-limits and the potential for success in prosecuting the offenders. As long as abusive behavior is held to be outside the parameters of public sanctions, it is unlikely to be subjected to the existing remedies within the criminal and civil courts of the state and even less likely to receive the necessary social supports to prevent and control its persistence. For some, bringing familial conflict into the public realm will continue to be viewed as an invasion of privacy and, therefore, be resisted. In effect, the argument is that the right of the family to be free of state intervention takes precedence over the rights of the individual members of the family, even when their rights are violated by inappropriate behavior within the confines of the family.

The growing number of laws and regulations for dealing with family and domestic abuse have resulted in a redefinition of intimate abuse from behavior that is viewed as wrong, but subject to informal interventions, to that which is not only wrong, but illegal, and thus subject to formal remedies of social control (Gelles, 1982; Pleck, 1987; Davis, 1988; Elliott, 1989). Today, family and intimate violence are recognized as national social problems. In addition to the previously mentioned changes, there are significant interventions by existing health and social service systems as well as law enforcement and criminal justice agencies. Most states, for example, have moved to make domestic assault criminal; close to forty states have enacted mandatory arrest statutes in cases of domestic violence and, in a number of states, prosecutors have established policies to provide greater support to victims filing complaints against their alleged abusers (Steinman, 1991; Ford and Regoli, 1993; Buzawa and Buzawa, 1990, 1996).

These legal changes, many of which have not yet been effectively evaluated, have played a major role in the growing acceptance of private violence as a public issue subject to the control of the state and the penalties of criminal law. Whether such policies will lead to significant reductions in the levels of intimate violence in the years ahead is difficult to determine; although, recent evidence indicates that criminal justice interventions have proved effective in reducing the prevalence of intimate violence among those offenders who have a stake in the community (Sherman and Smith, 1992).

On the other hand, the extension of state power into behavior traditionally viewed as falling within the realm of privacy is not without its problems (Davis, 1988). The arrest of abusers and the successful prosecution of violence against intimates as criminal offenses will not only necessitate the expansion of criminal justice facilities to control the offenders, but will likely require additional support services for the victims and their families (see Sullivan, chapter 9 of this volume; Lerman, 1986). Divorce and custody battles, welfare eligibility, and fear and retaliation are all potential consequences of the criminalization of private, intimate violence (Davis, 1988; Ford, 1991). Furthermore, the desires of some victims to have the offender rehabilitated through some form of mandatory counseling may be at odds with those people who are intent on reducing family violence through probation and jail time. As the chapters by Caringella-MacDonald and Sullivan show (this volume), the balancing of these needs is critical if prosecution policies are to deter batterers from future intimate violence (Ford and Regoli, 1993; Ford et al., 1996).

Summary

In recognition of some of the many issues raised above, the present volume brings together chapters on the varied patterns of violence between intimates, usually compartmentalized in other literature; and it also reflects the view that most individuals are involved in a continuum of intimate relationships over their life courses, from dating and courtship to marriage and divorce. Under these circumstances, it is essential to distinguish the similarities and differences in the kinds of abuse and violence that continue to occur along the continuum of intimacy. For example, do people who use verbal abuse as a means of control in dating relationships continue the behavior during cohabitation or in marriage, or does such behavior escalate to physical intimidation and attack once a greater level of privacy is assured? Similarly, do men who use violence while married continue to do so with other partners once the marriage is dissolved, or do they resort to other means of control? Achieving answers to these questions will better enable researchers to understand how violence is incorporated into everyday systems of social action, especially those systems involving intimate partners.

PART I

Patterns, Causes, and Conceptualizations of Intimate Violence

The following chapters provide a critical overview of the nature and extent of violence between intimate partners, as well as a discussion of recent and current research dealing with its onset and persistence. Taken as a whole, the chapters provide a strong argument that intimate violence is neither bound by the marital status of the partners nor by the partners' sexual preferences. Violence and abuse are not only commonplace among traditional married couples, but can be found among heterosexual and homosexual partners in varied stages of courtship and emotional commitment to one another. Each of the chapters contributes to the ongoing debate about the devastating effects of intimate violence to both the participants and social fabric of society. The authors detail the complex interactions between victims and perpetrators, as well as the incredible variety of violent actions to which offenders resort in order to maintain dominance over intimate partners.

In their overview of interpersonal violence in the United States, Miller and Wellford note the continued difficulties in establishing a reliable data base on the incidence and prevalence of violence among intimate partners. Intimate violence, as all of the authors note, may be a one-time event, a series of events occurring in some episodic fashion, or, worse, a chronic pattern of behavior with serious and sometimes lethal consequences. Furthermore, the private character of intimate violence makes it unlikely that one-time and episodic incidents will come to the attention of authorities. Thus, official rates of intimate violence, like interpersonal crime rates in general, vastly underestimate the true incidence of such behavior in any one year. Even as the movement to criminalize domestic violence continues to gain acceptance, it is unlikely to have much effect on the one-time or rarely abusive offender. Single or rarely occurring incidents are likely to be seen as aberrant events related to some situational stress or activity beyond the control of the perpetrator and, therefore, will remain private. This fact, however, does not diminish the potential consequences of even a single act of violence.

In recognition of these empirical issues, Miller and Wellford argue that there is a critical need to establish a typology of batterers that reflects the time-patterned violent events between intimate partners (Follingstad, 1991; Snyder and Frutchtman, 1981). Recent efforts by Saunders (1992) to develop a typology of men who battered their intimate partners resulted in three categories of batterers: (1) those who used aggression solely within the family, (2) those who generalized their aggression and were most likely to be violent outside the home as well, and (3) the emotionally volatile aggressors who were psychologically abusive and extremely jealous of their partners. While the typology is based mostly on psychological differences, it reflects the critical need to distinguish categories of offenders if intervention strategies appropriate to prevention and control are to be implemented.

The argument by Miller and Wellford for a multifaceted approach to intimate violence is further supported by Makepeace's analysis of courtship violence in chapter 2. In his critique of existing theory and research on dating and courtship violence, Makepeace points to the substantial variations in both the degree of maturity and levels of resources that individuals bring to the courtship stage. Such variations, he argues, become more complex as the courtship progresses, thereby affecting the patterns and meanings associated with intimate violence by the actors themselves. In distinguishing several stages of courtship—from pre-dating to cohabitation—Makepeace provides a framework for understanding how variations in the patterns and severity of courtship and dating violence are related to the intersection of psychological and sociological elements associated with youth and adolescence. In order to explain these variations, Makepeace proposes a developmental theory of courtship violence that posits aggression as an innate response to frustration and intimacy as an innate need. According to Makepeace, contemporary culture assigns the fulfillment of this need for intimacy within a socio-reproductive dialectic that includes parenting, courtship, and marriage. In each of these stages, a set of prescribed behaviors and attitudes are expected, the frustration of which may lead to violence and abuse (depending on a range of developmental and cultural issues associated with courtship including, but not limited to, age, family support, and available resources). To reduce courtship violence, Makepeace argues that it is essential to identify those issues that are conducive to policy-intervention strategies.

In this regard, Browne's chapter strengthens the argument that violence takes place along a continuum of intimacy, with marriage providing a new dimension in the dynamics of interpersonal violence. Thus, numerous women who are battered in marriage recall little, if any, violence taking place while they were in the courtship phase of their relationship. In her analysis, Browne not only examines some of the more critical controversies associated with spousal violence, specifically the extent of marital rape and mutual violence, but also looks at the continuum of violence itself—from its intrusion into everyday activities to instances of threats and lethal violence.

In examining the data on homicides, Browne notes that women rarely kill other people; when they do, they are most likely to kill their male partners. Furthermore, Browne argues that a significant proportion of homicides by women are in response to aggression and threats by their male partners. For the country as a whole, homicide remains a male-dominated form of behavior; 88 percent of all homicides are committed by males.

In terms of spousal violence, only a minority of men in the United States physically attack their wives or girlfriends (Straus and Gelles, 1990). This fact points to the need for more comparative research on those factors that explain why some men, presumably subject to the same levels of strain and conflict as abusers, refrain from such violence. In this respect, there is still a substantial lack of knowledge regarding (1) the frequency and severity of violence and the risk faced by women from male partners, (2) the persistence of both the violence and its risk, whether the women are living with or separated from their abusers, and (3) the number of women who instigate acts of abuse and violence against male partners.

That violence and abuse are not bound by the sexual preference of the partner is evident in Renzetti's research on the nature and extent of violence among same-sex couples. Until recently, the issue of intimate violence in gay and lesbian communities was virtually ignored by researchers in family violence, even though such behavior was common knowledge among the members of these communities. Renzetti cites widespread heterosexism in the social sciences as being one of the reasons for minimal interest in this area, as well as the belief that women are likely to be battered by men, not other women. Throughout her analysis, Renzetti compares the nature and extent of intimate violence among gay and lesbian couples with that of heterosexual couples. As with heterosexual couples, data on the incidence and prevalence of intimate violence among same-sex couples vary widely, from less than 20 percent to almost 75 percent in one study. While many of the studies presented are methodologically deficient, they demonstrate that partner abuse in same-sex relationships is as extensive and serious as that among heterosexual partners.

Unlike different-sex couples, however, gay and lesbian relationships are sometimes complicated by the high levels of AIDS among gay men and the threat of "outing" or public disclosure by an intimate partner. In a society where homosexuality is still frowned on by large numbers of people, the threat of "outing" may lessen the willingness of the abused partner to dissolve the relationship for fear of loss of employment and rejection by friends, relatives, and family.

Renzetti also provides an important analysis of the different meanings given by victims and offenders to their abusive relationships. In discussing abusive relationships, victims express intense shame and are frequently withdrawn. On the other hand, batterers legitimize their behavior, are self-righteous, and rarely express shame or remorse.

In presenting her findings on same-sex violence, Renzetti argues for more comparative research on heterosexual and homosexual couples, especially in terms of the incidence and dynamics of mutual battering. Overall, Renzetti's analysis of the extent and severity of violence among same-sex intimates provides further evidence of the need for a theoretical perspective that is limited neither by the marital status nor by the sexual preference of the partners.

As Miller and Wellford note in their chapter, one of the controversial issues associated with the study of intimate violence is whether some women are more vulnerable to victimization than others because of their socioeconomic status (Fagan, 1993; Schwartz, 1988; Gelles, 1980; Petersen, 1980). In addition, as Ferraro notes in chapter 7, economic dependence may be a major factor in preventing women from leaving abusive relationships. Given the growing number of families who live in poverty and receive some form of public assistance, the question of economic dependence may be especially important in establishing strategies directed to the cessation of family and intimate violence. In this respect, Moore (chapter 5) focuses on the relationship between intimate violence and socioeconomic status and argues that while violence exists across all social classes, there is growing evidence that it is more severe and persistent among intimate partners in the lower socioeconomic levels of the social structure. In her overview of research on the occurrence of abusive behavior in all social strata, Moore notes a shift by researchers away from socioeconomic status as a causal factor for explaining the existence of intimate violence (Straus and Gelles, 1990; Yllö and Bograd, 1988; Schwartz, 1988). One result of this de-emphasis, according to Moore, was the development of a "universal-risk" perspective, particularly by feminists, which contends that all women because of their gender are equally likely to experience interpersonal violence.

By advocating a universal-risk theory, feminists, according to Moore, avoid any note of classism while providing a corrective to the myth that violence is confined only to the lower classes and establishing a base to mobilize women from all classes against violence. Although a universal-risk theory is ideologically appealing, Moore notes that recent research does in fact show some association between intimate violence and family incomes, however, when compared with men, women are abused by intimate partners six to ten times more often than men are. In addition, Moore argues that intimate violence is more frequent and severe among lower socioeconomic women. Thus, singular approaches, rooted in the assumption that intimate violence cuts across all economic classes uniformly, are likely to yield inappropriate outcomes. To overcome this problem, Moore advocates a harm reduction approach that starts with the acknowledgment that intimate violence affects all women but that its occurrence varies across social strata.

Establishing an Integrated Theory of Intimate Violence

Throughout each of the chapters, the authors show an underlying concern for the direction theory and research is taking in order to explain the genesis and persistence of intimate violence. As Miller and Wellford note, recent trends show a greater willingness on the part of social scientists to develop integrated theoretical models that combine multiple levels of explanation (Messner et al., 1984; Williams, 1992; Parker and Toth, 1990; Eisikovitz and Edelson, 1989; Stith and Rosen, 1990). Such models not only increase our ability to include a range of factors in order to better interpret interpersonal violence, but they point to the need to establish multifaceted strategies to respond to the patterns of violence used by intimate partners within the continuum of intimacy from dating to marriage.

In addition to focusing on the need for an integrated understanding of the varied patterns of violence categorized as "intimate violence," the authors agree that unidimensional or mono-causal explanations do little to explain theoretically the complex issues associated with violence and abuse between intimate partners. For the most part, explanations of intimate violence have been broad based in scope, emphasizing ideological and psychological dimensions (particularly, asymmetry and misogyny). While the important and unequal distribution of power within intimate relationships cannot be ignored, the social-psychological elements of reciprocity, self-esteem, and dependence indicate the critical need for multiple-analytic perspectives to interpret the causal imperatives and meanings associated with intimate partners who experience abuse and violence. Because theory becomes the framework for seeking to explain the origins of behavior, it implicitly leads to suggested remedies for the control and prevention of the behavior. Thus, viewing battered women and their abusers as having psychological problems is unlikely to resolve some of the issues associated with the social inequality between men and women.

In rejecting psychological explanations that focus on individual pathologies to explain intimate violence, the authors are in agreement that more than the individual perpetrator needs to be addressed. Even the victim of abuse, for example, is part of a violent network in which the responses and effects of violence are related to the meanings attributed to violent and abusive events by both the victim and the offender. Based on this premise, it is important to address the influence of the social environment on the cognitive meanings given to violence. Because these meanings derive from the larger culture as mediated through the institutions and groups that make up the social order, they are likely to vary in content even when there is little difference in the end results. Chronic violence may become an interactive part of the relationship if couples are unwilling to view their abusive behavior as being a part of the larger phenomenon of violence. This avoidance is likely to decrease the willingness of victims to leave the relationship; rather, the abused partners are more likely to develop survival strategies for enduring the abuse.

In summary, the authors agree that much needs to be accomplished if the field of family and intimate violence is to move beyond current levels of analysis. Many of the existing paradigms have received limited support from empirical research and having failed to facilitate the prediction and control of violence and abuse between intimate partners. It is becoming increasingly important to understand how dominance in an intimate relationship can lead to physical violence, as opposed to anger and emotional abuse, under certain conditions. Theory building, as Miller and Wellford note, requires theoretical integration.

1

Patterns and Correlates
of Interpersonal Violence

SUSAN L. MILLER

Northern Illinois University

CHARLES F. WELLFORD

University of Maryland

In the past two decades, the media, practitioners, empirical researchers, and theorists have focused increased attention on interpersonal violence, forging new and more complete understandings through experiments dealing with criminal justice responses (Sherman and Berk, 1984; Hirschel and Hutchison, 1992; Berk et al., 1992; Dunford, 1992), as well as the development of new policies and strategies across social service, mental health, criminal justice, and legal agencies. Despite this unprecedented growth in interest and research, however, there is a dearth of comprehensive information concerning conceptual and methodological issues, as well as risk factors, associated with interpersonal violence. Part of this omission reflects the very nature of the behavior itself. Intimate violence, which accounts for a significant proportion of interpersonal violence, is neither uniformly nor universally defined. Furthermore, it is often surrounded by secrecy, as well as tacitly tolerated and reinforced by responses and inactions from criminal justice, medical, legal, social, and religious institutions.

This chapter, deals first with the patterns and trends in violent crime in the United States. Next it provides an overview of the patterns and correlates of interpersonal violence. This overview begins with an analysis of such violence and includes a summary of the literature on the correlates of interpersonal violence. Following this review, both the important variations of interpersonal violence and the diversity of populations affected by such violence are discussed, with particular emphasis on those populations that are examined in subsequent chapters. Finally, integrated models for understanding intimate violence are presented.

Unfortunately, it is now well established that relative to other societies, violence *is* as American as apple pie. When compared to other developed countries, the United States not only has higher rates of violent crime but "the more serious the crime, the greater the difference between the U.S. rate and those of other developed countries" (Reiss and Rhodes, 1993: 52). While national victimization surveys have documented a stable or declining crime rate over the past twenty years, rates of violent crime, especially for some groups and some types of victims, have been increasing (Bureau of Justice Statistics, 1993). Police reports show an even greater increase in violence in recent years, especially with homicide.

Throughout the last twenty years, the rate of violent victimizations reported by males twelve years of age or older has declined. During this same period, however, the self-reported rate of violent victimization of females did not decline, even with the substantial undercounting of sexual assaults against females (Bureau of Justice Statistics, 1994). A recent analysis of violence against women using national victimization data notes the following (Bureau of Justice Statistics, 1994):

- Although women were significantly less likely to become victims of violent crime, they were more vulnerable to particular types of perpetrators. Whereas men were more likely to be victimized by acquaintances or strangers, women were just as likely to be victimized by intimates, such as husbands or boyfriends, as they were to be victimized by acquaintances or strangers. The rate of violence committed by intimates was nearly ten times greater for females than for males.
- Over two-thirds of violent victimizations against women were committed by someone known to them: 31 percent of female victims reported that the offender was a stranger. Of those known offenders, approximately 28 percent were intimates such as husbands or boyfriends, 35 percent were acquaintances, and the remaining 5 percent were other relatives. In contrast, victimizations by intimates and other relatives accounted for only 5 percent of all violent victimizations against men. Men were significantly more likely to have been victimized by acquaintances (50 percent) or strangers (44 percent) than by intimates or other relatives.

In a society characterized by high rates of violent crime, women experience the majority of the violence directed at them by those with whom they have ongoing relationships. In effect, intimate violence—violence committed by those individuals one is more likely to trust and have continuing social relations with—represents the type of violence most likely to be increasing for women.

Incidence and Measurement Issues

The prevalence of spousal and non-spousal violence is well established (Mercy and Saltzman, 1989; Schulman, 1979; Straus and Gelles, 1986; Straus, Gelles, and Steinmetz, 1980; Teske and Parker, 1983; Pirog-Good and Stets, 1989; Hammond, 1989; Renzetti, 1992; Island and Letellier, 1990). However, estimates of the *overall* prevalence and incidence of intimate assaults are less accurate and complete, particularly in states and local areas (Saltzman et al., 1990). Even national statistical sources are incomplete. The current Uniform Crime Reports collected by the FBI do not include information regarding relationship status for nonfatal violent crimes, although design changes now underway may soon make this information available (Poggio, Kennedy, Chaiken, and Carlson, 1985). Definitional problems are also apparent with victimization data collected in the National Crime Survey, which defines *intimate* too broadly, as including neighbors, work associates, friends, and classmates (Saltzman et al., 1990). In addition, most research efforts and program development have focused on rates of violent crime in urban areas; it is even more difficult to estimate prevalence and incidence rates in rural areas, including smaller cities, towns, and reservations. These smaller areas create unique obstacles because of their greater geographic and social isolation (Edleson and Frank, 1991).[1]

Accurate estimates of the incidence rates of intimate violence are further compromised because of the nature of the offenses. Many victims are typically silent about their victimizations for multiple reasons: internalized shame, economic dependence, isolation, complications with children, fear of retaliation, religious or familial pressures to keep the family-relationship intact, unresponsiveness and even disbelief from police and other members of the criminal justice system, and, until recently, a lack of legal options or alternatives. Problems of invisibility and lack of support or resources may be compounded for homosexual, minority, and lower-income victims or others who are disenfranchised and thus even more unlikely to disclose information to researchers or to criminal justice and social service agencies.

Variations used in methodological strategies also affect incidence estimates. Estimates of the extent of interpersonal violence varies, depending on the methodology and the data source used. Incidence rates range from 16 percent, using nationally representative household surveys (Straus et al., 1980; Straus and Gelles, 1986), to 50 percent based on victimization surveys and interviews (Walker, 1979; Freize et al., 1980; Russell, 1982). National household survey data suggest that over 1.5 million women are battered each year (Straus et al., 1980; Straus and Gelles, 1986). A more

---

[1]What complicates the issue of "counting numbers" even more is that many researchers and activists caution against a heavy reliance on quantifying the incidence of intimate violence, fearing that it detracts from money, time, efforts, and resources that would be better spent on combating the violence, providing victims with legal and social support, developing treatment programs for batterers, and so forth. (Blackman, 1989). In addition, some fear that programs and financial commitments often are justified by large numbers, so they obscure the uniqueness of this kind of underreported—but very real—epidemic (Yllö, 1988).

recent national study of adult couples classified 14 percent of the male respondents as having used physical aggression toward their female partners (Williams and Hawkins, 1992). Based on victimization data, the National Crime Survey estimates that 2.1 million women are battered annually, with a recurrence of violence in 32 percent of the cases within six months of reporting (Langan and Innes, 1986). In victimization surveys conducted between 1978 and 1982, respondents revealed that only 52 percent of the time did they report the violent incidents to the police (Langan and Innes, 1986).

Physical violence occurring among intimate partners is not restricted to marriage. Violence in college dating relationships is estimated to be similar to incidence levels of marital violence (Pirog-Good and Stets, 1989; Arias et al., 1987; Cate et al., 1982; Makepeace, 1981; Rose and Marshall, 1985). In a review of over forty dating violence studies, 33 percent of male students and almost 40 percent of female students used violence against their partners (Sugarman and Hotaling, 1989). In one survey, data from respondents who were asked about their participation in relationship violence one month before their marriage indicated that 30 percent of the women and 35 percent of the men reported violent victimizations at least once in the past year (Arias and O'Leary, 1984). While these studies begin to demonstrate the high levels of intimate violence between non-married partners, they neither differentiate between aggressive and defensive violence, nor consider gender differences in the potential for injurious outcomes. In the following chapter, Makepeace provides a critical overview of some of the issues surrounding dating and courtship violence.

Some research has examined incidence rates for subsamples of victims, such as battered lesbians and battered gay men (see Island and Letellier, 1990; Hammond, 1989; Renzetti, 1992; and Renzetti, chapter 4 of this volume). Accurate incidence estimates are even more difficult to obtain given the social "taboos" of being a domestic violence victim as well as a homosexual.[2] The unreliability of the existing estimates is due to sample limitations, such as nonrandomness, self-selected samples (snowball, convenience, referrals through newspaper recruitment, advertisements, fliers, and contacts with psychotherapists), and thus may tend to reflect higher rates than actually exist. One sample of lesbian couples found close to half of the partners noting they had experienced interpersonal violence (Coleman, 1990), while another survey of 1,566 lesbians uncovered a figure of only 17 percent (Loulan, 1987). Using extrapolations from estimates of the incidence of heterosexual intimate violence and estimates of the gay male population, Island and Letellier (1990) use 10.9 percent as a conservative estimate of gay male battering, setting an upper limit at approximately 20 percent. Incidence rates are also affected by cultural expectations. In one of the most comprehensive

---

[2]Battered lesbians and battered gay men may see disclosure as too risky, particularly if their relationships are not socially desirable or institutionally sanctioned. Reporting rates are also affected by isolation from traditional sources of help, such as shelters and laws, which have been designed primarily to benefit women engaged in heterosexual relationships. In addition, the police have not always been helpful to gay members of the population—trivializing their complaints, not following enforcement actions, and sometimes even perpetuating and escalating violence against them (Comstock, 1991).

analyses to date, Rasche (1988) examines the unique problems faced by battered women of color and why measurement strategies could be significantly affected by how different racial, ethnic, or cultural minority groups define *abuse*. For example, some evidence suggests that certain ethnic groups are more tolerant or approving of intimate violence based on cultural expectations (see Carroll, 1980; Segovia-Ashley, 1978, for Mexican Americans; Skurnick, 1983, for Latin Americans; Spiegel, 1980, for Italian Americans; Loizos, 1978, for rural Mediterraneans) these are all groups "where 'family honor' supersedes all other values" (Rasche, 1988: 155). Similarly, Cazenave and Straus (1979) and Williams (1981) found approval or toleration of intimate violence higher among blacks in their surveys, and Shoemaker and Williams (1987) report that Native Americans are more tolerant than both blacks and Hispanics. Low rates of intimate violence reported for Asian American communities may reflect cultural prohibitions against "loss of face" for oneself or one's family, including revealing the abuse to an anonymous victimization surveyor (Rasche, 1988). Language barriers faced by immigrant women (Eng, 1985; Skurnik, 1983) and Latinos (Zambrano, 1985) also hinder reporting. At times, these silences are further reinforced by the lack of assistance from religious institutions (Fortune, 1981; Zambrano, 1985; White, 1985). An unwillingness to report incidents of intimate violence is also reinforced by those minority communities who "place an extremely high value on setting forth a positive racial-ethnic identity and seek to avoid anything which might reinforce stereotypical images" (Rasche, 1988: 163).

Although it has long been recognized that intimate violence cuts across all racial, ethnic, religious, and income groups, a disproportionate number of minority and lower socioeconomic status victims are reflected in criminal justice statistics, sustaining the view that battering is predominantly a minority or lower-class phenomenon. An alternative interpretation suggests that the higher reporting rates reflect unequal access to formal law-invoking alternatives or economic resources (Miller, 1989). Comparative research across groups is often flawed and relies on false assumptions that "all groups in this country are homogeneous, regardless of their political, socio-historical, and economic experiences," which causes "serious methodological and theoretical errors" (Lockhart, 1985: 40).

Disclosure issues are particularly salient for minority groups who have a long history of uneasy relations with the police (see Overby, 1971; Rossi et al., 1974). African Americans and other people of color as well as persons with lower socioeconomic status are more likely than whites and individuals with a higher socioeconomic status to perceive injustice operating against them by police, juries, and court personnel (Hagan and Albonetti, 1982; Yates, 1985; Carter, 1985). Victims who perceive or have experienced injustice may be reluctant to call on the police to protect them and may be more ambivalent about seeking assistance from the criminal justice system (Goolkaisian, 1986; Hearing on Violence Prevention Act, formal testimony, 1978).

An early study using national household samples (Straus, Gelles, and Steinmetz, 1979) revealed higher rates of intimate violence by men against women for minority groups than for whites. Other studies have also been in agreement with this finding.

Shoemaker and Williams (1987), Gelles (1980), Staples (1976), and Cazenave and Straus (1979) all found African Americans to have rates twice that of other minority groups and four times that of whites. These findings, however, are inconsistent with other rese   eveals no significant racial group differences (Lockhart, 1984; Berk et   nd Schumacher, 1979; Walker, 1979; Smith and Snow, 1978). In addi-tio   ered women's shelters consistently report racial and ethnic distri-bu   to the general characteristics of the populations in that area (Walker, 1983; Kun, 1982, Crisson, 1981; LaBell, 1979; Rounsaville, 1978–79; Gelles, 1972).

Because minority groups are overrepresented in the lower socioeconomic groups, and socioeconomic status affects options, social class may be inextricably linked to race in the study of intimate violence (Lockhart, 1985, 1987). Women with higher incomes not only have greater access to resources to assist them in keeping their abuse private, but have the ability to afford private physicians and safe shelters. Furthermore, they are more likely to have the needed resources to procure a separation or divorce. Such opportunities allow these women to avoid any detection from law enforcement agencies, hospital emergency rooms, or social service agencies (Prescott and Letko, 1977; Stark et al., 1979; Washburn and Frieze, 1981; Asbury, 1987).

More reliable methods to measure the degree, magnitude, and intensity of intimate violence, as well as the instruments to examine patterns of behavior, motive, and consequences, are clearly needed (Hudson and McIntosh, 1981; Rosenbaum, 1988; Yllö, 1988; Shepard and Campbell, 1992). While the Conflict Tactics Scale (CTS), developed by Straus and his associates for use in mass surveys to measure multiple types of family violence, remains the most widely used instrument (Straus, 1979), it has not been without criticism. The major objections are that the scale ignores the content of the conflict and the unequal physical strengths of combative partners, as well as the injurious outcomes (Dobash and Dobash, 1988). Existing research not only suggests that the extent and severity of injury is far greater for women than men (Freize and Browne, 1989), but that the violence by women is primarily defensive rather than offensive action (Saunders, 1988). The CTS has been further criticized on the grounds that it does not adequately address psychological abuse (Tolman, 1989) and that it inappropriately combines threats, attempts, and actual violence (Dobash and Dobash, 1988). Despite these criticisms, the CTS continues to be the most widely employed instrument, although other indexes have been introduced (Tolman, 1989; Hudson and McIntosh, 1981; Gondolf, 1987; Shepherd and Campbell, 1992).

Causes and Correlates

Most of the studies associated with the first wave of intimate violence research focused on victim needs and attributes, concentrating on identifying the patterns, extent, and consequences for victims as well as available or needed institutional responses and remedies from the social services and criminal justice systems. More recently, a growing body of research has begun to examine the actual batterers, including causation theories and treatment issues. Multiple theoretical perspectives have been formulated in the attempt to answer the question, "what causes battering?"; nevertheless, there is little solid evidence about what factors are highly correlated with intimate violence. For the most part, theories have not been adequately tested; most studies have used small, unrepresentative clinical samples in their tests (Schwartz, 1990).

Factors suggested as correlating with intimate violence range from an emphasis on individual-level and family factors to a recognition of structural and cultural variables (Morash, 1986). Micro-level research, often involving clinical samples, tends to focus on interpersonal and situational dynamics, ignoring the larger social systems and institutions that may impact on battering. Other researchers, concerned with macro-level approaches, view violence in a more expansive context, that is, as encompassing social conditions (patriarchy, economics, legal status of women, and so forth) that are related to intimate violence. Regardless of the ideological or methodological approaches employed by researchers, however, there remains much ambiguity surrounding the question of whether the factors of interest are related to or directly cause intimate violence. Three of the most consistent themes or explanations for intimate violence present in the literature are reviewed here.

Individual Pathology

Individual-level explanations focus primarily on personality disorders and traits, mental illness, self-image problems, stress, and problems with drugs or alcohol. Violence is seen as resulting from various psychological abnormalities, such as inadequate self-control, sadism, and psychopathology (Gelles and Straus, 1979). To date, however, the available scientific evidence provides little, if any, support for these assertions. In addition, these theories are unable to explain which abnormal personality traits are directly associated with violence, especially since only a very small proportion of mentally ill persons are violent (Burgess and Draper, 1989). Another popular theme in the explanation of intimate violence focuses on the correlation between substance use-abuse and battering; the primary suggestion is that alcohol and drugs act as disinhibitors, thereby releasing violent tendencies within an individual. Again, there is little scientific evidence to support this premise. Although violent abusers are often drinking when they engage in abuse, this behavior does not in and of itself explain where these violent tendencies originate or why alcohol and drugs do not lead to similar results for everyone who uses alcohol (Burgess and Draper, 1989). Other researchers have in fact suggested that alcohol abuse might provide an excuse for abusers to justify the violent behavior, but not serve the function of disinhibiting behavior (Gelles, 1974). Overall, when alcohol and drug abuse are examined as factors in intimate violence, the consensus is that the relationship of drugs and alcohol to battering is not a causal one; most batterers are neither alcoholics nor drug addicts (Herman, 1988; Edleson et al., 1985; Gelles and Cornell, 1985).

Batterers themselves often suggest that they were provoked; they view their partner's verbal aggressiveness as equivalent to their own physical aggressiveness (Ptacek, 1988; Lion, 1977; Faulk, 1977), a position that has received some support from clinicians (see Deschner, 1984; Margolin, 1979). In his review of treatment models for batterers, Adams (1988) discusses the common assumption of personality disorder: "impaired ego functioning (e.g., poor self-concept, emotional dependency) leads him to overreact to real or imagined threats in a violent matter." This loss of control is exacerbated for individuals with low frustration tolerance, fear of intimacy, fear of abandonment, dependency, and underlying depression (Adams, 1988). In this respect, some studies reveal batterers to exhibit depression and poor self-concepts, while others find no significant differences between batterers and non-batterers (see review by Edleson et al., 1985). It may be that instead of depression causing battering, battering may in fact result in depression (Tolman and Bennett, 1990).

Some researchers contend that violence stems from sex role identity in which "exaggerated, hypermasculine behaviors are rooted in men's unconscious anxiety about the 'psychologically feminine' parts of their personalities" (Adams, 1988: 179; see also Biller and Borstelman, 1967; Winick, 1968). Feminist researchers are especially critical of these individual-level explanations; they argue that researchers ignore how many men are socially sanctioned to develop misogynistic values and controlling behavior as appropriate (Pleck, 1981). As shown by recent exploratory research, male friends of abusive husbands are more likely to approve the batterer's violence against his wife than male friends of non-abusive husbands (Smith, 1991).

Other researchers have used demographic indicators to explore the nature and extent of intimate violence within relationships. In an early study, Gelles (1972) focused on social structural theory and the role of social class, arguing that lower-class individuals engage in violence because of their limited opportunities for educational and occupational attainments. The study hypothesized that when these opportunities are blocked, stress and frustration will result, which in turn will lead to abusive behavior. In one of the few studies to use a national sample, Schwartz (1990) used National Crime Survey data to explore resource equality, work status, and unemployment and their relationship to intimate violence. The results show employment status to be unrelated to intimate violence or injury, particularly since most of the abusers identified in the data set were employed.

The major problem associated with individual-level explanations results from the likelihood that batterers with the most pathological problems are precisely the ones who will either volunteer for or be ordered by the courts to attend treatment programs. Thus, in their recent review of the quantitative research on men who batter, Tolman and Bennett (1990: 89) conclude that the overrepresentation of psychopathology in clinical samples of batterers "does not directly implicate psychopathology as a causal factor in battering."

Family Dysfunction

This perspective places violence against the family background and experience of the batterer. According to one widely held view, intimate violence is essentially learned behavior. Thus, if children witness or experience physical violence in their family of origin, they will begin to see violence as an appropriate way to handle problems and frustrations that arise. One outcome of this learning process is that violence as a means of resolving conflict is replicated in adult relationships. This viewpoint is alternatively described as the intergenerational transmission (IGT) of violence, the cyclical hypothesis, or the cycle of violence. Empirical evidence to support this hypothesis, however, is mixed. Straus et al. (1980) found that children witnessing parental violence are three times more likely to be violent to their own partners than those who were raised with nonviolent parents. While the effects of witnessing violence vary according to the gender of the witness, some studies demonstrate that intimate violence is even more likely to develop if, as children, the batterers both witnessed parental violence and endured victimization (Caesar, 1988; Pagelow, 1981; Rosenbaum and O'Leary, 1981). O'Leary (1988) found that males who witnessed violence between their own parents were more likely to abuse their own partners. Kalmuss (1984) also reports an increase in violence by both men and women who witnessed parental violence. On the other hand, others have noted no enduring intergenerational effects on subsequent violence (see Frieze and Browne, 1989; Weiss, 1989).

A recent reanalysis of the Straus et al. (1976) national data by Cappell and Heiner (1990) suggests that spousal violence in the family of origin increased the likelihood of victimization for both men and women, but it was not related to the learned role of the perpetrator for either sex. While these same authors include both mildly and severely violent acts in their aggressive scale, they do not differentiate between aggressive and defensive actions by respondents, a common problem identified with the use of the Conflict Tactics Scale (CTS). Overall, however, the research by Cappell and Heiner (1990) and Herzberger (1983) begins to challenge the widespread acceptance of the intergenerational transmission hypothesis.

Another hypothesis related to family dysfunction suggests that the batterer's developmental skills are not sufficiently developed because of parental neglect, inappropriate or missing role models, inept teaching, and the like; these factors result in the inability on the part of the batterer to refrain from violence in interpersonal situations (Ptacek, 1988).

Structural Conditions/Feminist Approaches

In these perspectives, the pervasive subordination of women associated with patriarchal societies becomes the key to understanding intimate violence (Bograd, 1988). Researchers argue that there has been an historical toleration and sometimes even encouragement of abuse against women by male members of the religious, medical, criminal justice, and legal systems. Therefore, it should come as no surprise that violence is tolerated in the family as well (Kurtz, 1987). Because women are viewed as property, subject to the whims and rules of first the father and then the husband, this patriarchal ideology is reinforced by both explicit and tacit toleration by social institutions in which most of the power and authority over the decision making is wielded by men. In addition, many women who bring their cases to court will be subjected to credibility challenges and character attacks, victim blaming, and inadequate protection laws (Schechter, 1982; Dobash and Dobash, 1988). Within the feminist perspective, these challenges and attacks are viewed as taking place within a patriarchal (male-dominated) context in which the subjugation of women into subordinate roles is accomplished through societal discrimination and ideological beliefs that women are innately inferior (Yllö, 1988). The result is that men exercise all power and privilege in society at large and women are systematically excluded from business, legal, political, and religious leadership; the use of male domination, power, and authority in the home are similarly used to establish and maintain control over women.

Sexual inequality is viewed by some researchers as a causal factor in intimate violence because a sexist society provides few opportunities for economic independence for women who would otherwise leave violent marriages (Pogrebin, 1974; Schuyler, 1976; Straus, 1976). On the other hand, some researchers have argued that sexual equality and domestic violence are negatively related (Toby, 1974; Whitehurst, 1974; Marden, 1978). Husbands may feel threatened by marital conflict because there are increasing alternatives to marriage.

Martin (1976) and Dobash and Dobash (1980) present feminist perspectives on wife abuse; they argue that battering is a manifestation of the long-standing historical tradition of male domination of women. In extending this perspective, Martin (1976) focuses on the economic dependence of women on men and argues that this dependence is the result of the organization and history of marriage, along with the economic, legal, and religious systems, that relegate women to subordinate roles. In a similar vein, Dobash and Dobash (1980: 24) assert that: "men who assault their wives are actually living up to cultural prescriptions that are cherished in Western society—aggressiveness, male dominance, and female subordination—and they are using physical force as a means to enforce that dominance."

A recent, but fruitful, avenue of exploration derives from Eisikovitz and Edleson's (1989) ecological model. Its usefulness in explaining intimate violence rests on the assumption that there is no single-level explanation, but rather a need to address the "interaction of multiple variables from the individual to the society" across a backdrop of the social inequality of women.

Toward an Integrated Model for Explaining Intimate Violence

While the various explanations noted previously have been offered to account for the level, type, and distribution of intimate violence, more recent analyses have focused on a clarification of the types of intimate violent offenders and the development of integrated models for the explanation of this behavior. The focus on offender variation and theory integration in the explanation of intimate violence loosely parallels efforts to explain other kinds of violent and deviant behavior and to develop meaningful typologies of violent behavior that are theory driven.

As Terrie Moffitt has recently observed (1993), "There are marked individual differences in the stability of antisocial behavior. Many people behave antisocially, but their antisocial behavior is temporary and situational. In contrast, the antisocial behavior of some people is very stable and persistent." In a study of juvenile delin-quency, Wolfgang et al. (1972) observed that approximately 5 percent of a delin-quency birth cohort accounted for as much as 50 percent of the official delinquency attributable to that birth cohort, including 80 percent of the violent delinquencies committed by that same birth cohort. Similar studies by Farrington (1991), Loeber and LeBlanc (1990), and others have documented the clear pattern of a small group of individuals committing a disproportionate amount of delinquency, violence, and antisocial behavior. This same model most likely applies in the area of intimate vio-lence. Undoubtedly, many acts of intimate violence are temporary and situational in the sense that the violence occurs only occasionally and is not an integral part of the interactions that occur between intimate individuals. While such acts are no less seri-ous, explanations of this type of intimate violence may require more emphasis on sit-uational, time-transient characteristics. On the other hand, there is strong evidence that a core of individuals are violent in a variety of situations, including intimate sit-uations, and that their violence extends to multiple intimate partners (Reiss and Roth, 1993). These individuals reflect the chronic, stable, and persistent antisocials referred to by Moffitt and observed in other analyses of crime, delinquency, and deviance. Because of these differences, explanations of the behavior of these two general types of intimate offenders will undoubtedly vary. In the broader area of antisocial behav-ior, the explanation of the sporadic antisocial behavior places greater emphasis on situational and temporary life-course dimensions. On the other hand, persistent, vio-lent behavior is better understood in terms of broad cultural dimensions and clear patterns of personality that lead an individual toward violence.

In analyzing intimate violence, it will become increasingly important to make at least this basic distinction in trying to explain and respond to this kind of behavior. The typology of intimate violent offenders that is suggested by this broader literature needs to be further developed, but, at this point, the distinction between temporary-situational intimate violent offenders and long-term offenders is likely to prove use-ful in developing better models of explanation and in using those models to guide interventions and policy.

Increasingly, social science explanations of behavior, including violent behavior, have supported the development of integrated theoretical models. As noted earlier in this chapter, previous explanations of intimate violence have tended to focus on spe-cific factors or domains of explanation, such as individual factors, social dimensions, family stress and family characteristic dimensions, and structural conditions. Consistent with the more general trend in social science theory, emphasis is increas-ingly being placed on the development of integrated models that combine multiple levels of explanation. While general models of intimate violence should include both situational-life-course components and broader cultural and personality components, the weighting of these components will vary in explaining this occurrence of tran-sient and stable intimate violence.

For many years, social scientists have attempted to identify the individual factors or dimensions (e.g., personality, social structure, or culture) that might differentiate the violent person from the nonviolent one. These efforts have proved to be only partially successful; as a result, there is a clear need for models that incorporate the many levels and types of explanation that have been offered. These more recent works in theory development (e.g., Messner et al., 1984) place emphasis upon notions of theory integration. While theory integration can take a variety of forms, in the area of interpersonal violence and intimate violence, it is increasingly taking the form of identifying the interrelationships and individual and joint contributions of different levels of explanation. For example, Eisikovitz and Edleson's (1989) ecological model stresses the need to address "the interaction of multiple variables from the individual to society in a general theory of intimate violence." Their work examines these factors, particularly, across the backdrop of social inequality for women in American society and the way this cultural and structural condition may modify a variety of other explanatory variables. More recently, Stith and Rosen (1990) have developed what they refer to as an interactive model of domestic or intimate violence. Their work identifies various elements they postulate as being the important dimensions of an explanation of intimate violence. These elements include stressors, vulnerabilities, resources, and the social and cultural context in which interactions occur. Stith and Rosen emphasize the way these multiple dimensions interact to explain some forms of intimate violence. Riggs and O'Leary (1989) also propose an integrated or multilevel theory. Their model (applied to courtship aggression) demonstrates the trend toward more comprehensive theoretical explanations. While stressing personality and interpersonal social-learning approaches, it includes situational, individual, social, and cultural dimensions in a theory of one prominent form of intimate violence.

Works such as those of Eisikovitz and Edleson (1989), Stith and Roth (1993), and Riggs and O'Leary (1989) bring to our attention the multiple levels of explanation that may be used to explain intimate violence: the characteristics and experience of individuals—their personalities and developmental and biological characteristics; social dimensions—the economic, social, political, and community environments in which they are socialized and live; and cultural conditions, including subcultures—that is, the values and mores of the individuals and the significant groups to which they belong. Such factors provide a comprehensive analysis of the elements that may explain intimate violence.

Integrated or multi-level theories of intimate violence clearly reveal that the response to intimate violence must be multifaceted. Focusing on any particular dimension of the intimate relationship to the neglect of other characteristics, or the social and cultural context in which it occurs, will not provide a complete analysis of the problem. The development of effective interventions and strategies to respond to intimate violence will increasingly depend on the extent to which our understanding of what violence is, is informed by a comprehensive integrated model.

Summary

In sum, it is important to remember the distinction offered in this chapter about the types of intimate offenders. Explanations of situation-temporary offenders may emphasize stressors in the person's life or factors that exist for some limited period of time. The clear involvement of alcohol, for example, in many institutional violent events is one indicator of this element. The interventions in these cases may be more difficult to develop in a preventive sense but may be easier to implement when appropriate contexts are identified. On the other hand, the response to those individuals with histories of chronic acts of intimate violence may require interventions that address all levels of explanation for this behavior. Focusing on individual change—without attention to family dynamics, social and cultural factors, and the structural conditions operating to account for the emergence and persistence of chronic interpersonal violent offenders—may encompass too narrow a focus.

Finally, we contend that work in the area of intimate violence should focus on better understanding the extent and distribution of this type of violent behavior, differentiating intimate violent offenders into a meaningful typology, and developing integrated models of explanation that can better guide research, effective policy, and intervention. Further attempts to explain intimate violence without an understanding of the differences in offender types and without the development of integrated models to explain those different types may prove of limited value.

2

Courtship Violence as Process: A Developmental Theory

JAMES M. MAKEPEACE

College of St. Benedict

Much current literature on courtship violence views the behavior as being undifferentiated in content. Yet, a major trend in the twentieth century has been the expansion and differentiation of the courtship process, a factor that has had an important influence on both the nature and extent of courtship violence. Thus, in the early part of this century dating was rare or nonexistent; the process of courtship generally took place later in life with marriage not long after. Today, heterosexual recreations, such as dances, parties, and sporting events, typically begin during junior high school and continue throughout adolescence and early adulthood. Given that the average age of first marriage is now in the mid-twenties, courtship has become an extended process for most young people in today's society.

A major characteristic of the courtship ritual is the continued need for intimacy between partners, the frustration of which is an enduring cause of personal stress, aggression, and at times violence. In addition, there are substantial variations across the continuum in the maturity and resources that individuals can command and in the relationships in which they are involved within the primary social institutions such as the family, school, and economy. Associated with these variations are changes in the normative expectations about courtship and in the frustrations that courting couples experience when their efforts to fulfill these expectations are obstructed. These developmental issues tend to accumulate and become more complex as courtship progresses. Offsetting the violence-generating potential of these issues are developmental maturation and an accrual of resources that may be helpful for coping with frustration.

Courtship, including its violent aspects, is a distinct stage in a larger social process, the socio-reproductive dialectic, some form of which all societies construct to ensure their own survival. The desire for intimacy may have organic foundations as well, but certainly culture magnifies and romanticizes intimacy so that as members of society consider entry into parenting, courtship, and marriage, the principle gratification they anticipate receiving for the involved obligations is one of intimacy. When the need and expectation of this intimacy are unfulfilled, however, personal frustration is likely to occur. Moss and Schwebel (1993: 33) describe this process as follows:

> The level of intimacy . . . individuals experience within relationships exerts a profound influence on their social development, personal adjustment, and physical health. . . . intimacy plays an integral role in individual's successful passage through developmental stages, solidification of friendships, attainment of marital happiness, and success in psychotherapeutic encounters (Erickson, 1963; Fisher and Stricker, 1982; Schaefer and Olson, 1981; Sullivan, 1953) . . . failure to obtain satisfactory levels of intimacy in a romantic relationship has been identified as the largest category of problem behavior which motivates people to obtain psychotherapy (Horowitz, 1979) and as the most frequent reason given by couples for their divorce (Waring, 1988). . . . intimacy is particularly sought in romantic relationships. In fact, people typically evaluate their romantic relationship in terms of its level of intimacy (Frankel, 1982; Greenberg and Johnson, 1986).

The attainment of a satisfying level of intimacy, then, is taken as the fundamental, enduring individual need and social prescription for courtship; the frustration of this need is taken to be the most frequent and enduring cause of courtship abuse and violence. In keeping with this thesis, studies have found jealousy, which is anxiety over perceived loss of intimacy, to be the most frequently cited reason for courtship violence (Makepeace, 1981; Fallingstad et al., 1991) and that many unmarried males and females agree that hitting is an acceptable response to jealousy (Carlson, 1990).

Incidence and Research Trends

For some years after the problem of spouse abuse had been recognized, most scholars continued to overlook violence among couples before marriage. In 1978, Makepeace (1981) found that 21.2 percent of a sample of 202 college students had at some time physically assaulted or been assaulted by a courtship partner. Based on these results, a follow-up national study of over 2,700 students on eight American college campuses was undertaken. The results indicated that 16.7 percent of the students had experienced at least one incident of courtship violence. Since three of the eight campuses were located in one of the least violent urban areas of the nation, the results likely underestimated the actual volume of such behavior.

Most often courtship violence occurred with only one partner (69.3 percent of participants), though most of these (70.6 percent) reported multiple experiences.

Violence was most often bilateral, each participant both inflicting and sustaining violence at some point (Makepeace, 1986), and most often resulted in less rather than more serious injury (Makepeace, 1988). Additional findings have been reported elsewhere (Makepeace, 1983, 1984, 1986, 1987, 1988, 1989) and will be referred to at appropriate points in this chapter.

In a review of courtship violence studies conducted during the 1980s, Sugarman and Hotaling (1989) found an average courtship violence rate of 30 percent across all studies. While most studies of courtship violence are based on samples of U.S. high school and college students, a recent study of males at a Canadian university, found that 42 percent of the respondents had used violence within a courtship relationship (Barnes, Greenwood, and Sommer, 1991). Another study, which focused on youths (ages 13 to 16) in residential treatment, found 42 percent of the girls but only 7 percent of the boys to have been involved in courtship violence (Carlson, 1990).

One of the most unexpected findings to emerge from courtship violence research is the involvement of both genders. Early reports seemed to labor under the preconception that males are always perpetrators and females victims. Evidence now indicates, however, that both males and females inflict and sustain courtship violence—indeed, that females may more often inflict violence, though most incidents are bilateral (Makepeace, 1986; Burke, Stets, and Pirog-Good, 1988).

Nor, at least among youth, is courtship violence necessarily proscribed. Several studies have found many youth view force as an acceptable response to emotional injury, and even consider it at times to be an expression of love (Henton et al., 1983; Carlson, 1990). This "acceptance" is undoubtedly related to how participants respond to violence. Thus, few incidents are ever reported to authorities or parents, and this is particularly true when sexual disagreement is involved (Pirog-Good and Stets, 1989).

In one of the earliest studies of courtship violence, a link to earlier family violence (having been abused by or having witnessed abuse between one's parents) was hypothesized as a major causal factor for this behavior (Makepeace, 1981). While the weight of evidence supports the assumption, it now appears that this relationship is not as powerful as earlier expected and is subject to important variations according to gender, victimization versus precipitation, and other factors (Sack, Keller, and Howard, 1982; Alexander, Moore, and Alexander, 1991; Gwartney Gibbs, Stockard, and Bohmer, 1987).

Although most of the early research on courtship violence focused on the nature and extent of this behavior among college students, recent research shows its existence among younger daters (Cate et al., 1982; Carlson, 1990; Stets and Henderson, 1991) and its highest level to be among cohabiting couples (Lane and Gwartney Gibbs, 1985; Makepeace, 1989; Stets and Straus, 1989).

An important direction of research has been the closer study of variables that initially received attention primarily as "correlates." Several studies have given careful consideration to the interconnections of courtship violence with jealousy (Fallingstad et al., 1991); alcohol (Makepeace, 1988; Stets and Henderson, 1991); sexuality (Lane and Gwartney Gibbs, 1985); romanticism (Henton et al., 1983; Fallingstad et al., 1992; Lloyd, 1991); and interactive style (Bird, Stith, and Schladale, 1991). The reexamination of courtship violence correlates and increased emphasis on the development of courtship violence theory are important developments regarding the patterns and causes of courtship violence in American culture.

Finally, there is a growing concern about how to prevent and control this behavior. During the last few years, public awareness of courtship violence has been greatly increased by television programs and popular magazine articles: Educational materials have been produced; law enforcement and criminal justice agencies are now much more cognizant of the problem; high schools and colleges are greatly sensitized to and have numerous programs addressing intimate abuse and exploitation; and lastly education, counseling, and social work professions are rapidly developing their own knowledge bases in this area.

Patterns of Courtship Violence

Although intimacy anxiety is viewed as the principle abiding source of violence during courtship, much additional violence is related to frustrations more specific to particular phases of courtship as described here.

Pre-Dating Courtship

In the earliest phase of courtship (generally ages 12 to 14) individual identities are typically insecure, emotions are immature, and most norms do not endorse dating. Yet, the desire for intimacy is generally aroused at this time both by biology and by numerous encouragements and enticing depictions of dating that culture presents through family and peer encouragement and modeling, television programming, teen magazine fare, and so forth. Extensive evidence documents the high rates of sexuality and pregnancy that result from inappropriately early dating. Thus, according to Rosa (1991: 370):

> Each year in the U.S. there are over 1 million pregnancies, almost 500,000 births, and over 400,000 abortions to women under 20 years old (Hayes, 1987; Moore, 1990). . . . Almost one half of these pregnancies are to women under 18 years old . . . the birthrate among 15–17 year old adolescents now appears to be increasing (Moore, 1990). . . . the U.S. has one of the highest adolescent fertility rates among developed nations (Jones et al., 1986).

The substantial adverse consequences that such "out of prescribed sequence" reproduction has for the individual and for society have been well documented (Popenoe, 1988, 1993; Miller and Teaton, 1991; Adams, Adams-Taylor, and Pittman, 1989; Rosa, 1991). In addition, the temptation to use violence to vent frustration, to punish the partner, or to attempt to terminate unwanted pregnancies may also be evident. These adverse consequences, it is hypothesized, constitute a significant proportion of the association of courtship violence with younger age dating (Henton et al., 1983;

Makepeace, 1987; Stets and Henderson, 1991). Sexuality-related problems continue, of course, through the ensuing years of courtship, although, as time passes, the adversity of the consequences is mitigated by resource accrual and developmental maturation.

Another important factor to consider is runaway behavior, with which early teen pregnancy and related family conflict are undoubtedly associated. In this respect, it is hypothesized that the intimate associations formed by runaways are an important source of particularly dangerous courtship violence (Garbarino et al., 1986).

High School Courtship

Somewhere around age 15 or 16, a shift of norms from relative proscription to relative prescription of dating and limited sexual intimacy takes place. During this stage, it remains difficult to engage in sexual intimacy without adverse and potentially violent consequences occurring. The couple is permitted more time alone (implicitly for intimacy expression), but many are still lacking in developmental maturity, self-control, and resources (particularly money and contraception) needed for effective management of sexuality. This is *not* to say that full sexual relations are acceptable or that youngsters at this age should be using contraceptives. Rather, it is a recognition of the problematic asynchrony of cultural norms that are permissive of sexual activity but simultaneously restrictive of access to resources needed for effective management of the risks involved.

It is, of course, members of the adult culture—particularly parents and those in the decision-making positions of the schools, government, and economy—who determine the availability of these resources on the one hand and of aggressive marketing of highly eroticized television, magazine, and musical fare on the other. Such adult ambivalence that this represents results in relationship difficulties, pregnancies, running away, courtship violence, and other painful situations among young people.

In addition to the sexual dilemma, the economy presents two extremely problematic forces: automobiles and drugs, particularly alcohol. These forces are so pandemic that it may be asserted that *high school dating culture is a car, sex, and alcohol-party culture.* It is difficult to imagine how such a cultural scripting could be enacted without the terrible and epidemic consequences—such as accidents, fights, depression, anxiety, school and job failures, pregnancies, suicides, dependencies, etc.—that are known to ensue (Garbarino et al., 1986). The frustration that grows out of these problems is hypothesized to be a paramount source of courtship violence and abuse during this period.

During the senior year and particularly its final months, the potential for courtship violence is compounded by yet additional forces, including greatly accelerated emancipation, intensified social activity, and educational–economic transitions. The approach of the eighteenth birthday is felt by many young people to signify liberation from parental accountability and compliance. There is simultaneously an intensification of social activity—proms, banquets, dances, parties, outings, and so forth—that are incipient occasions for sexual, alcohol, drug, and automobile involvements that test many courtship relationships.

At the same time as these activities are taking place, young people are faced with major mobility decisions (such as moving to new jobs or attending college) that are precipitated by our educational and economic institutions. These transitions may arouse abandonment anxiety and conflict among couples who find themselves deficient in the maturity and resources requisite for the peaceful resolution of these difficult issues. Not surprisingly, the rate of courtship violence has been found to be high among eighteen-year-olds in their senior year of high school (Makepeace, unpublished manuscript).

College Dating

The connections of courtship with sexual behavior, mobility, substance abuse, and youth culture continue to exist through college. But, perhaps because of campus social controls, increasing maturity, and an abundant availability of affordable and enjoyable diversions, the rate of courtship violence appears to be lower among college daters than among those who are younger or those who are cohabiting or married (Makepeace, 1989; Stets and Henderson, 1991; Yllö and Straus, 1981).

Willard Waller's famous article, "The Rating and Dating Complex" (1937), depicted college dating as a dalliance arrangement marked by frivolity, thrill bartering, exploitation, and aggression; it promoted the view that instead of dating, young people should be proceeding to the socially useful activities of marriage and family. Alarm about college dating has been sounded again in recent years as awareness of relationship victimization has heightened, and new ameliorative programs have been implemented on many campuses. However, the true magnitude of these problems, the objectivity of the documenting research, and the necessity of such programs has been questioned (Felten, 1991; Morgenson, 1991).

It may well be that the college years are the time when dating is at its functional best in providing for enjoyable diversion, while marriage is delayed in favor of higher education. Although it is true that much of the dating activity of this period is frivolous and thrill oriented, this is not necessarily a negative experience. While competitive "rating," gold digging, and crude sexual aggression such as Waller described are no doubt still present to some degree, and more contemporary indications of acquaintance rape and courtship violence are also problems, a proper assessment would look at these problems in comparative perspective and weigh them against the benefits of the system. It is possible that careful comparative analyses of violence during college with that during high school dating, noncollege dating, and marriage would yield a relatively more benign portrayal than some current reports suggest.

Marital Anticipation

As the college years transpire, the delay of marriage yields to more active marital anticipation; an increasing sense that education is nearing completion; and a rising awareness that it is time to move from parental dependence to adult independence, including marriage, moving away from home, and economic self-sufficiency. Hopeful of these goals, daters increasingly scrutinize partners as potential spouses with whom they might be engaged over the long term in economic provision, lovemaking, parenting, and homemaking. The concerns of previous phases remain, but they are viewed in a changed light. The alcohol consumption that facilitated merriment at college parties may now raise questions about a partner's capacity for sobriety. Speeding tickets or low grades that may earlier have bemused may now signal concern about responsibility. The flirtatiousness that was initially attractive may now cause anxiety about a partner's capacity for monogamous commitment. Because such issues are highly personal and volatile, they may generate acute conflict among dating partners. In some cases, these assessments may result in a view that the relationship is unlikely to work, and painful and violent breakups may ensue.

Engagement Courtship

At some point in the courtship process, a decision to marry may be made and the couple enters an engagement phase. Revised perspectives are likely to evolve at this time regarding such long-standing issues as alcohol use, sexuality, and automobile operation. With regard to sexuality, there is another major change in that the decision to commence sexual relations is much less likely to be an issue than in earlier decades, because the great majority of today's engaged couples are sexually active. Thus, a recent study of 526 couples engaged to be married in the Catholic church and taking mandatory premarital instruction found 94 percent of the couples actively engaged in sexual relations (Faurre and Maddock, 1994). It is to be expected, then, that sex-related disagreements during engagement would more often be about issues of sexual responsiveness, forms, or frequency, rather than about the choice to engage in sexual behavior.

To the extent that engaged partners know one another well and have a long-standing relationship, the issue of predatory courtship violence also seems unlikely to arise as the evidence suggests this to be a habituated disposition that tends to be expressed early in the courtship continuum (Makepeace, 1989). As some older issues wane in relevance, however, new issues once again arise. Among these are the numerous concerns leading up to the wedding, such as the time and place of the wedding, who is to pay for the related expenses, and establishing relationships with one another's families.

Finally, as engagement is a stage of anticipation, couples now imaginatively rehearse their futures and negotiate an implicit marital contract. Many of the matters considered during this "blueprinting" phase are potentially conflictual. Couples must arrange where they will reside, how their home will be furnished and provisioned, whether and when to have children, who will work at what jobs, and how they will support themselves if one or both decide to pursue additional education. They are likely, too, to consider issues of contraception, child care, housekeeping, career paths, the "fit" of their families, possible honeymoons and vacations, savings, and religion. Additional conflicts may arise from matters such as employment opportunities, graduate school admissions, housing availability, and pregnancy because the matters are often beyond the couple's control.

Though these issues are enormously important to the engaged couple's welfare, involve fundamental issues of personal philosophy and life aspiration, and are subject to chance forces, there appears to be a relatively low incidence of engagement violence (Makepeace, 1989). Reasons for this may be that engaged couples are of relatively established compatibility, have routinized their interactive and decision-making styles, and have already implicitly taken many of these matters into consideration via numerous forces that have evolved them toward homogamy. Furthermore, the looming "master issue" during engagement is *pending marriage*, not actual marriage, and it is far easier to "blueprint" how happiness and need satisfaction will be achieved in marriage, than to actually achieve them. In addition, relationships at this stage are undoubtedly fortified by the idealism of the romantic love myth. Although this mythology has been criticized for contributing to courtship violence (Henton ct al., 1983; Lloyd, 1991), it may nevertheless be functional in motivating and sustaining couples to proceed hopefully with the difficult work that, in fact, lies ahead and that may disenchant soon enough.

A comparison of the findings of courtship violence during engagement (Makepeace, 1989) with other phases of courtship corresponds with the foregoing interpretation. Specifically, violence was less likely to have occurred during engagement than during any other stage of courtship; disagreements about sexuality and alcohol also take place less often. Jealousy, the most volatile issue, precipitated more engagement violence than any other behavior. When engagement violence did occur, it was particularly traumatic emotionally.

Cohabitation

Rindfuss and Vanden Heuvel (1990) and Schoen and Weinick (1993) provide overviews of two major themes of cohabitation present in the literature on marriage and the family. The first theme argues that cohabitation is distinct from marriage with "different goals, norms, and behaviors, the relationship more a part of courtship, and the participants more like single people" (Schoen and Weinick, 1993). The second perspective sees cohabitation as more like marriage, albeit informal, or "loosely bonded."

The view adopted here is that cohabitation is simply the sharing of a residence by an intimate heterosexual couple and is distinct from either courtship or marriage, though it may be coincident with either. This view corresponds to the perspective held by young people themselves. Thus, in a recent study, Ford (1994) presented 462 university students with 11 scenarios and asked them if each represented a "family." All respondents considered the traditional nuclear unit as a family and the majority perceived marital status and parental status to be important features when defining a family, and, they tended to exclude cohabiting couples without children, same-sex partners, and certain extended groups. Thus, the majority of these young people did not view cohabitation as a form of marriage.

Empirical research also shows cohabitation to be different from courtship or marriage alone. Although Bumpass, Sweet, and Cherlin incline to the view that cohabitation is like marriage when they state "in many ways currently cohabiting couples resemble married families" (1991: 925), the confusion that results from this view is revealed by the facts that they present. Sixty percent of cohabiting households have no children present; in the 40 percent that include children, many are children from prior marriages and are neither socially nor legally the progeny of the "live in" partner; and many cohabitors do not intend to marry. Indeed, these same authors find (1) that there is a surprisingly high level of disagreement about whether marriage is ever intended; (2) that normative pressures toward marriage are weak; and (3) that cohabitors exhibit less certainty about their relationships than do married couples. This is not to deny that cohabitation is like marriage in some ways. It is, rather, to stress that it is unlike marriage in other important ways, and that the view that cohabitation is courtship or is marriage diverts attention from features of it that may contribute to violence.

If cohabitation were rare and unproblematic, distinguishing it from courtship and marriage might not be important; but there has been a great increase in the practice in recent years, and considerable evidence indicates that it is often dysfunctional—both in its high rate of violence and in the dissatisfaction of marriages that follow it. Thus, whereas cohabitation was rare only twenty-five years ago, 40 percent of U.S. women born from 1958 to 1962 had cohabited before marriage (Schoen and Owens, 1992). Furthermore, the practice is highly characteristic of minority teenagers who have not completed high school and who have borne children. Indeed, normative pressures against unmarried childbearing appear very weak among cohabitors (Bumpass, Sweet, and Cherlin, 1991).

Studies also indicate that rates of violence are high in cohabitation, both in relation to marriage and to other stages of courtship (Lane and Gwartney Gibbs, 1985; Yllö and Straus, 1981; Makepeace, 1989; Stets and Henderson, 1991). This may seem anomalous in the face of the assumption that patriarchal marriage is the principal cause of violence against women, and that liberal, equalitarian alternatives are less violent (Dobash and Dobash, 1979; Walker, 1978). Perhaps for this reason, some scholars have argued that such violence is unrelated to cohabitation per se. Thus, Stets (1991a) attributed her findings of more severe violence among cohabitants not to differences between cohabitation and marriage, but to the different demographic profiles of cohabitants; that is, cohabitants are more often violent because they possess demographic characteristics (black, youthful, and psychologically and behaviorally troubled) that are associated with greater violence in general, not because of the nature of cohabitation. This view, however, is not supported by the empirical and theoretical considerations that will be discussed next.

Cohabitation is, first of all, coincident with various stages of courtship—that is, cohabitants are often also dating or engaged. It is reasonable to assume, then, that cohabitation would be susceptible to a double dose of problems. Cohabitating couples would experience many of the same courtship-stage frustrations as other daters and, in addition, would be susceptible to conflicts that derive from living in close association under one roof, such as disputes about housekeeping, noise levels, space utilization, furnishings, bill paying, meal preparation, socializing, and entertaining. While such difficulties are also experienced by many married couples, they do not derive solely from the marital status itself. Rather, they come from living together under one roof, and they apply whether the couple is married or not.

Finally, a form of frustration more particular to cohabitation is its normative ambivalence. The National Survey of Families and Households found that a surprisingly high proportion of cohabitants not only disagree about whether they will marry, but express concern about the stability of their relationships (Bumpass, Sweet, and Cherlin, 1991: 925–926). Similarly, Faurre and Maddock examined the sexual meanings of cohabiting partners and found them to be significantly more discrepant than those of noncohabiting or married couples. They write, "if individual meaning systems are in significant conflict, the resulting hostile environment might contribute to . . . violence" (1994: 59). Presumably this reasoning would apply not only to sexual meanings, but to the many areas of normative discord that characterize cohabitation.

In short, the rate of violence among cohabitants is high—higher than in marriage or in any other stage of courtship except "first dates" during which the special case of predatory violence is concentrated. And, cohabital violence is not anomalous; it has distinct features that would logically predispose it to greater frustration and aggression.

Correlates and Perspectives

Until recently, the study of courtship violence tended to be largely atheoretical, with little systematic testing of theory. As with interpersonal violence in general (Miller and Wellford, chapter 1), many early studies attribute courtship violence to psychopathology, family dysfunction, conflict, and multifactor perspectives. Although there is insufficient space to review or critique these perspectives properly, this section briefly describes the central insights and some limitations of each perspective.

Psychopathology

According to the psychopathology perspective, courtship violence is caused by mental abnormality. While a wide variety of recognized perceptual and mood disorders—such as dysphoria, schizophrenia, paranoia, anxiety, and illusions—could be causally related to courtship violence, little research on specific disorders exists. The few studies that have been done, along with related work on spouse abuse, however, are of some help. Bernard and Bernard (1984) examined Minnesota Multiphasic Personality Inventory (MMPI) profiles of abusive males and found that such men exhibit significant pathology, including abnormal levels of jealousy, anger, and control. Their interpretation of the data was, however, impressionistic; they did not indicate rates of specific diagnoses or address whether the problems had preceded the violence. Still, their findings correspond with this summary of the literature on wife batterers:

> As a group, batterers have an identifiable set of personal characteristics: dependent, anxious, low self-esteem, paranoia, dissociation from . . . feelings, poor impulse con-

trol, antisocial tendencies, hostility toward women. . . . there is psychopathology in many men who batter (Vaselle-Augenstein and Ehrlich, 1992: 139).

Yet, methodological and theoretical questions may be raised about this conclusion. First of all, most of the evidence cited consists of statistically significant differences between groups of men who had battered and men who had not. Yet, such differences could easily be of statistical but not of substantive significance; particularly with large samples, statistically significant intergroup differences may be found even though the differences between members of the two groups are quite small. Secondly, such statistical differences could easily be due to the presence in the "batterer" groups of only small proportions of highly deviant men, while the overwhelming majority of the men in the two groups may not differ at all. Finally, even if the "batterers" do differ from the "nonbatterers," the question of causal direction still remains. As Rosenbaum and O'Leary (1981) and Telch and Lindquist (1984) have indicated, the troubled personality characteristics that have been ascribed to batterers are found among most men who experience marital difficulty. Therefore, both psychological difficulties and violence may be consequences of the relationship difficulties rather than the violence being caused by psychopathology. Vaselle-Augenstein and Ehrlich counter with the observation that when concurrent marital difficulty has been controlled in a number of studies, batterers were still found to differ significantly "on some measures from nonbatterers who were maritally unhappy, and the differences were always in the expected direction" (1992: 147). While this lends some weight to their position, however, it is also the case that batterers *did not* differ from nonbatters in some of the asserted directions, and the remaining differences could still be due to the other methodological difficulties indicated above.

One study of courtship violence took a somewhat different approach to this problem. Rather than examining the traits of the participants, Makepeace (1989) investigated the nature of the violent events and compared these across different types of relationships. The findings show some courtship violence to be distinctly methodical, habituated, sexual, and brutal. Described as "predatory," this violence is particularly prevalent in first-date situations and relatively rare in later stages of courtship. Some studies of spouse abusers have found similar character types: Hamberger and Hastings's (1986) "Group 4" batterer—angry, aggressive, and antisocial; Gondolf's (1988) "sociopathic" batterer; and Hanks's (1992) Type III, "habitual violent interpersonal style." Gondolf (1988) estimates that these types account for only about 7 percent of batterers.

Attention has also been directed to the psychological makeup of female victims. In this respect, Hanks argues that (1992: 160) "There is no direct evidence that battered women have a clinically diagnosable character disorder to a greater extent than non-battered women." In contrast, Makepeace (1986) compared the profiles of males and females who had experienced courtship violence and found a wide variety of characterological problems to be as prevalent among female victims as among male assailants.

Lastly, the association of low self-esteem with courtship violence has been considered in a number of published reports, with mixed results. Self-esteem was not significantly related to courtship violence in Makepeace (1987) or in Burke, Stets, and Pirog-Good (1988). Conversely, inverse associations of esteem with courtship violence have been found by Deal and Wampler (1986) and Stets and Pirog-Good (1987).

Family Dysfunction

This perspective views courtship violence as being a product of adverse features of the home environment, particularly a family background in which violent values and behaviors were taught or modeled or from which skills and resources needed for coping with frustration were not acquired. Most important in this vein is the learning theory that proceeds from the central insights that violence is learned via observation and imitation of role models and that imitated behavior which is reinforced will tend to be continued (Bandura, Ross, and Ross, 1961; Bandura, 1973).

Learning theory has been the most widely used perspective in the courtship violence literature. Its most prominent formulation, the intergenerational transmission (IGT) hypothesis, proposes that persons who engage in partner abuse do so because they learned abusiveness from parents who abused them or one another. In reviewing this research, Sugarman and Hotaling concluded that there is little evidence in support of intergenerational transmission (1989: 17). In fact, however, the weight of the evidence is quite supportive, though the relationship is not as strong and direct as the hypothesis suggests, and the effect may vary considerably depending on gender and whether inflicted or sustained violence is considered. Thus, for example, seven of the twelve studies they reviewed found a positive relationship between childhood maltreatment and later use of dating violence; those studies that did not tended to be characterized by use of multivariate statistical techniques and relatively small samples, a combination that may make statistical significance extremely difficult to attain, even when relationships are real and relatively large. Nevertheless, the intergenerational transmission hypothesis does not explain why some violent daters do not come from violent homes or why there are so many nonviolent persons who do come from violent homes. Furthermore, important questions remain about intervening factors, such as the degree to which offspring model the behavior of same versus opposite gendered parent as well as the relative influence of parents versus other possible role models, for instance, peers, partners, or figures in the mass media. (For a review of these issues, see Bernard and Bernard, 1983; Cate et al., 1982; Gwartney Gibbs, Stockard, and Bohmer, 1987; Kalmuss, 1984; Roscoe and Benaske, 1985; Malone, Tyree, and O'Leary, 1989; and Barnes, Greenwood, and Sommer, 1991.)

Conflict/Patriarchy

General conflict theory begins with the premise that conflict is normal and that the central question for theory is how groups use power to maintain social order and control (Coser, 1956). This perspective was employed by Collins (1971) in a brief consideration of courtship violence, but then lay dormant for some years.

A version of conflict theory in the spouse abuse literature holds that violence against women is the result of *patriarchy,* the institutionalization of male privilege that is maintained by the legally and socially supported right of men to use violence to enforce the subordination of women (Dobash and Dobash, 1979). Walker's (1978) patriarchy theory also explains that repeated exposure to violence results in a condition of depression and incapacity to act self-defensively called "learned helplessness." In an examination of the help-seeking behavior of victims of courtship violence, however, the findings showed that victims of severe courtship abuse were not less likely than victims of less severe abuse to seek help. The authors thus conclude that they found "no evidence . . . to support the hypothesis of learned helplessness" (Pirog-Good and Stets, 1989: 123). Technically, however, it is repetition of violence over time that Walker sees as producing learned helplessness, not simply the severity of the abuse.

Applying patriarchy theory to courtship violence, Lloyd (1991) and Rosen and Stith (1993) focused on male control and the romantic love myth. In Lloyd's formulation

> two features of courtship . . . encourage the use of exploitative behavior. . . . First, the different context of courtship for males vs. females encourages male control of relationships and female compliance. . . . Second, the highly romanticized nature of courtship encourages partners to stay together. . . . Patriarchy as used here refers to the financial and emotional dependence of women on men. . . . Romanticism allows violence to be easily downplayed, as violence is attributed to external factors and not to a fundamental flaw in the relationship (1991: 14).

While intuitively satisfying, some research on gender, attitudinal, and relationship correlates is not confirmatory. Patriarchy theory holds that women are the principal victims of courtship violence, and that this is due to male control. Yet, research indicates that women neither less often inflict nor more often sustain courtship violence, nor are they less controlling of dating relationships than men (Plass and Gessner, 1983; Makepeace, 1986; Carlson, 1990; Stets, 1991b; Stets and Henderson, 1991; Barnes, Greenwood, and Sommer, 1991; Fallingstad et al., 1991). Therefore, "to say that patriarchy . . . helps us understand dating aggression says nothing about why women are aggressive" (Stets and Henderson, 1991: 35).

Similarly, the assumption that romantic values contribute to courtship violence seems contradicted by research showing that daters who are more romantic and traditional are less, not more, often involved in courtship violence (Makepeace, 1987; Alexander et al., 1991). Furthermore, as the theory of patriarchy holds couple violence to be caused by gender inequities of power and resources, it would be expected that relationships that are more equalitarian would be less violent. In her review of the cohabitation literature, Macklin (1983) found cohabiting couples to be more unconventional in their roles, to hold more liberal attitudes, and to view themselves as androgynous and more liberated from traditional sex roles than non-cohabitors. Yet, cohabitors have consistently been found to be *more* violent than either non-cohabiting or married couples (Makepeace, 1989; Lane and Gwartney Gibbs, 1985; Yllö and Straus, 1981).

Finally, systems therapists following the perspective of Bateson have argued that the indictment of male control is epistemologically invalid (because unidirectional causation is impossible in any system) and inherently destructive of the goals of therapy (Dell, 1989). Coinciding with this, a recent study found that women who had sought to redress dating difficulties by focusing on power and blaming their partners had more often experienced violence in relationships (Bird, Stith, and Schladale, 1991).

A recent direction in conflict theory has been to focus upon violence as a negotiating strategy and on the factors that lead partners to employ it. Lloyd, Koval, and Cate (1989) found, for example, that conflicted couples who resorted to violence were characterized by a belief that change was possible, high investment in their relationship, and persistence of attempts to get their partners to change.

Multi-Analytic Approaches

Theories which include multiple-analytic perspectives seem most promising since it seems unlikely that all courtship violence can be explained by any single factor such as psychopathology, intergenerational transmission, stress, or patriarchy. Systems and exchange-resource theories are examples of multifactor approaches that have been prominent in the family violence field. Systems theorists view behavior as the result of multiple factors that are inextricably interrelated and exist at a number of different levels, for example, at the biological, the microsystemic, the mesosystemic, the exosystemic, and the macrosystemic levels in the Garbarino (1977) formulation. Other family violence systems theory efforts include those of Bateson (previously discussed) and Steinmetz and Straus (1974). Whereas systems theories explain human behavior "from the outside" and at multiple levels, exchange-resource theories are social and psychological in nature and focus on the person as "economically" calculating—that is, as perceiving options and interacting and engaging in exchanges with other people that they perceive will be most profitable and least costly (Goode, 1971; Gelles, 1983).

Formal efforts at integrated theories of courtship violence have begun to appear, but may suffer the same difficulty of such theories in other—that is, of being too complex to be testable or predictively useful. A recent (untested) effort by Riggs and O'Leary (1989) sought to overcome this problem by separating factors into two tiers: contextual factors to predict who will behave aggressively against a partner and situational factors to predict situations in which aggression will occur. Another model (Burke, Stets, and Pirog-Good, 1988) appears more manageable for testing and prediction. Each of these, however, lacks the comprehensive scope that seems the greatest (but difficult to test) promise of systems theory.

Finally, there are numerous studies that examine the separate associations of multiple factors with courtship violence without regard to their integration in theoretical or statistical models. While it would be impossible to provide a comprehensive review of these studies in the space available, such research has identified many relationships that merit mention. As a compromise, the following section will review findings of what, in scale of the study and comprehensiveness of the factors considered, is one of the most definitive of such studies (Makepeace, 1987). Factors are categorized according to background, life experiences, and character variables, although obviously the factors (italicized) sometimes overlap the categories.

Background Factors. Involvement in courtship violence commences at an early age—the majority of respondents (54 percent) reported their first experience to have occurred at age 16 to 18. Courtship violence varied substantially according to *racial/ethnic group*, being moderate to moderately high among the three largest groups in the United States (whites, 16.1 percent; blacks, 28.9 percent; Hispanics, 23.9 percent), exceedingly high (45.5 percent) for the "other" category, and exceedingly low for Asians (4.8 percent). Those identifying with well-established Christian *religions* (Protestant, Catholic, Mormon) had moderate courtship violence rates, while the rate was high (28.8 percent) among those indicating no religion and exceedingly low for Jewish respondents (5.9 percent). Rates increased steadily with *community size. College type* was important, with the rate lowest at a small, residential, church-related college (8.2 percent), intermediate at midwestern land-grant universities (13.3 percent; 11.4 percent), and highest at open enrollment public institutions (22.0 percent; 22.2 percent). *Family income* was of only marginal importance.

Life Experiences. Those with the following life experiences had more involvement in courtship violence: family backgrounds involving *absent, emotionally distant, or harsh parents; school difficulties* (low grades, suspensions, expulsions); difficulties in *employment;* and having begun *dating at an early age.*

Character Dispositions. The recent lives of those with courtship violence experience had involved more *stress.* Courtship violence was also more prevalent among those holding equalitarian *gender role values. Social isolation* (having relatively few active social relationships with friends, family members, and neighbors) was associated with greater involvement in courtship violence. *Low self-esteem* and *support for other forms of social violence* (such as capital punishment and war) were not related.

In general, the most important of the factor groups was life experience, that is, difficulties in the family, school, and employment. The most highly associated individual factors were ethnicity (Asian) and religion (Jewish), each being inversely related. These were analyzed as background factors but may be reflective of life experience factors, namely, family cohesiveness and the belief in the value of educational and occupational attainment.

Towards a Developmental Theory of Courtship Violence

Humans exhibit little evidence of innate dispositions to mate, bear, or rear offspring, though these activities are necessary for the continuation of society. Society, therefore, devises institutional arrangements that include them and induce participation in them via socialization and social control. The major forms of intimate relationships are stages in this larger integrated process termed the socio-reproductive dialectic—socio-reproductive because it is concerned with the regeneration of society's membership; dialectical in that it cycles, or "spirals," through the lives of individuals and through history. This dialectic is composed of the three familiar stages of mate selection, reproduction, and socialization. Each has identifiable points of inception and termination and is the focus of the activity of a minimal social group.

Mate selection is the stage of seeking and selecting a heterosexual partner. The minimal unit, which may be formed and dissolved many times, is the courting pair. Its inception is at the "coming out"—the gradual, but nonetheless real, entry of the young person into active partnering activity. It terminates, typically, with marriage.

Reproduction involves sexual union, gestation, prenatal caring, anticipatory arrangement making, and childbirth. The acting social group is the married couple—the male and female who together undertake and accomplish these events. This stage begins with the reproductive sexual act and ends with conception.

Socialization involves the extraordinary complex of activities necessary for human offspring to survive and eventually function in society. The minimal unit is the parent–child relationship, though there are compelling societal and individual advantages for cooperation of two parents, a mother and a father. This stage commences with conception and concludes with emancipation—another imprecise but real transition event.

Again, this process is real, integrated, and compelled by natural facts of human biology and societal need, and society's endurance depends on its social construction of courtship, marriage, and parentage, and induction of participants into them. Toward that end, society romanticizes and idealizes the entire dialectic, encourages the young in its direction, sanctifies and civilly binds it, and dispenses a wide variety of sanctions that encourage perseverance through it.

In general, the socio-reproductive script that prevails in American courtship calls for sober, affectionate, romantic, heterosexual, monogamous relationships that are focused in early phases on recreational pleasure and, increasingly in later phases, on anticipatory socialization for marriage. Fulfillment of this script is taken to be in line with the needs of American society (Scanzoni and Marsiglio, 1993; Ganong, Coleman, and Mapes, 1990; Bernardes, 1986; Mintz and Kellogg, 1988; Hogan, 1978, 1980); in providing for affection (Bellah et al., 1985; Popenoe, 1988, 1993); reducing individual insecurity "by making past events more readily understandable and future events more easily predictable" (Orbuch, Veroff, and Holmberg, 1993: 815); and helping participants avoid the adverse consequences of deviations (Mancini, 1978, 1984; McLaughlin et al., 1986; McLanahan and Adams, 1987).

Socio-reproductive activity is inherently rewarding in many respects. In others, though, it is complex and difficult. Particularly challenging is the abiding tension between society's need for its members' perseverance in the dialectic and various hedonistic and brutal inclinations that they may feel, such as aggression and polygamy, but that may be disruptive of that perseverance. Strategically, then, a major problem confronting society is to induce sufficient numbers of people to participate in need-ed socio-reproductive activity while controlling contrary or disruptive dispositions such as violence. Much toward this end is accomplished via socialization, which con-ditions in numerous ways the expression of violence in later life. For example, the young person is taught that one may gain satisfaction of desires by exchanges of affec-tion, goods, services, or honor-conferring symbols, but that the use of force is gener-ally not acceptable (Goode, 1971; Gelles, 1982).

While it is learned that violence is proscribed, the proscription is only partial in that numerous counter-norms tacitly endorse, authorize, and even honor violence (Viano, 1992: 3–7; Goode, 1971). It is readily observed, for example, that the state maintains a preparedness at all times to engage in the most severe forms of violence, if necessary, to maintain social order and its own power. Even parents are given the authority to spank, paddle, restrain, and withhold food from their children as they rea-sonably deem necessary to render them compliant. Specific skills and information supporting interpersonal violence are also continually taught in society. Thus, chil-dren observe violence and its rationales modeled by their parents, see it in television programming, and are trained via sports in such skills as restraining, pushing, tack-ling, clubbing, kicking, wrestling, throwing, punching, and shooting.

Socialization is simultaneously very much about inculcating the prescription of participation in the socio-reproductive dialectic. Most fundamentally, it is taught that appropriate intimate relationships are among society's most honored social arrange-ments, as are all customs that mirror or dispose people toward them. This includes courtship, because it involves the rehearsal of pair relationships, and eventually, the selection of a partner for marriage. Moreover, it is taught that "respectable" people devote most of their lives to fulfilling the dialectic—indeed, that it is life's "master script."

Reaching adolescence, then, youth have been conditioned to two related com-plexes of norms—one partially proscribing the use of force; and the other prescribing participation in courtship. Unfortunately—and this is crucial to the etiology of courtship violence—there are numerous occasions when simultaneous compliance with both bodies of norms is difficult. The cultural pressure is to enact courtship rela-tionships of a highly idealized type the attainment of which is, at times, beyond the capabilities and resources of many young people. These pressures are generally benign in intent, but not always so in their effects. Thus, most parents wish their chil-dren well and partners hope for the best in one another. An abundance of television and magazine fare depicts courtship as harmonious and enjoyable; participants as con-fident, attractive, and socially skilled; and all problems as surmountable. Yet, more real for many during these years are loneliness; not being asked out; fear of approaching potential partners; painful rejections; inadequate resources for gaining attention and favorably impressing; and difficulty resisting the powerful temptations of sex, alcohol, and automobiles, which the economy presents in the most alluring manner possible.

Young people frequently find themselves, then, confronting two somewhat con-tradictory normative complexes: first, the expectation of establishing and maintaining the prescribed courtship relationships and, second, the expectation that they will do so only with socially approved resources. When it seems very difficult or impossible to comply with both of these norms, as often happens, there arises a tendency to "compromise" the second norm in order to fulfill the first. When, in this compromise, the illegitimate resource of physical force is deployed against the courtship partner, the event is courtship violence.

Summary

The preceding pages have adumbrated the beginnings of a developmental model that would integrate both theoretical insights and empirical information about courtship violence. The model posits aggression as an innate response to frustration, and intimacy, the giving and receiving of affection, as an innate need. Contemporary American culture assigns the fulfillment of this need primarily to relationships within the socio-reproductive dialectic—parenting, courtship, and marriage. The attainment of intimacy thereby becomes an incentive among members of the culture to accomplish the activities needed for society to endure.

The normative prescription for courtship is the pair relationship with the previously indicated qualities. These qualities both reflect and anticipate similar affectional bonds and recreational orientations that are prescribed for marriage and parenting. More specifically, the norms prescribe the expected attitudes, behaviors, and forms of courtship according to age, development, and standing relationship to collateral institutions of family, education, and economy. Culture members internalize these prescriptions as personal desires. It is the frustration of the desire to fulfill these developmental prescriptions that, when the preconscious and innate disposition to aggress in response to frustration has not been sufficiently extinguished via socialization, is the principal cause of courtship violence.

Courtship violence builds upon normative foundations concerning violence and intimacy that are established during parent–child relationships. It contributes, in turn, to a repository of skills and cognitions that condition the occurrence of violence and the corrosion of affection in later marriage (O'Leary et al., 1989; Roscoe and Benaske, 1985; Kelly, Huston, and Cate, 1985).

The model is advanced as integrative. It supplements rather than rejects other perspectives. It accepts the innate disposition to violence of frustration-aggression and biological theorists; it posits psychopathology, learning, and family dysfunctionality as important influences on the manner of expression of aggression; it grants the strategizing and resource exchanging disposition of the person; and it recognizes that macrological arrangements have an important influence on the rates and nature of violence within society (though, to take account of current empirical evidence, the theory of patriarchy, per se, is in need of revision).

While the foregoing description of courtship is somewhat idealized (that is the nature of the norms of a dominant culture) and reflects the author's impression of the current "master scripting" of American courtship, it is recognized that society has, in reality, multiple scripts that have varying degrees of social support and that change over time. Rejected, however, is the view that there has been an "irremediable collapse of cultural . . . consensus on a normative family ideology" (Stacey, 1993: 546) in the United States. No society can endure without the normative foundation of a socio-reproductive dialectic.

A central implication of this perspective is the need for a theoretical and research agenda that specifies the developmental interconnections between socio-reproductive scripting and violence. On the basis of such process-oriented work, developmental issues that are most viable for policy interventions to reduce courtship violence could be identified and thus contribute to the scientific goal of full and detailed understanding of this problem and the humanitarian goal of relieving it.

3

Violence in Marriage: Until Death Do Us Part?

ANGELA BROWNE

The Better Homes Foundation

Individuals who are dating or living together often look forward to marriage and the security that the more formal legal, financial, and social ties can provide. Sometimes, however, the very links that bind married couples together make it more difficult to disclose aggression or safely escape from an intimate partner. Abuse in couple relationships may include intense criticisms and put-downs, verbal harassment, name-calling, sexual coercion and assault, physical attack and threat, restraint of normal activities and freedoms, and denial of access to resources such as money, employment, transportation, and friendships (Sonkin, Martin, and Walker, 1985). This chapter focuses primarily on acts of aggression with the potential to cause physical injury, sexual force or threat, and threats to kill or to harm.

Incidence, Prevalence, and Severity of Marital Violence

Physical Assault

Until the mid-1970s, very few researchers and policymakers inquired about the prevalence of violence between husbands and wives. Families, it was assumed, provided shelter and support for their members. It was thought that women, in particular, were protected by the presence of a husband and were safer inside rather than outside of the home. Today we know that physical assault and threat has been, all along, the hidden

48

subtext in the lives of many married and formerly married couples. In the first national representative survey of violence in families conducted in 1975, over one-quarter—28 percent—of married couples reported at least one physical assault occurring between them (Straus, Gelles, and Steinmetz, 1980). A Harris poll during the same period found that over one-fifth of all women surveyed had been physically attacked by a male partner at least once as an adult (Schulman, 1979). This number was much higher for women who were recently separated or divorced. The National Crime Survey for 1980 indicated that individuals assaulted by their intimates were more likely to sustain physical injury than those accosted by strangers and that three-fifths of the attacks by family members occurred at night, when the victims were "home safe."

Although the succeeding years have seen a dramatic increase in national awareness of violence between partners and in legal and social responses, rates of marital violence remain high. A second National Family Violence Survey, conducted in 1985, revealed that nearly one out of every eight husbands had physically assaulted their wives during the twelve months prior to the survey (Straus and Gelles, 1990). Despite the popular idea that "domestic" assaults are relatively minor, one-third of these assaults involved severe aggression, such as punching, kicking, beating up, and threatening with or using a knife or gun. These figures would mean that at least two million women are severely assaulted by male partners in an average twelve-month period in the United States, based solely on acts of violence that individuals are willing to report.

As high as these figures seem, they actually underestimate the problem. National statistics on marital violence are based on self-reports obtained through telephone surveys or in-person interviews with individuals who are at home at the time interviewers call and who are willing to talk with strangers about such a sensitive topic. Estimates are based only on those respondents willing to report to an unknown interviewer—even anonymously—acts of aggression they have experienced or perpetrated in their intimate relationships. In addition, nationally "representative" surveys omit the very poor; those who do not speak English fluently; all individuals who are hospitalized, homeless, institutionalized, or incarcerated at the time the survey is conducted; and all military families living on base. Experts now believe that the true incidence of violence between married partners might be double the existing estimates—or four million women severely assaulted each year—and that one in every three women will be physically attacked by a male partner at least once during adulthood.

Sometimes it is easier to grasp the dimensions of a problem by breaking it down into smaller segments. In 1991, over 21,000 assaults, rapes, and murders of women by their male partners were reported to the police every week (U.S. Senate Committee on the Judiciary, 1992). These numbers leave out the majority of physical and sexual assaults by men against intimates, which occur in private, often without witnesses, and rarely become known to the police. Types of physical abuse reported by women with violent mates range from being slapped, punched with a fist, kicked, or thrown bodily to being hit with objects, scalded with hot liquid, cut, choked, or bitten (Browne, 1987; Pagelow, 1981; Walker, 1984). In relationships with ongoing male violence, assaultive incidents often involve a combination of physical intimidation, physically or sexually assaultive acts, verbal abuse, and threats. Abusive episodes may range from a burst of aggression that lasts only a few minutes to an ongoing ordeal that continues for hours or even days.

Sexual Assault

Like physical assaults, most sexual assaults on women are perpetrated by current or former male intimates. A recent survey of a national sample of 4,008 women indicated that over 13 percent (or the equivalent of twelve million women) had experienced at least one forcible rape during their lifetimes. *Seventy-eight* percent of the forcible rapes identified in this study were perpetrated by family members or acquaintances. In-depth studies further document the risk of sexual assault by male partners, as opposed to acquaintances or strangers (Russell, 1982; Finkelhor and Yllö, 1985; Wyatt et al., 1992). Using a conservative definition of rape (vaginal intercourse only), a random sample study in California found that 62 percent of all rapes and attempted rapes identified in the study were perpetrated by current or former husbands, boyfriends, lovers, or male relatives (Russell, 1982). *Fourteen percent* of ever-married women reported at least one rape by a husband or ex-husband; more than twice as many as were sexually assaulted by acquaintances or strangers. A representative sample in an East Coast city yielded similar results; more than twice as many women were raped by marital or cohabiting partners than by other types of assailants (Finkelhor and Yllö, 1985).

Rape by male partners seems to occur most frequently as a form of physical domination in relationships in which other forms of physical aggression are ongoing (Frieze and Browne, 1985). In studies of relationships in which male violence occurs, from 35 to 59 percent of their female partners experience sexual as well as nonsexual attack. Contrary to the assumption that violence perpetrated by strangers is more serious than violence by intimates, the closer the relationship between rapist and victim, the greater the level of aggression and the potential for injury (Pagelow, 1984). Research on assaults by men against their wives indicates that the most violent incidents often include sexual as well as physical attacks. Women with sexually aggressive partners have a higher risk of experiencing more severe and injurious nonsexual aggression than women with male partners who are physically but not sexually violent (Frieze and Browne, 1989; Browne, 1992; Shields and Hanneke, 1983).

The Question of Mutual Violence

Of course, both women and men can be verbally or physically aggressive. Some surveys indicate that just about as many women as men have perpetrated at least one of the behaviors listed on a scale (shove, slap, punch, kick, beat up, etc.) at least one time during their current relationship. Based on these reports, some researchers contend that women are about "as violent as men" in couple relationships (Straus and Gelles, 1990;

Stets and Straus, 1990). However, the potential for severe bodily harm when being kicked, punched with a fist, choked, or beaten up by a typical unarmed woman versus a typical unarmed man simply cannot be equated. To adequately assess the "equality" of violence, it is important to know the relative size and strength of the perpetrator and the victim, the force with which an action was carried out, and the impact in terms of injury (Browne, 1993). Finally, assertions that women and men are "equally violent" in couple relationships fail to include the prevalence or impact of forcible sexual assaults, virtually all of which are carried out by men. The same surveys used to assert that women and men are "equally violent" in marriage relationships identify the following (Straus et al., 1980; Stets and Straus, 1990):

- Men perpetrate more aggressive actions against their female partners than women do against their male partners.
- Men perpetrate more severe actions, at least by the name of the action (e.g., punch, kick, choke, beat up, threaten with or use a knife or gun).
- Men are more likely to perpetrate multiple aggressive actions during a single incident.
- Women are much more likely to be injured during attacks by male partners than men are during attacks by female partners.

Simplified equations regarding intimate violence also fail to incorporate information on physical intimidation or on the role that unequal strength plays in the options available to the targets during an assault. As Pagelow (1984: 274) has observed: "Men are, on the average, larger and muscularly stronger than women, so if they choose to strike back they can do greater physical harm than is done to them, they can nonviolently protect themselves from physical harm, or they can leave the premises without being forcibly restrained."

A recognition of the potential for severe physical harm deeply affects the way in which women respond to actual or threatened assaults by opposite-sex partners. It is unlikely that very many unarmed women, even with a punch or a kick, would put their mates in fear of severe bodily harm or of death. Yet physical danger is a powerful dynamic in assaultive male/female interactions (Browne, 1987, 1993).

Physical Outcomes of Partner Violence

In terms of severity of injury for victims of violence, national surveys show sharp gender differences in the physical outcomes of partner violence. The greatest risk for men of injurious or life-threatening physical or sexual assault by intimates is during childhood and adolescence—primarily from siblings, adult relatives, and close family friends. As adults, men are at greater risk of violence from acquaintances and strangers than from their wives or girlfriends, with the majority of their assailants being other males. Compared to the dangers men face from the violence of other men, the risk of severe physical injury or death from their wives is quite low.

In contrast, a woman's risk of injurious or life-threatening assault at the hands of a male partner is higher than from any other type of assailant (Browne, 1992). Women assaulted by male partners are more likely to be repeatedly attacked, injured, raped, or even killed in contrast to women accosted by acquaintances or strangers (Browne and Williams, 1989, 1993; Langan and Innes, 1986; Stets and Straus, 1990). This repetition and severity of aggression is facilitated by the fact that an intimate partner is readily available, the amount of time at risk is high, assaults can be carried out in private when the target is completely off-guard, and assaults against a wife are still a relatively low-risk behavior for a perpetrator in terms of identification or severe sanctions (Gillespie, 1989).

Injuries sustained by women as a result of marital violence range from bruises, cuts, black eyes, concussions, broken bones, and miscarriages to permanent injuries—such as damage to joints, partial loss of hearing or vision, scars from burns, bites, or knife wounds, or even death (Browne, 1987; Walker, 1984). Women assaulted by male partners may have medical evidence of old injuries such as fractures, strained or torn ligaments, and bruises in various stages of healing. Multiple injuries and injuries to the head, chest, and abdomen are also frequently seen in women who have been attacked by male partners, but are rarely seen in males who are victims of assaults by their wives (Browne, 1992; Burge, 1989).

Studies in medical settings give some idea of how serious partner violence is for women. A records review of 3,676 randomly selected patients in a large urban hospital in the late 1970s, funded by the National Institute of Mental Health, led to estimates that 21 percent of all women using emergency surgical services were there for physical outcomes of partner violence, that one-half of all injuries presented by women occurred in the context of partner violence, and that over one-half of all rapes to women over the age of thirty were partner rapes (Stark et al., 1981). Studies conducted in medical settings more recently confirm these early findings and often yield even higher estimates. In a recent study conducted in a large, community-based family practice clinic, more than one-third (39 percent) of all women coming into the practice for regular appointments during a two-month period had experienced at least one physical assault by a male partner as an adult. One-quarter (25 percent) had sustained injuries (Hamberger, Saunders, and Hovey, 1992). Among those women living with, or recently separated or divorced from, partners during the twelve months prior to the study, 25 percent had experienced a physical assault from that same partner and 15 percent had been injured.

Assaults During Pregnancy

Women who are pregnant and involved with an assaultive partner face the risk of especially severe outcomes (Saltzman, 1990). Although we do not know if the incidence of marital violence increases during pregnancy, we know it does not cease. In the 1985 National Family Violence Survey, 154 of every 1,000 pregnant women were assaulted by their mates during the first four months of pregnancy, and 170 of every 1,000 women were assaulted the fifth through the ninth month (Gelles, 1988). Studies based in medical settings yield higher estimates. Medical sources now suggest that up to 37 percent of obstetric patients—across all class, race, and educational lines—are physically attacked by an intimate partner sometime during the three trimesters (Helton, McFarlane, and Anderson, 1987, 1992). Pregnancy is a particularly high-risk time for physical injury. Advanced stages of pregnancy leave a woman less able to avoid blows or escape attacks and more at risk for injuries to herself as well as to the fetus.

Lethal Outcomes of Partner Violence

Data on homicides in the United States further illustrate the potential severity of partner violence, as well as the differential risks for women and men. During the four years from 1988 through 1991, the deaths of 7,168 individuals age sixteen and over were the result of one partner killing another; this figure includes currently and formerly married, common-law, and dating partners. Of these deaths, nearly *two-thirds*—64 percent—were women killed by male partners, and 36 percent were men killed by women partners. Men are overwhelmingly the perpetrators of homicide in the United States. They account for 88.5 percent of all homicides committed by adults—most of these directed against strangers and acquaintances—and have higher rates of all types of homicide, including partner homicide. In contrast, women rarely kill other people, accounting for only 11.5 percent of homicides committed by adults. When women do kill, they are most likely to kill their male partners, but their rates of partner homicide are only about half the rate for men. Whereas most male homicide victims are killed by strangers and acquaintances and usually by other men, women face the greatest risk of lethal assault from men and from their intimates. Again, some groups of minority women are at especially high risk for lethal assault. For example, during the period from 1976 to 1984, the homicide victimization rate for African American women exceeded not only that for Caucasian women, but for Caucasian men as well (O'Carroll and Mercy, 1986).

National statistics on homicide are derived from Supplementary Homicide Reports, and are a compilation of incident reports filed by police at the time of the incident and collected by the FBI as a part of its Uniform Crime Reporting program. These reports contain only a brief description of the context of the homicide (e.g., domestic argument or drug-related), the means used to kill, and the relationship between victims and perpetrators if known to the police. Because these reports do not contain information about prior interactions of specific couples, no national estimates are available on the number of partner homicides that involve a history of physical assault and threat prior to the lethal incident. More detailed studies of homicides in cities and counties do indicate that a significant proportion of partner homicides by women are in response to their partners' aggression and threats. For example, women are much more likely than men to kill during an incident in which their partner was the first to use violence or to kill to avert an incident in which they believe that they or a child will be seriously hurt or killed (Browne, 1987; Jurik and Winn, 1990; Maguigan, 1991).

Because of the link between homicides by women and violence against women by male partners, researchers have theorized that the presence of resources to allow threatened women to escape or be protected from a partner's violence may act to off-set at least some of the killings that otherwise occur in desperation and self-defense. An analysis of national trends in partner homicide from 1976 through 1984 in fact revealed a sharp decrease—over a 25 percent decline—in the numbers of women who killed male partners during this period (Browne and Williams, 1989). This decrease began in 1979, at about the same time that domestic violence legislation and community resources for battered women were becoming established in most of the fifty states (Schechter, 1982). Further investigation revealed that states with more domestic violence legislation and other resources for abused women (e.g., funding for battered women's shelters, crisis lines, legal aid) had lower rates of homicide by all women against male partners; moreover, the presence of resources for women in danger from male partners was correlated with the general decrease in partner homicides by women during these years.

Unfortunately, this sharp decline in women killing male partners was not matched by a similarly steep decline in partner homicides by men. In fact, from 1976 through 1987, the rate of men killing nonmarital intimate partners (women they were or had been dating or living with) increased significantly (Browne and Williams, 1993). This increase occurred despite the domestic violence legislation and other resources for women with violent mates that were established during those same years. Although the national rate of husbands killing wives has declined since the mid-1980s, the decline has not been as sharp as the decrease in wives killing husbands.

Special Risk Factors: Poverty and Ethnicity

As a group, ethnically diverse women and women living in poverty are at especially high risk for all types of violence, but particularly for severe and life-threatening assaults (Belle, 1990; Merry, 1981; Steele et al., 1982). However, research based on nationally randomized samples has revealed that race alone does not distinguish violent and nonviolent couples. When factors such as family income and husband's occupation are controlled, rates of partner assault for African American couples are not significantly different than rates for Caucasian husbands and wives (Koss et al., 1994). Much of the increased risk faced by minority women seems to be associated with poverty and isolation.

Restrictions of choice and vast increases in the risk of early death characterize all economically oppressed populations. For women, a lack of economic resources can be devastating to their ability to alter their environments or live in safety. In many areas, women living in poverty reside in communities in which the levels of assault across all relationship categories are high. Furthermore, availability of protective services is usually low. In examining the effects of poverty on the risk of violence for minority women, Harvey (1986: 168) observed that poor African American women may be "virtually imprisoned in settings where they are most likely to be victimized and where the personal and institutional safeguards that they would be privy to in other places may not exist." In rural areas, resources for poor women are often many miles away and transportation to those resources is nonexistent. For these women, isolation with a male partner and his violence may be virtually complete.

Although some research has been conducted within the African American community (e.g., Lockhart and White, 1989), there is little knowledge on physical violence between adult partners in Hispanic American or other minority populations (Rivera, 1994). One of the few comparative analyses, based on Epidemiological Catchment Area survey data for Los Angeles, found no significant differences in physical violence toward a spouse or other intimate adult partner between Mexican American and Caucasian couples. However, Mexican-born Mexican Americans had significantly lower rates of partner violence than either Caucasians or U.S.-born Mexican Americans (Sorenson and Terres, 1991). This finding is, in itself, troubling because it suggests that early socialization in the United States plays a critical role in the development of aggressive behaviors toward family members. Immigrant status and little knowledge of the English language are critical factors in the responses of some minority women who face violence from their male partners (Torres, 1991). For many immigrant women, maintaining residency and attaining citizenship depend on remaining married to their husbands. Women who reside in the United States without legal documents are particularly inhibited about seeking help because identification could lead to arrest and deportation. In addition, many immigrant women may be in the United States without friends or family who might otherwise provide important sources of protection and psychological or financial support.

No systematic studies have been conducted on family violence in Native American or Asian American populations, and the rate of violence between partners is unknown. Many Asian Americans consider marital problems to be highly private matters that must remain within the family; self-restraint and preventing "loss of face" are strongly held values. If an Asian American woman brings her husband's violence to public or official attention, she is likely to be completely ostracized and isolated (Ho, 1990). Divorce is also uncommon among Asian American families, and separation is not typically considered to be an option. Language and citizenship barriers may be especially difficult for Asian Americans. Although most police forces, hospital settings, and social service agencies have Spanish-speaking staff, interpreters for other languages are not readily available in most locales.

Information on male violence against Native American women comes primarily from anecdotal data and descriptions of tribal reactions and mores. Physical violence against women appears to be at frightening levels throughout most Native American populations (e.g., Allen, 1990). However, with few exceptions, tribal councils and official agencies are unwilling to discuss or document the extent of the problem (Koss et al., 1994). Some experts contend that abuse of Native American women and children by Native American men was almost unknown until the introduction of alcohol and of patriarchal beliefs that sanctioned subservience of women to men (Allen, 1990). The relationship between the extreme subjugation and isolation of Native Americans within the United States is also viewed as a critical variable affecting the high levels of violence in many Native American communities (Duran, Guillory, and Tingley, unpublished).

The Continuum of Marital Violence: From Intrusion to Homicide

Abuse in couple relationships may range from verbal put-downs and harassment to episodic or chronic physical assaults and threats. Little is known, however, about relationships in which physical assault by male partners occurs only rarely; violence that occurs only occasionally often goes unreported and is especially likely to be attributed to particular causes, not to be viewed as a problem with aggression itself. However, the impact on a woman of even a single incident of violence should not be underestimated. Although women who are assaulted "only once" are rarely labeled as "battered" and still less often studied, any use of violence in a relationship can dramatically alter the balance of power, destroying a sense of openness and trust on the part of the woman and resulting in a permanent sense of inequality, threat, and loss.

Once assaultive behavior occurs in a relationship, it often becomes chronic (Straus, Gelles, and Steinmetz, 1980; Walker, 1984). As Straus (1990) noted after analyzing data from two national surveys, "when an assault by a husband occurs, it is not usually an isolated instance. In fact, it tends to be a recurrent feature of the relationship." In light of the greater severity of aggressive acts by men against their wives—and of the outcomes of these actions in terms of injury, death, and societal costs—this section focuses on patterns reported in relationships in which a man's aggression toward his wife is ongoing.

Onset of Violence

Of course, patterns of onset, types of abuse and threat, and changes in patterns over time vary across relationships. Even in relationships in which assaults by a male partner become chronic, the onset of physical aggression is often preceded by nonviolent verbal abuse and restrictions, as well as by attentive and loving behavior. Many women who have lived with violent and threatening mates report that—early in their relationships—these men were the most attentive and romantic partners they had ever had.

> One woman remembered that her partner was "a wonderful man" when she first met him, "very observant and gentlemanly." She did know he "liked women" and that he was used to "stepping out"; she caught him in an affair once and nearly left him. But he was so sorry and so charming; his intensity over her convinced her she was really the one he cared for. He pressed her to move in with him, and then to marry him, and she felt they had worked through their problems. In those early days, he laughed easily and drank lightly; it was three years before she realized he was an alcoholic. His temper started to change in the second year: You could say one thing and he would laugh at it, and then later become angry over the same thing. She learned that much of the time he was lying to her about his past and his activities; he quit his job two months before she found out he wasn't going to work. The third year they were married he began "dating"; the physical abuse started soon after (Browne, 1987: 41).

Warning signs of a potential for future violence are often found in the very behaviors that initially seemed so attentive and caring (Browne, 1987). Early and intense interest, a constant concern with the women's whereabouts and activities, wanting to do everything together, jealousy over any activity or relationship outside of the relationship with the partner, and pressure for an early commitment are frequently mentioned as characterizing relationships in which the male partner later becomes violent toward his partner. Women, however, often interpret a new partner's intensity or pressure for early commitment as indications of love, and fail to recognize the warning signs of future trouble embedded in these behaviors (Browne, 1987).

It is often difficult to separate early warning signs from more typical romantic or social interactions. Couples who are newly in love think primarily of one another, want to spend time alone together, and, in the process, may become isolated from others outside of the relationship. Moreover, the society in which intimate couples grow and learn supports men in maintaining decision-making power, financial control, and physical dominance over others. Since the romantic tradition has historically been based on gender stereotypes of male dominance and ancient property laws in which the wife was the possession of the husband, a potential for violence may be hidden within behaviors culturally sanctioned as appropriate for men in relation to their female partners. Patterns of intrusion, isolation, and possessive control are particularly important to identify in assessing the possibility of later aggression (Sonkin and Dutton, 1988; Sonkin, Martin, and Walker, 1985; Wilson and Daly, 1993).

Early Warning Signs

Intrusion. A constant desire by a male partner to know a woman's whereabouts and activities—which at first makes the woman feel valued and cared for—is often described by women with violent mates as escalating over time into an insistence that they account for every hour, with violent reprisals if their explanations are not believed. Women with abusive partners report being followed to or from work or school, receiving frequent phone calls to make sure they are where they said they would be, intensive questioning about daily activities, and sudden appearances to check up on them. Arriving home a few minutes late, insisting on going out alone, or being seen talking with someone (especially a man) become triggers for suspicion and assault, regardless of the explanation.

Isolation. Early in romantic relationships, a partner's desire to spend every moment alone together may seem understandable and endearing. However, the tendency of abusive men to discourage their partners from maintaining relationships with others frequently leads to severe restrictions in later contacts and activities (Frieze and Browne, 1985; Walker, 1984). Women involved with violent mates may increasingly isolate themselves from friends and family even before the onset of physical aggression, in an effort to avoid upsetting their partners. Sometimes such women quit their jobs or leave school because of their partners' negative reactions; or else in later stages of the relationship, they are ordered or forced to quit activities outside the home. In many of these cases, however, prior warnings are evident. The man may have shown little interest in, or even expressed jealousy of, friends and family; he may have seemed to resent the woman's involvement in work or school. However, this discomfort with the woman's involvement in a larger network is often overlooked in the initial intensity of being together.

Possession. Belief that a girlfriend or wife "belongs" to the man with whom she is involved is supported by the cultural traditions of romance and marriage, as well as, until recently, many U.S. laws that applied to husbands and wives (Gillespie, 1989). In the early stages of a relationship, a woman may experience a man's belief that she is "his" as more protective than controlling. However, beliefs of ownership underlie the justification of many acts of violence by men toward their women partners. Abusive men insist that they have the right to tell their wives what they may or may not do, to punish them for misbehavior, to force sexual activity on them if they choose to, to violently retaliate if they believe their wives have been with another man, and—sometimes—to murder their wives if they leave (Bowker, 1983).

Jealousy. Jealousy is another warning sign imbedded within our romantic tradition. People expect jealousy to be a by-product of infatuation and love and often mistake it as a yardstick by which to gauge affection. However, in abusive relationships, jealousy typically far exceeds the bounds of reason and, except for attempts to end the relationship, tends to underlie the most violent and life-threatening assaults (Wilson and Daly, 1993). Jealousy fuels many of the intrusive behaviors described previously and contributes to the severity of retaliation for imagined misdeeds during times of physical separation or estrangement. Women with violent and jealous mates describe extreme situations such as being unable to shop at the supermarket because of the presence of male employees or having to keep their eyes lowered while riding in the car with their partner to avoid the appearance of making eye contact with people on the street. As with other warning signs, there are often early indications. Constant jealous reactions by a male partner that generalize to all types of relationships—or to all contacts with men, regardless of relationship—are particularly serious, and suggest that reasoning or increasing the level of commitment will not be enough to reduce the threat of violence and isolation that extreme jealousy presents.

Prone to Anger. Retrospective analyses of relationships in which men physically assault their wives suggest other early warning signs less confounded with the conception of romantic love, although supported by cultural stereotypes of acceptable male behavior. Even before the onset of violence, many women noticed that their partners not only were easily angered, but that their moods could change without warning and what might set them off was difficult to predict. More importantly, the anger was often completely out of proportion to the circumstance that occasioned it. This pattern of out-of-proportion rage later puts a woman at risk of physical attack for something as minor as forgetting to buy beer or leaving the checkbook in the car (Browne, 1987).

History of Violence. Finally, although other warning signs may be hard to separate from more typical romantic interactions, a prior history of aggression should never be ignored. Some women become involved with men with known histories of violence and believe that, with them, it will be different. Yet aggressive responses in one area of life often spill over into another. Although initially this aggression may be directed against other people or against objects, women whose partners have a past or current history of reacting violently to their environments should consider themselves at risk for similar actions. A potential for violence also may become evident in driving behaviors. Women survivors recount occasions during which the man seemed to deliberately put both of their lives in danger; abusive partners deliberately ran into stop signs or parked cars, drove the car toward pedestrians or cyclists, or over curbs and lawns to frighten them. Such behaviors demonstrate a willingness to endanger and to do damage; they are an indication that a potential mate may someday direct this destructiveness against his partner as well.

As noted previously, physical assaults by male partners before marriage are frequently triggered by the man's jealousy or the woman's attempts to end the relationship. Often, the violence is seen as atypical of the partner and unlikely to happen again. Both partners may believe that if they make a stronger commitment—quit seeing other people, move in together, or get married—the man will be reassured and his physical aggression will cease. However, it is often at the point of a major commitment or soon after that the onset of chronic violence occurs. Empirical studies of women with violent mates indicate that, in 73 to 85 percent of the cases, women experienced repeated assaults only after they had married the abuser (Frieze and Browne, 1989).

Verbal Abuse and Threats as a Prelude and Accompaniment to Violence

In many relationships in which a man is assaultive toward his woman partner, verbal abuse and threats constitute an important dimension of abuse patterns (Pagelow, 1984; Walker, 1979, 1984). Verbal abuse, lectures, and name-calling often precede the onset of physical violence in relationships and accompany physical attacks when assaultive behavior becomes chronic. Sometimes a male partner assumes the role of an angry teacher or parent. Under these circumstances, an incident, once begun, can be difficult to diffuse. One woman described her relationships with her partner Roy as follows:

> "He felt I was a child. He'd say, 'I'm going to teach you a lesson, raise you right.' He'd make himself angry, lecturing me. I was always caught off guard by his attacks. They seemed to be mainly dependent on his mood, rather than on things going on around him. He would slap me, hit with his fists, twist my arms behind my back, call me names . . . And then he'd tell me it was for my own good. If I tried to say anything, he'd call that 'talking back' and I'd get hit. But if I kept quiet, he'd say I was ignoring him. No matter what I did, it just got worse and worse, once it got started. He'd say, 'You're going to dance to my music . . . be the kind of wife I want you to be . . .'" (Browne, 1987: 60).

Even in cases in which physical assaults become quite severe, women often report the verbal abuse and derogation as being more painful and damaging than the physical attacks and injuries (Jones and Schechter, 1992; Walker, 1979).

Threats also exist along a continuum, and often parallel the themes previously discussed in "Early Warning Signs." In relationships with ongoing violence, threats to do harm or even to kill are reported by nearly 50 percent of women involved with physically assaultive mates (Browne, 1987; Walker, 1984). Threats to harm may include warnings against "misbehavior" (e.g., leaving the house without permission, using the telephone or car, or talking to neighbors), telling someone about the abuse, or attempting to leave the relationship. Threats to kill are most often related to attempts on the woman's part to separate from the abuser or being with another man. In warning partners against leaving, threats of harm sometimes extend to those individuals from whom a woman might seek shelter, such as relatives or friends. Some women are also warned that they will lose custody or that their children will be kidnapped or harmed if they attempt to end the relationship. Because of prior experiences with their partners' capacity for aggression and willingness to do harm, women with assaultive mates often take these warnings quite seriously. Over time, threats may become one of the most important dynamics in a couple's ongoing interactions—as they intensify the woman's perception of danger, limit her perception of alternatives, and provide a means of control by the abuser even when physical aggression is not used.

Threats—even extreme threats—may also be implied by actions. Destruction of personal property such as clothing, pictures, and family mementos is frequently reported as part of an escalation of assault and intimidation. Coming home to find pictures of herself or her children shredded or singed may be far more frightening to a woman than physically assaultive actions. Extreme violence against family pets is also reported and is often seen by women as a representation of what the abuser may do to them. Threats with weapons also form a part of the pattern of intimidation used by some severely abusive partners. Some women report waking up to find a gun facing them on the pillow and the abuser standing by the bed; others describe having gunshots fired into doorjambs just above their heads or having guns held against their bodies while the trigger is pulled only to find the gun was unloaded (Browne, 1987). Even if the weapon is never actually used and no words are spoken, these actions carry a clear message of extreme and unpredictable danger.

Sexual Violence

While marital rape also forms a part of the pattern of aggression in many abusive relationships, women may be unwilling to define even forced sexual acts as assaultive when the acts are perpetrated by their husbands. In some studies, women described physical aggression during sexual activity as being so severe that they were injured or lost consciousness (Pagelow, 1981); yet these same women did not define these acts as "sexual" assaults. The association of violence and sexual activity is demonstrated in the following narrative:

Jim Johnson quit his job during a fight with his boss and couldn't get another one. He wouldn't hear of Molly going back to work, telling her he had married her and would support her. . . . As the weeks went by, Jim began coming back later at night, often drunk. When drinking, Jim was different than Molly had ever seen him—yelling at her, calling her names, accusing her of not loving him or of wanting to leave him. And sometimes he raped her. Molly didn't think you could call it rape when it was your own husband, but he was very rough during lovemaking—pinching and biting and treating her with anger. At these times, he was like another person; he didn't seem to know her or realize what he was doing. Molly began to have constant bruises and bite marks. But Jim was always cold sober by morning—quiet and depressed and terribly sorry. He would apologize and stroke her face, and drink less and spend more time with her for the next several days. Molly prayed he'd find work soon. She kept telling herself that things would be alright, once he got a job . . . (Browne, 1987: 38–39).

Husbands who rape are more likely to associate sex with violence, have extramarital affairs, and be extremely jealous of their wives than husbands who are not sexually assaultive (Frieze, 1983). Interestingly, research indicates that a wife's refusal to have sex with her husband by itself is not typically a cause for rape. A willingness to rape is part of the characteristics of the perpetrator, and—if nonsexual violence is not already occurring—is a warning that other forms of serious aggression are possible. Women are extremely reluctant to report rapes by their husbands because of an extreme sense of shame and humiliation, an expectation that they will not be believed, and a belief that even forcible sexual relations are the "right" of a husband or lover (Russell, 1990). However, although it is almost always trivialized, sexual assault by a male intimate is an extremely serious form of violence. It is possible to inflict an intense level of physical pain and to cause a wide range of injuries—from superficial bruises to serious internal injuries and scarring, as well as to cause great mental anguish (Koss and Heslet, 1992). As one survivor noted:

It was as though he wanted to annihilate me. More than the slapping, or the kicks . . . as though he wanted to tear me apart from the inside out and simply leave nothing there (Browne, 1987: 103).

Patterns of Violence over Time

In relationships with recurring aggression, typically there is a pattern to the violence, both within incidents and over time. This pattern often involves verbal or other actions that precede the physical assaults, types of physical aggression used during assaults, and expressions of contrition and remorse after abusive episodes are over.

Abuse usually started when Billy was drinking. Kim didn't know when the beatings were going to happen; Billy's mood would change and they would begin to argue, but there usually was not much talking. It became physical very quickly. Billy got a certain look on his face—jaw set, mouth tight—he would turn and stare at her and then begin hitting. He rarely said anything, once the violence began. It was as though something inside of him had to run its course. Then he would stop suddenly, usually when Kim was down. During these attacks, Kim would plead with him, "Billy, please quit. Please quit. I love you, Billy. Please quit." She didn't know if it had any effect, but it was the only thing she knew to try (Browne, 1987: 149).

Contrition and Remorse. Based on early interviews with battered women, Walker (1979) proposed a "Cycle Theory of Violence" in relationships with ongoing violence. This cycle consists of three phases: (1) the *tension building phase,* during which there is a gradual buildup of tension, verbal or physical intimidation, and physical aggression by the abusive mate; (2) the acute *battering incident,* when the abuser unleashes his aggression at his partner and physical assault occurs; and (3) a period of *loving contrition* following the incident, when the abuser may apologize, show kindness or remorse, and promise that the violence will not occur again (Walker, 1984).

Violent assaults often leave victims shaken and especially vulnerable to the abusers' expressions of love and apology. Especially early in a relationship, women may base all their hopes of improvement on their partners' expressions of regret. In relationships in which the woman has already become isolated, the abuser may be the only source of comfort available. Yet, in a relationship with a violent mate, even periods of contrition hold danger. In addition to apologies, these periods often include intense pressure to forgive and forget. Thus, women are frequently blamed by the abuser for "holding a grudge" when they continue to react with hurt or anger to the violation they experienced (e.g., "I said I was sorry!"). Typically, there is also much pressure to minimize the seriousness of what has occurred (e.g., "It wasn't so bad" or "You're not really hurt") and to have the victim accept responsibility for the abuser's behavior (e.g., "If you hadn't made me so angry" or "You were involved, too"). In many instances, refusal to make up or to respond to the partner's sexual overtures may lead to renewed anger and assault.

In most cases—regardless of the partner's reassurances and remorse, violent episodes continue to recur. Even with expressions of intense sadness over the harm done to the woman, an abuser's callousness about doing damage may reassert itself soon after the incident as shown in the following example:

Early in the relationship, Billy seemed sorry when he hurt Kim. After an especially bad beating, he would sit and look at her with tears in his eyes. Kim remembers once, when she was badly hurt, Billy rocked her in his arms . . . holding her against his chest like he was mourning a dead child. Sometimes she would come to after being hit and hear Billy saying, "Be okay. Be okay, baby. I didn't mean to. Oh God, please be okay!" Yet he would force her to go out with him after beatings, even when she was badly bruised and her face was swollen. He didn't seem to care what others thought . . . (Browne, 1987: 150).

Further study of this third phase of the cycle revealed that loving contrition is most in evidence early in abusive relationships. In relationships with chronic violence, aggression by male partners often becomes more frequent or severe over time, while expressions of regret and affection diminish (Walker, 1984). Especially with severely violent abusers, love and empathy may completely disappear:

> Toward the end of his life, Duke no longer seemed sorry about hurting Maggie. He became increasingly violent and trying to talk about it could set off another angry attack. Maggie felt she was more like a punching bag or a sexual outlet than a person to him; the only time he noticed her was when she got in his way. Violent assaults just "occurred" in the course of his day. Maggie didn't think he thought about them at all (Browne, 1987: 64).

The Role of Alcohol and Other Drugs. Women with assaultive mates frequently report that the violence seems to be more related to internal factors in the man than to events in the external environment (Dutton, 1992; Walker, 1984). Descriptions of male violence against wives often include reports of heavy drinking or the use of drugs on the part of the abuser. Because of the prevalence of alcohol and other forms of drug abuse among men who are physically aggressive with women partners, women (as well as others who hear about the attacks) often believe that without the use of alcohol or drugs, such assaults would not occur. Besides providing women with some explanation for their partners' aggression, believing that alcohol is responsible gives them hope that the violence will cease if only their mates would stop drinking.

Research on marital aggression indicates a strong association between substance abuse and the perpetration of violence by intimate partners (Hotaling and Sugarman, 1986). However, although men who are violent toward their women partners are more likely to abuse alcohol or other drugs than are non-abusive men, episodes of violence do not necessarily occur only when an abuser has been drinking. In an in-depth study of 532 relationships in which men were violent toward their wives, only 20 percent of the abusers were consistently intoxicated when violent. More than half of all the assaults by male partners were perpetrated by an abuser who was sober at the time (Walker, 1984). Even during the most serious incident reported for each relationship, only 54 percent of the assailants were under the influence of alcohol or drugs. A history of substance abuse does have a significant impact on the severity of abuse the partner will suffer, however. Abusive men with alcohol or drug problems attack their wives more frequently, are more apt to inflict serious injuries on their partners, are more likely to be sexually assaultive toward their partners, and are more likely to be violent outside the home than abusers without a history of substance abuse.

Although women assaulted by male partners may also abuse alcohol or other drugs, research shows no consistent relationship between substance abuse by women and the experience of violence by marital partners (Hotaling and Sugarman, 1986). While some women in abusive relationships cease drinking completely at the onset of severe or chronic violence in order to remain alert to impending danger, others show a marked increase in their intake of alcohol or other drugs as a way of coping with the terror of assaults, grief over changes in the relationship, anticipation of future attacks, and physical pain or injury (Browne, 1987; Walker, 1984). Unfortunately, this response works against immediate or long-term protection and plans, and it greatly increases the risk of serious emotional and physical damage.

Lethal Violence

Studies of partner homicide by women and men reveal quite different patterns in (1) circumstances prior to and at the time of the homicide; (2) motivations for the assault; and (3) location where the homicide is committed (Browne, 1987; Jurik and Winn, 1990; Wilson and Daly, 1993). Like assaults that occur prior to marriage and threats to kill or to harm, homicides by men against their female partners most often center around issues of jealousy or attempts by the woman to end the relationship. In some cases, homicides by male partners are batterings that go too far. Especially when drinking or under the influence of other drugs, serious physical damage may be done during assaultive incidents with the perpetrator unaware of how badly the woman is being hurt. Men are much less likely than women to have been physically attacked by the victim prior to the homicide or to kill in self-defense. Because men who kill their partners are often motivated by separation or the threat of separation, they are more likely than women to commit the homicide away from a shared dwelling, either on the street or in the victim's private residence. These men are also much more likely to kill others in addition to their wives at the time of the homicide (e.g., the wife's children or other relatives), and more likely to kill themselves after the homicide is completed. In interviews with men who have killed their wives, either threats of separation or actual separation itself are most often cited as the precipitating event and are taken to represent "intolerable desertion, rejection, and abandonment" (Bernard et al., 1982: 278). Men who have killed their wives often report that the violence was in reaction to previous behaviors, such as leaving, on the part of their wives (Wilson and Daly, 1993).

In contrast, women rarely track down and kill male partners from whom they are separated (Jurik and Winn, 1990; Wilson and Daly, 1993). Partner homicides by women most typically occur in the couple's shared residence, or in the woman's private residence if the estranged partner threatens her there. One explanation for why women primarily kill their male partners, not strangers or acquaintances, is that it is their partners from whom they are the most at risk. Homicides by women are likely to be preceded by an escalating pattern of assault, sexual assault, and threat (Browne, 1987; Jurik and Winn, 1990). In contrast to the common assumption that women kill partners while they are sleeping or otherwise incapacitated, most partner homicides by women occur during an assaultive incident against the woman or a child (Maguigan, 1991).

Women who kill male partners often are experiencing a very severe level of violence and threat by the time a homicide occurs. In comparing the relationships of women charged with the death of their assaultive mates and women in violent relationships in which no such incident occurred, Browne (1987) found several distinguishing factors between the two groups:

- Women who killed their mates were assaulted much more frequently than women in the "abuse only" group. Nearly *40 percent* of women in the homicide group reported that physical assaults were occurring more than once a week by the end of their relationships, whereas only 13 percent of women in the non-homicide group reported that assaults were occurring that often.

- Women who killed their mates sustained more, and more severe, injuries than women in the non-homicide group.
- Women who killed their mates were subjected to a much higher frequency of rape and other forced sexual activities by their partners than women in the non-homicide group. *Sixty-one percent* of women in the homicide group had been sexually assaulted by their male partner more than three times in contrast to only 13 percent of the non-homicide group.
- The men who were killed were much more likely to abuse alcohol or drugs severely than men in the non-homicide group. In the homicide group, *80 percent* of the abusers were intoxicated nearly every day by the end of their relationships, compared to 40 percent of men in the non-homicide group who became intoxicated that often.
- Finally, 80 percent of the men who were killed had threatened to kill the woman or others, compared to 59 percent (still a high number) of men in the non-homicide group.

As danger escalates and contrition disappears, women with violent partners become exhausted by repetition, fear, and injury. Hopes for improvement not only are crushed, but are replaced by a sense of desperation and entrapment (Browne, 1987; Totman, 1978). Over time, a combination of exhaustion, numbing, and panic may make effective long-range planning or escape almost impossible. Women kill when they feel hopelessly trapped in desperate situations in which staying may mean being killed but attempting to leave also carries with it the threat of reprisal or death. By the end of the relationships, women in the homicide group were subjected to frequent and injurious attacks from partners who were likely to be drinking heavily, using drugs, and threatening murder. Among those women who observed their partners' patterns of violence for years, their was the view that the abusers were beyond the point at which they would be able to stop short of murder. For these women, it seemed only a matter of time before they or a child would be killed. While most women in these violent relationships had no history of violent behavior, their attempts to survive with increasingly violent and unpredictable partners eventually resulted in acts of violence on their part as well (Browne, 1986, 1987).

Women's Responses to Assaults by Partners

Discussing serious forms of violence raises important questions. Stories of severe aggression make us wonder why women with violent mates endure such brutality: Why don't they just walk out one day when the abuser is away? Why would anyone let violence reach such a severe level that a homicide occurs? Although not apparent to many observers, most women with assaultive mates are actively engaged in coping with the violence even though such coping may be more related to surviving within the relationship than to leaving or initiating legal action against the abuser (see Browne, 1987; Gondolf and Fisher, 1988; Herman, 1992). In contrast to theories that interpret such responses as indicative of a personality disorder, the reactions to violence and threats are what one would expect from any individual confronted with a dangerous or life-threatening situation (Browne, 1993; see also Ptacek and Ferraro, Part II of this volume). Overall, the characteristics of male partners are better predictors of the risk of women being assaulted than are the characteristics of the women themselves (Hotaling and Sugarman, 1986).

Human Responses to Trauma

The responses by women to violence by intimate partners parallel the reactions of survivors across a variety of traumatic events (Browne, 1987, 1993; Symonds, 1979). Similar to survivors of natural disasters, crime, or war, women assaulted by male partners react with shock, denial, fear, confusion, a sense of helplessness, and a sense of self-blame (Bard and Sangrey, 1986; Browne, 1992; Dutton, 1992; Herman, 1992; Walker, 1979). During and even after an assault, victims sometimes offer little or no resistance in order to minimize the threat of injury or renewed aggression, while at the same time adapting their behavior so that abuse will not occur again. Such adaptions typically have little effect on the chronicity of partner assaults, however, and may even facilitate repeated violence (Browne, 1987; Browne and Harvey, in press). Women who are sexually attacked by male partners suffer many of the same reactions as other types of rape victims, including shock, numbness, withdrawal, a long-term sense of vulnerability, and a lowered sense of self-worth. Because these women have close relationships with their assailants, however, these effects may be particularly severe (Browne, 1987; Pagelow, 1984; Walker, 1984). Women report being stunned by the sexual attack on the part of someone they trusted, and they often experience permanent changes in the perception of their partners and their relationships. Long-term effects of marital rape include severe depression, anxiety, suicidal feelings, and fatigue (Goodman, Koss, and Russo, 1993; Stark et al., 1981; Randall, 1990; Russell, 1982; Walker, 1979).

Cumulative Effects of Trauma

As with survivors of other types of trauma, women who are assaulted, may become dependent and suggestible and find it difficult to carry out long-range planning or make decisions alone (Bard and Sangrey, 1986). Survivors of ongoing assaults often narrow their focus to dealing with the immediate threat and regaining or maintaining strength between assaults (Browne, 1987). Like victims of disaster, women in chronically violent relationships may voice unrealistic expectations about recovery, while convincing themselves that they can either "rebuild" the relationship or that, somehow, everything will be all right. Similar to individuals caught in hostage situations or concentration camps, women with violent mates learn to weigh all alternatives against the perception of their assailant's ability to control or to harm (Browne, 1993). As levels of threat and violence escalate, these perceptions of alternatives become increasingly restricted; acting on any of these alternatives may seem too dangerous to pursue. For those women whose assailants are husbands or other intimate partners, predictable effects of attack are further compounded by the fact that the assailant is someone they may love, someone they are supposed to be able to trust, and someone on whom they may depend for shelter and other components of survival.

Although even one assault can have permanent negative effects, severe and repeated violence leads to especially serious outcomes. Typical reactions to ongoing aggression include chronic fatigue and tension, intense startle reactions, disturbed sleeping and eating patterns, nightmares, and physical illness (Goodman, Koss, and Russo, 1993; Herman, 1992). Women who are assaulted frequently, sustain physical injuries, are sexually assaulted, or experience death threats evidence some of the most extreme effects. Women who experience *both* physical and sexual aggression in a marital relationship also manifest more serious aftereffects than women whose partners are physically but not sexually assaultive (Browne, 1987; Frieze, 1983; Pagelow, 1984; Walker, 1984).

The Continuum of Threat and Danger

The perceptions by women of danger, as well as the risks attendant in various alternatives, are often supported by external reality (Browne, 1993). For example, the fear among women that if they leave, their abusers will find them and retaliate is often justified (Mahoney, 1991; Ptacek, chapter 6 of this volume). In some cases, threats and aggression by abusive men against their partners continue to escalate after separation. Violent men may nearly kill their partners, but they don't want to lose them. Many of these men search desperately for the partner once separation takes effect. They spend day and night calling her family and mutual acquaintances; phoning or showing up at places of employment; and haunting school grounds, playgrounds, and grocery stores. She is "theirs," they insist. She cannot leave and refuse to talk to them! Some women who leave violent men are followed and harassed for months or even years; and some are killed (Jones, 1994; Jurik and Winn, 1990; Wilson and Daly, 1993). While studies indicate that the several months immediately after estrangement are especially high-risk times for homicides by abusive male partners, homicides by estranged male partners may occur months or even years after couples are separated or divorced (Wilson and Daly, 1993).

For women married to their assailants, decisions about their relationships are also complicated by legal and financial ties, overlapping family and support networks, and issues related to the care and custody of children. Behaviors that outside observers may interpret as "helplessness"—such as not separating from the abuser or refraining from initiating legal actions—may simply be accurate evaluations of the assailant's potential for violent responses as well as the inability of others to intervene in time to guarantee safety (Browne, 1993). Living in hiding is incompatible with maintaining employment, raising and educating children, and other components of normal life. Involvement in legal actions against an aggressive mate may only anger and upset him, increasing the tension and danger. Orders restraining the assailant from entering the home or neighborhood of the victim work only if the assailant respects those orders, or at least does no harm during times of violation.

Disputes related to children are a particularly effective, long-term way for abusers to maintain contact with their wives; abusers threaten their wives emotionally and physically with the loss of the children. Women frequently find themselves attempting to obtain protection orders or shelter from violent and threatening mates, while at the same time complying with required court appearances, visitation procedures, or mandatory mediations that put them in constant proximity to dangerous assailants (Pagelow, 1993; Jones, 1994). Economic circumstances also play a role in the choices facing a woman living with violence at home. If, in leaving an assaultive mate, a woman lacks adequate financial resources and must live in an unsafe dwelling in an unsafe part of town, a survivor may only change the type of danger to be braved while adding the risk of assaults by strangers to the risk of reprisals by her partner.

Given the severity of threats against leaving made by many abusers, and the possibility of severe or even lethal reprisals, some women choose the known danger and hope for improvement. For many women, leaving their mates and living in constant fear of reprisal or death seems more intolerable than remaining with them, despite their fears of further harm. Women in hiding talk about how they are afraid to go into their apartment when they get home (what if he is there?), to go to work in the morning or leave at night, to approach their car in a parking lot, or to visit their friends (Browne, 1987). They know if their estranged partner finds them, he may simply retaliate and not wait to talk. If he does begin a conversation and they do not agree to go home, that may trigger an attack as well. Every sound at night, every step in the hall, every pair of headlights pulling up behind them, might be him. Accomplishing even daily tasks against this wall of fear becomes an exhausting process.

Summary

The level of violence and aggression in the United States is unique among industrialized nations. Not only are rates of assault, homicide, and victimization between strangers significantly higher in the United States than in other Western nations, the rate of family homicide itself is higher than the total homicide rate in countries such as Germany, England, and Denmark. Similarly, the rape rate in the United States is ten to thirty times higher than rates in Western European nations—and this does not include the majority of rapes by intimates, which typically go unreported (Whatley, 1993). The use of guns in the United States is also radically different than that in other Western nations and is particularly implicated in the recent increases in severe assault and homicide. In some states, shooting deaths now exceed all deaths due to motor vehicle accidents. Furthermore, the continued representation of these events in the daily media is one of the reasons why many people live much of their lives with a sense of danger, even while being assured that their personal fear of being victimized far exceeds the risk.

Although the past two decades have witnessed sweeping policy changes and legal innovations to protect women from violence by their male intimates (Browne and Williams, 1989), many responses to the victims who are still based primarily on a lack of knowledge about (1) the frequency of partner violence in women's lives, (2) the severity of risks faced by women involved with threatening or assaultive mates, (3) the persistence of these risks whether women are living with or separated from the abusers, and (4) the actual outcomes for women who pursue approved strategies for dealing with violence and abuse.

Given this state of affairs, there is a critical need for integrated theories that take into account differing types of perpetration by male intimates, in order to provide better assessments of risk and a more informed basis for protective interventions for threatened women and children. Until more is known about the realities of what happens to women when they take the steps society now recommends, we cannot effectively tailor social and legal alternatives to address these realities. Findings on male violence after separation, as well as before, highlight the need for an integrated response to the continuum of threat and danger. An enhanced awareness of the prevalence, severity, and tenacity of violence by men against their female intimates would not only lead to a different understanding of the legitimacy of the reactions by women to trauma and life-threatening situations and the choices they make, but would provide different bases for initial and long-term responses by policymakers, mental health and legal practitioners, and community representatives.

4

Violence and Abuse among Same-Sex Couples

CLAIRE M. RENZETTI
St. Joseph's University

E stimates that the incidence of intimate violence among heterosexual couples ranges from 12 to 33 percent, depending on the sample size and measures of abuse (Straus, 1993; Koss, 1990; Straus and Gelles, 1990), are familiar to most researchers. In contrast, many are surprised to learn that a number of studies show the rate of partner abuse among lesbian and gay couples to be comparable. The problem of intimate violence in the lesbian and gay communities has been virtually ignored by researchers until recently. This lack of attention stems from a number of factors, but certainly two of the most important are widespread heterosexism in the social sciences (as well as other academic disciplines) and, in the case of lesbians at least, the belief that women are not aggressive and do not batter other women. Intimate violence has been studied—and service responses have been structured—as if partner abuse is something only men do, and then, only to women.

The present chapter focuses on intimate violence among same-sex couples, including a review of the extant (and still limited) research on this problem, as well as an examination of the factors that may contribute to partner abuse among lesbians and gay men. In doing so, comparisons will inevitably be drawn between same-sex and heterosexual couples. Issues unique to lesbian and gay relationships will also be considered in this analysis.

Rates of Partner Abuse among Same-Sex Couples

It was noted at the outset that some studies have found that partner abuse occurs among homosexual couples at about the same rate as it does among heterosexual couples. Nevertheless, incidence statistics with respect to homosexual couples should be interpreted cautiously. For one thing, most reports are based on anecdotal evidence. Even in empirical studies, however, samples are self-selected, not random.[1] In addition, the majority of studies have focused on lesbian relationships; partner abuse in gay male relationships has been less studied.

One study that involved a self-selected sample of 48 lesbians and 50 gay men who completed a 17-item version of Straus's (1979) Conflict Tactics Scale (CTS), found that 95 percent of the respondents reported having been verbally abusive at some point in their relationships with lovers; 47 percent had been physically aggressive in these relationships; and 3 percent had been violent (Kelly and Warshafsky, 1987). Although lesbians and gay men in this study reported similar rates of verbal abuse and violence toward their partners, lesbians had lower reported rates of physical aggression.

A study comparing 75 heterosexual women and 55 lesbians reported experiences of victimization from four types of physical aggression (pain inflicted beyond consent when practicing sadomasochism, physical abuse, attempted rape, and completed rape) (Brand and Kidd, 1986). Overall, male partners of heterosexual women perpetrated a greater number of physically aggressive acts than did female partners of lesbians. However, with respect to two of the four types of aggression, no significant differences in the reported victimization rates of the heterosexual and lesbian respondents were reported: 25 percent of the lesbian respondents and 27 percent of the heterosexual respondents said that they had been physically abused by intimate partners; 7 percent of the lesbian respondents and 9 percent of the heterosexual respondents said that they had been raped by dates.

In studies dealing with lesbian couples, estimates of the rate of partner abuse vary widely. Loulan (1987) in her study of 1,566 lesbians, reported that 17 percent had been involved in violent relationships. In contrast, most other researchers have found significantly higher rates of abuse. Coleman (1990) considered 42 (46.6 percent) of the 90 lesbian couples she studied to be violent. Lie, Schilit, Bush, Montagne, and Reyes (1991) surveyed 169 lesbians and found that 73.4 percent said that they had experienced physical, sexual, or verbal-emotional aggression in at least one previous lesbian relationship; 26 percent had these experiences in their current relationships. Lie and Gentlewarrier (1991) in their survey of 1,099 lesbians found that 52 percent had been abused by a female lover or partner. At the same time, of those who had been victimized, 51.5 percent also reported that they themselves had been abusive toward their partners; whereas 30 percent of the sample admitted having abused a lesbian lover or

---

[1]Researchers cannot draw random samples of the gay and lesbian populations at this time. Given the stigma attached to homosexual relationships and, consequently, homosexuals' strong motivation for hiding their sexual identities from others including researchers, complete or even adequate sampling frames needed for drawing random samples are simply unavailable.

partner without also being victimized. In a similar study utilizing a considerably smaller sample ($n = $ 174), Bologna, Waterman, and Dawson (1987) found that 26 percent of their respondents had experienced at least one act of sexual violence at the hands of their lesbian partners; 59.8 percent had been victims of physical violence; and 81 percent had been verbally or emotionally abused. In terms of mutual battering, the authors also discovered that 68 percent of their sample had not only been victimized by a partner, but also had themselves used violence against their current or most recent partner.

Finally, in discussing gay male relationships only, Island and Letellier (1991) attempted to gauge the rate of gay male intimate violence by extrapolating from estimates of the gay male population and the rate of heterosexual domestic violence. Based on their calculations, anywhere from 330,000 gay men (or 10.9 percent of the gay male population) to 650,000 gay men (or 20 percent of the gay male population) are abused by their partners each year. Such estimates are, of course, only as reliable as the statistics on which they are based, and certainly there is reason to question most estimates of the number of gay men in this country (e.g., see Cronin, 1993).

Although none of these studies is a true prevalence study because of the nonrandom nature of the samples as well as other methodological difficulties, they raise several important issues. First, they show quite convincingly that partner abuse in same-sex relationships does indeed occur and that it is not so infrequent as to be anomalous. Moreover, given these frequency estimates, it is unlikely that most violence in same-sex relationships is a one-time situational event, as Leeder (1988) has argued. To the contrary, research involving a self-selected sample of 100 battered lesbians (Renzetti, 1992) indicates that only 8 percent of the respondents had been involved in abusive relationships that could be considered situational by Leeder's criterion (i.e., that they had experienced only one or two abusive incidents).

The majority of the lesbians (Renzetti, 1992) had been involved in what Leeder (1988) called chronic battering and emotional battering relationships. A chronic battering relationship is one in which physical abuse is recurrent and becomes increasingly destructive, with the violence escalating over time. In Leeder's (1988) typology, the emotional battering relationship is the same as the chronic battering relationship except that the abuse is verbal or psychological rather than physical. Seventy-nine percent of the participants (Renzetti, 1992) were involved in an abusive relationship with a lesbian lover for one or more years. However, for more than three-fourths (77 percent) of the participants, the first incident of abuse occurred less than six months after the relationship began; 89 percent reported that the first incident occurred before the relationship was two years old. Fifty-four percent of the participants experienced ten or more abusive incidents during the course of the relationship; 74 percent experienced six or more abusive incidents.[2] In addition, 71 percent of these women reported that

---

[2]It is important to note that, when respondents discussed "abusive incidents," they were referring to instances in which there was what might best be described as an "explosion" of anger and violence. Virtually all of the respondents indicated that verbal abuse, including insults and belittling remarks, occurred more frequently—for many, on a daily basis—particularly after the first incident of physical abuse had occurred.

the abuse grew more severe in successive incidents. At the same time, however, these relationships cannot be classified simply as either chronic or emotional battering relationships. Although psychological abuse was most common, only 11 percent of the women reported experiencing psychological abuse by itself. In contrast, 87 percent said that they were subjected to both physical and psychological abuse.

These findings with respect to partner abuse in lesbian relationships are similar to those reported by Island and Letellier (1991) in their study of gay male intimate violence, although they relied extensively on anecdotal evidence and secondary data. Thus, while it is still difficult to pinpoint with much accuracy the prevalence of abuse in same-sex relationships, it is clear from a variety of sources that in those relationships that are abusive, the abuse is recurrent and tends to grow more severe over time.

This raises a second important issue: the seriousness of the abuse. Straus (1993) has argued that most abuse occurring between heterosexual couples is relatively minor and rarely results in serious injury to either partner. It is the chronic abuse, he claims, that is most severe and injurious, and this type of abuse is picked up not in studies utilizing large, randomly selected community samples, but rather in those that draw on clinical populations, such as residents of battered women's shelters. Perhaps then, the self-selected nature of the samples in studies of partner abuse among same-sex couples accounts for the seriousness of the abuse that has been uncovered.

In this respect, Renzetti (1992) found that two of the most important (and disturbing) results derived from questions about the forms of abuse respondents experienced at the hands of their partners. Respondents were given a list of sixteen different forms of physical abuse and seventeen different forms of psychological abuse and were asked to indicate which types they had experienced and how often. The most common forms of physical abuse involved being pushed and shoved; being hit with fists or open hands; being scratched or hit on the face, breasts, or genitals; and having things thrown at them. The least common forms of physical abuse included the carving of numbers, figures, or words into their skin; having guns or knives put into their vaginas; being deliberately burned with a cigarette; and being stabbed or shot. The most common forms of psychological abuse involved verbal threats; being demeaned in front of friends, relatives, and strangers; having sleeping or eating habits disrupted; and having property damaged or destroyed. It also was common for the partners of these respondents to abuse others in the household (i.e., children or pets), which in turn usually constituted another form of psychological abuse inflicted on the respondents.

While these findings are notable in themselves, the two more significant findings that emerged were (1) that every type of abuse listed was experienced by at least two participants in the study and (2) that despite its length and variety, the list was not exhaustive. With respect to the first point, it should be emphasized that while some of the most severe forms of violence (e.g., being stabbed or shot or having guns or knives inserted into one's vagina) were relatively rare, the fact that these occurred at all and that they occurred more often than rarely in even a tiny fraction of the relationships is cause for alarm. Regarding the second point, we should note that on the questionnaires and during subsequent interviews with a subsample of the respondents, numerous additional forms of abuse were described (e.g., being physically restrained, being forced to sever all ties and contacts with relatives and friends, and having property stolen by partners). Abusers would sometimes harm themselves, or threaten to harm themselves, as another means to control or manipulate the respondents. In addition, abusers frequently tailored the abuse to the specific vulnerabilities of their partners. Especially chilling examples of this were reported by two women with physical disabilities. Their partners would abandon them in dangerous settings (e.g., an isolated wooded area) without their wheelchairs. Another woman who was diabetic stated that her partner would "punish" her by forcing her to eat sugar.

Island and Letellier (1991) recount numerous equally disturbing examples from their discussions with gay male victims of intimate violence. They also explore how AIDS complicates the problem of gay male intimate violence. This issue, while not totally unique to gay male relationships, is nevertheless especially relevant to them, since gay men constitute the largest percentage of people with AIDS. Island and Letellier (1991) are concerned that AIDS—or, more accurately, the stress caused by the fear of contracting AIDS, dealing with the disease if one has contracted it, or trying to care for an infected partner—is becoming an excuse for gay male intimate violence. According to the authors, the real impact of AIDS on cases of gay male intimate violence is that it increases the difficulty abuse victims confront in trying to leave their batterers. On the one hand, abused partners who also have AIDS may be so dependent on their batterers for financial support and health care assistance that they decide to remain in the relationship rather than risk living alone. On the other hand, abuse victims whose batterers have AIDS may feel tremendous guilt about leaving dying partners with no one else to care for them.

One form of abuse unique to same-sex relationships also merits attention: the threat of "outing" or the public disclosure of one's homosexuality. Although blackmail may sometimes be a form of abuse in heterosexual relationships, it does not appear to be common. Moreover, it carries criminal penalties if the victim decides to prosecute. In a society in which homophobia is widespread, however, "outing" may result in abandonment by relatives and friends, the loss of a job, and a wide variety of other discriminatory behaviors, about which the victim has little legal recourse. In Renzetti's study (1992), 21 percent of the respondents reported that their partners rarely, sometimes, or frequently threatened to "out" them. Several women stated that they quit their jobs before their partners carried through on the threat to "out" them at work. Their rationale was that if they left on their own and resolved their problems with their partners, they could find another job more easily than if they were "outed," subsequently fired or laid off, and surreptitiously blacklisted by an employer.

A final issue raised by research on the incidence of partner abuse in same-sex relationships involves the problem of mutual battering. With respect to heterosexual intimate violence, there appears to be a growing call among some researchers (e.g., Straus, 1993; McNeely and Robinson-Simpson, 1987) to recognize that most abusive relationships are "mutually combative" and that women are perpetrators in a significant number of abusive relationships. In at least two of the studies on same-sex intimate violence reviewed here (Bologna et al., 1987; Lie and Gentlewarrier, 1991), the findings indicate that a large percentage of abuse was reciprocal. In more than half the cases, the respondents were both perpetrators and victims.

The subject of mutual abuse is a highly controversial one. Straus (1993) has claimed that his work in this area has been extensively criticized simply because it is "politically incorrect." While he is probably right in some instances, the research of others, especially those who have studied same-sex intimate violence, indicates that there is good reason to be extremely cautious in leveling charges of mutual abuse. Straus (1993) himself recognizes that the context in which the behavior occurs is a crucial variable. The mutual battering perspective often assumes that all violence is the same when, in fact, there are important differences between initiating violence, using violence in self-defense, and retaliating against a violent partner. This goes beyond the question of who hit first, since individuals may be motivated to strike first because they believe violence against them is imminent, or they may be provoked by prolonged and severe verbal or psychological abuse. In Renzetti's study (1992), several women reported that their abusive partners persistently goaded them with insults and taunts, such as "Hit me; you know you want to hit me for what I'm saying to you" (see also Island and Letellier, 1991: 86–87).

Simply asking people if they ever behaved violently towards a partner, "fought back" during an abuse incident, or defended themselves when abused by a partner is not sufficient for determining whether a particular relationship is mutually abusive. Nor is it adequate to simply ask research participants to characterize their own behavior as self-defense, retaliation, or mutual battering (e.g., see Lie et al., 1991). There are several reasons for this. First, individuals who have been abused frequently accept the label "mutual battering," even if they were violent toward their partners only once, because they typically feel guilty about doing any harm to their partners and have come to accept responsibility for the abusive relationship. The second reason is closely related to the first: Abuse victims frequently adopt the mind-set of the batterers. "Often batterers use the survivor's self-doubt to their advantage. Batterers are notorious for labeling the survivor 'mutually abusive' in order to avoid taking responsibility for their actions" (Asherah, 1990: 57). Third, many batterers, while acknowledging they were abusive, also claim their partners left them no choice. In discussing their own actions, they often begin with the words, "If she [or he] hadn't . . . then I wouldn't have. . . ." To paraphrase Hart (1986), batterers often see themselves as the victims of those they batter.

Researchers as well as help providers have been especially quick to attach the label "mutual battering" to abusive same-sex relationships. It is typically assumed that battering is something men do to women; therefore, in cases of homosexual intimate violence, researchers sometimes claim that it is impossible to determine which partner is the perpetrator and which, the victim. In a culture in which men are expected to be aggressive and assaults on men by other men are commonplace, it is not surprising to find partner abuse in gay male relationships usually labeled "just a fight between two guys" rather than intimate violence. Partner abuse in lesbian relationships often gets reduced to a "cat fight." If the sexual orientation of the individuals involved is known to the police, judges, counselors, or others, the incident often is not taken seriously because of widespread homophobia and heterosexist stereotypes (e.g., "Who cares if two fags beat each other up?" or "It's just a couple of dykes acting butch"). Because they are well aware of this rampant homophobia, lesbian and gay male victims of partner abuse remain closeted in their interactions with officials and help providers, or forgo seeking help altogether (Renzetti, 1992; Island and Letellier, 1991).

In interviewing both perpetrators and victims of lesbian battering, Renzetti (1992) concluded that only rarely is the distinction between perpetrator and victim a difficult one to make. For one thing, the behavior of the two is typically quite different. In this respect, 78 percent of 100 respondents stated that they had defended themselves against the battering, fought back, or retaliated against their batterers (Renzetti, 1992). However, in elaborating on specifically what they had done, only 18 described behavior that could be characterized as fighting back—that is, trading blow for blow, insult for insult—and only 5 actually retaliated (1 by interrupting her partner's attempts to study, 2 by hitting their partners first, and 2 by emotionally withdrawing or withholding sex from their partners). Instead, in most cases (64) the behavior described was clearly self-defensive: pushing their partners away, holding their arms or wrists to keep from being hit, or blocking punches with their own arms or with an object. In 23 instances, the self-defense was indirect: The women simply covered their faces or their heads with their hands and arms to protect themselves, they tried to talk their way out or negotiate with the batterer, or they tried to escape (e.g., by locking themselves in a room). In comparing these behaviors to the forms of abuse inflicted on them (discussed earlier), it is not difficult to detect a difference.

There is also a difference in the way victims and perpetrators discuss their abusive relationships and the violent behavior in which they have engaged. Victims express intense shame, particularly if they have defended themselves or fought back, but also because they are embarrassed by their victimization. They are quiet and frequently withdrawn. In addition, they express concern for their partners' well-being and often continue to accept responsibility for the relationship long after it has ended. Batterers, in contrast, are quite vocal in legitimating their behavior. They are typically self-righteous and assert a claim to the label "victim." With indignation and undisguised anger, they will recite a litany of partner "transgressions" that justified their violence. They rarely express shame or even remorse, and while they may be willing to accept partial responsibility for the relationship, the abuse is never entirely their fault (Renzetti, 1992).

This discussion underlines the need for more research with both heterosexual and homosexual couples in order to better understand the incidence and dynamics of mutual battering situations. Based on available evidence, such cases are far fewer than some researchers currently are claiming. Researchers who examine this problem should be encouraged to develop a methodology that allows for longitudinal analysis of partner interactions as well as the motivations or "vocabulary of motive" underlying specific behavior. The mutual battering perspective gives considerable attention to the behavior itself, while overlooking for the most part the potential for diverse goals or purposes in each partner's actions. The victims' actions, for example, are typically aimed at pleasing their partners (in order to stop the abuse) and ensuring self-preservation. In contrast, the goals of the perpetrators' actions are to control or punish their partners. Indeed, as argued elsewhere (Renzetti, 1992), it is not the abusive behavior per se, but rather the factors that give rise to the abuse and the consequences of the abuse for both victims and batterers that are central to understanding battering relationships.

Correlates of Abuse

Most of the factors studied as contributors to partner abuse in homosexual relationships have been suggested by studies of partner abuse in heterosexual relationships. As noted in the earlier chapters, these include an imbalance of power between partners; substance abuse; violence or abuse in at least one partner's past, usually his or her family of origin; overdependency on one partner by the other; and personality disorders. Others, such as internalized homophobia, have been suggested largely by research on lesbian and gay couples, although not necessarily those involved in abusive relationships. In any event, some of these are structural-level variables and some are individual-level variables. However, as will be noted, these factors, rather than being distinct, appear to be interrelated and to work in combination to increase the risk that abuse will occur in a given lesbian or gay relationship.

Substance Abuse

As Gelles (1993: 182) points out, the "demon rum" theory of violence and abuse "is one of the most pervasive and widely believed explanations for family violence in the professional and popular literature." Certainly, this explanation has intuitive appeal. Most readers would probably agree that alcohol impairs the drinker's judgment and lowers his or her inhibitions, which, in turn, may lead him or her to become aggressive, perhaps even violent. Most people know a few "bad drunks," individuals who inevitably start a fight when they drink. Interestingly, however, while some researchers still maintain there is a direct causal link between alcohol consumption and domestic violence (e.g., see Flanzer, 1993), a preponderance of research on the relationship between alcohol and violence indicates that expectations of what alcohol will do, rather than the pharmacological effects of alcohol itself, appear to produce aggression and violence in some drinkers. Moreover, with the exception of amphetamines, other drugs such as marijuana, LSD, heroine, and cocaine do not appear to cause users to become violent. Because amphetamines increase the excitability and muscle tension of the user, they may produce impulsive behavior that is violent or aggressive, but this outcome depends on the amphetamine dosage consumed and the prior personality of the user. A user who already has an aggressive personality before consuming a high dosage of amphetamines is likely to become more aggressive while under their influence (Gelles, 1993).

Most research on substance abuse and intimate violence has focused on the effects of alcohol consumption; the results show that a number of variables intervene in the relationship between alcohol and intimate violence. Researchers have reported

that in as few as 6 percent and as many as 85 percent of incidents of heterosexual partner abuse, at least one of the partners, usually the male batterer, had been drinking
(Manzano, 1989; Kaufman, Kantor and Straus, 1987). However, additional research indicates that alcohol's effect on behavior is mediated by such factors as the amount of alcohol consumed, the pre-consumption personality of the drinker, and the expectations by
both the drinker and others as to how alcohol influences behavior.

In making sense of research on alcohol and substance abuse with respect to intimate violence, Gelles (1993) argues that the expectations of the drinker regarding the
effect of alcohol on behavior derive from wider cultural norms. Drawing on work by
MacAndrew and Edgerton (1969), Gelles notes that when people in American society drink or believe they are drunk, they give themselves, and others give them, a
"time-out" from the normal rules of social behavior. At the same time, "[b]ecause family violence is widely considered deviant and inappropriate behavior, there is a desire
to 'hush up' or rationalize abusive behavior in families. The desire of both offenders
and victims to cover up family violence and the belief that alcohol is a disinhibitor
combine to provide a socially acceptable explanation for violence" (Gelles, 1993: 184).
In other words, rather than causing intimate violence, alcohol consumption facilitates
and legitimates such violence. Gelles (1993) provides an extensive review of research
to support this position (see also Kaufman, Kantor, and Straus, 1987).

The relationship between alcohol and intimate violence has been of particular
interest to researchers who study partner abuse in same-sex relationships because of
reports that substance abuse, but especially alcoholism, is a serious problem in the gay
and lesbian communities. Several factors appear to put homosexuals at high risk for
substance abuse. One of the most significant of these is the centrality of bars in the
social lives and leisure activities of homosexuals (Weathers, 1980; Fifield, 1975). In
addition, societal homophobia and oppression of homosexuals generate feelings of
alienation and isolation among gay men and lesbians which, in turn, are associated
with increased alcohol consumption and other forms of substance abuse (Nicoloff and
Stiglitz, 1987; Weathers, 1980; Diamond and Wilsnack, 1978).[3]

In several studies of same-sex partner abuse, the use of alcohol (and other drugs)
was found to be prevalent. Kelly and Warshafsky (1987), for instance, report that alcohol or drug use was related to violence in 33 percent of the cases they studied. Coleman
(1990) found that almost 71 percent of the lesbian couples she characterized as violent used alcohol or drugs compared with only 29.4 percent of the lesbian couples she

---

[3]Researchers have offered two additional reasons for a greater likelihood of alcohol problems among lesbians as opposed to gay men. The first is that some lesbians, like some heterosexual women, drink because
they are depressed and feel a sense of loss, but that in lesbians, depression and isolation may be intensified
by societal homophobia (Diamond and Wilsnack, 1978). Second, recent medical research indicates that
women who drink suffer greater impairment than do men who drink, even when controlling for physical
size. This is because women have less of a specific stomach enzyme that helps in the digestion of alcohol
before it passes into the bloodstream. Consequently, women absorb more alcohol in their bloodstreams than
do men (Freeza et al., 1990).

classified as nonviolent. Schilit, Lie, and Montagne (1990) found that in 64 percent of the 39 abusive lesbian relationships they studied, alcohol or drugs were involved prior to or during battering incidents and that respondents' frequency of alcohol consumption was significantly related to their perpetration of partner abuse as well as their likelihood of being victimized by their partners. Island and Letellier (1991), however, apply Gelles's (1993) argument to gay male relationships and maintain that alcohol and drug abuse typically are used as excuses that allow batterers to avoid full responsibility for their actions. They cite research showing that some batterers decide to batter even before they decide to drink, and that men who batter do so whether or not they are under the influence of alcohol or drugs.

Recent research with battered lesbians (Renzetti, 1992) supports Gelles's (1993) position. When asked if they or their partners were ever under the influence of drugs or alcohol at the time of a battering incident, 33 of the respondents answered in the negative and 67 answered affirmatively. Among the 67 respondents, 35 reported that only their partners were under the influence, 28 that both they and their partners were under the influence, and 4 noted that they themselves were the only ones under the influence at the time of a battering incident.

In early statistical tests of these data, there appeared to be a strong positive relationship between substance abuse and the frequency and severity of partner abuse that these women experienced. However, in a subsequent stepwise regression analysis, the relationship between substance abuse and partner abuse disappeared if the variable that measured the batterer's dependency on her partner was removed from the equation (Renzetti, 1992). This suggests that both substance abuse and partner abuse in lesbian relationships may actually be caused by a third factor, dependency of one partner on another. In fact, the literature on alcohol abuse among lesbians indicates that, for many lesbians, drinking is a means of feeling powerful in order to compensate for feelings of dependency. "Studies that describe lesbians as independent and self-sufficient . . . suggest that, as a group, lesbians may accept dependency needs less readily than heterosexual women do. Through its ability to enhance feelings of personal power, drinking may offer lesbians a way to overcome their needs for dependency" (Diamond and Wilsnak, 1978: 136). Abusing a partner may also be a way to feel powerful and to overcompensate for feelings of dependency.

While data (Renzetti, 1992) do not support a direct relationship between substance abuse and partner abuse in lesbian relationships, data from interviews with a subsample of 40 of the research participants indicate that substance abuse may facilitate partner abuse in these relationships by becoming a basis on which the abusive partner's aggression is excused. In the majority of cases in which one or both partners drank or used drugs, abuse victims and others "explained away" the violence by attributing it to the substance abuse (e.g., "She didn't know what she was doing; she was drunk," or "I know I wouldn't have been beaten if I hadn't been drinking").

There was a strong inclination on the part of the women who had been victimized to rationalize the seemingly irrational behavior of their partners, and substance abuse was a logical and widely accepted means to do this in those cases in which alcohol or drugs had been used. However, it must be kept in mind that in one-third of the cases studied, neither partner was under the influence of alcohol or drugs at the time of the abusive incidents and, in some of these cases, respondents indicated that both they and their partners rarely used alcohol or drugs. These women sought other reasons to account for the battering, and one of the most frequently cited was a history of abuse in their own or their partner's family of origin.

Intergenerational Transmission of Violence

Based on social learning theory, the intergenerational transmission position maintains that individuals who as children witnessed or experienced violence in their families of origin are more likely as adults to be abusive toward their own partners (or children). As the old adage goes, "Children learn what they live." Like the substance abuse explanation, this hypothesis also has intuitive appeal, and as Akers (1985: 46) has pointed out, modeling is "a more complicated process than 'monkey see, monkey do.'" Consequently, research that has tested the intergenerational transmission hypothesis has produced equivocal results (Simons et al., 1995).

In one of the most frequently cited studies of heterosexual couples, Straus, Gelles, and Steinmetz (1980) found that men and women who had witnessed their parents physically attack one another were three times more likely to have been violent toward their own partners than men and women who grew up in nonviolent households. As the severity of the violence they witnessed increased, so did their probability of being violent toward their partners. Moreover, Straus et al. (1980) discovered what they called a "double whammy" effect; that is, individuals in their study who had both witnessed and been victimized by parental violence were five to nine times more likely to be violent toward their own partners than were individuals who grew up in nonviolent households.

Many researchers studying heterosexual intimate violence, however, have been unable to replicate these findings. Some researchers have found no association, or only a very weak one, between having been victimized by parents and current aggression against a partner (O'Leary, 1993; Demaris, 1990). Others report that individuals who have witnessed abuse between their parents are more likely to abuse their own partners than individuals who had experienced abuse at the hands of their parents (Straus and Gelles, 1990; Hotaling and Sugarman, 1986). Still others have found that the "witnessing effect" holds only under specific circumstances or with certain groups (compare, for instance, Demaris, 1990, with Forsstrom-Cohn and Rosenbaum, 1985, and O'Leary, 1988). Finally, Kalmuss (1984) has argued that witnessing parental abuse not only increases the likelihood that one will later be abusive toward one's partner, it also increases the likelihood of becoming an abuse victim in an adult intimate relationship (see also Cappell and Heiner, 1992).

In studies of partner abuse among same-sex couples, the findings with respect to the intergenerational transmission hypothesis are no less confounding. For instance, Lie et al. (1991) found that lesbians who had been victimized in the home as children were significantly more likely to be victimized in an intimate relationship as an adult or to become abusive themselves than lesbians who grew up in nonviolent families. Lie and others (1991) also found support for the "double whammy" effect: Lesbians who had both witnessed and experienced intimate violence as children were significantly more likely than lesbians from nonviolent households to be victimized in an intimate relationship as an adult or to abuse their own partners. In contrast, neither Coleman (1990) nor Kelly and Warshafsky (1987) found support for the intergenerational transmission hypothesis in their studies of partner abuse in gay and lesbian relationships.

Support for the intergenerational transmission hypothesis was also not forthcoming from a study of 100 self-identified battered lesbians (Renzetti, 1992). The data do not indicate a high incidence of abuse in the personal histories of either the research participants or their abusive partners. While the study participants had a lower incidence of victimization in their families of origin than did their abusive partners, there were almost as many abusers who grew up in nonviolent households as abusers who grew up in violent ones. An interesting finding that did emerge, however, involved those cases in which abuse had been present in either the respondent's or her partner's family of origin. In these cases, the history of abuse was subsequently used by respondents, their batterers, and others to excuse or legitimate the current violence.[4]

Thus, while a good deal of research indicates that for both heterosexuals and homosexuals, a history of abuse may increase the risk of being both an abuser and victim of abuse by an intimate partner, some research also shows that family-of-origin violence may contribute to current battering in much the same way that substance abuse does—that is, as a facilitator. If one believes that childhood exposure to abuse "preprograms" one to become a perpetrator or a victim, then such a belief may be utilized to rationalize a batterer's current abusive behavior and even to exonerate the batterer (see also Gelles and Cornell, 1990). Clearly, more research is needed to better understand the role of childhood exposure to intimate violence in the etiology of both heterosexual and homosexual partner abuse.

The Balance of Power

A major contribution of feminist theory to our understanding of intimate violence has been its focus on partner abuse as a means of coercive control through which the batterer displays power and enforces the subjection of the victim (Yllö, 1993). The focus of the feminist model, however, has been almost exclusively on heterosexual relationships in which men batter women. In this view, men batter women because they benefit from the violence: "He gets his way, feels strong and manly, and has a partner catering to him in hopes of avoiding further violence" (Yllö, 1993: 57).

---

[4]Interestingly, one woman reported that she was not abused by her partner until after she confided to her partner that she had been abused as a child (Renzetti, 1992).

Feminists have recognized some of the limitations of their model. Yllö (1993) points out that the feminist paradigm has fallen short of providing a full or complete explanation of intimate violence. For instance, it does not explain why a relatively small percentage of men choose to batter, despite the rewards that battering seems to bring. In addition, while the feminist perspective highlights the gendered nature of power and entitlement within heterosexual relationships, this emphasis overlooks the problem of partner abuse in same-sex relationships, especially lesbian relationships. Unless we accept the notion that in abusive lesbian relationships one partner (the batterer) plays the masculine role and one partner (the victim) plays the feminine role, the feminist premise that intimate violence is a manifestation of unequal gender relations in American society does not seem to apply to these relationships. There is, in fact, no evidence to support the "gender role-play" explanation of lesbian partner abuse. Lesbian batterers are, as often as not, physically smaller than their victims, and they also are frequently described as "more feminine" than their partners (Renzetti, 1992).

Still, this is not to say that the feminist model cannot enrich our understanding of partner abuse in same-sex relationships. The feminist emphasis on domestic violence as coercive control—as a means to exercise power, to get one partner to do what another wants even if he or she doesn't want to do it—clearly applies to abusive same-sex relationships. The goals of homosexual batterers are the same as those of heterosexual batterers. Modifying Yllö's (1993) words a bit, these goals include getting one's own way, feeling strong and powerful, and having a partner who caters to one's needs.

The difficulty empirically is how to measure the role of power as a contributor to intimate violence. Traditionally, power has been measured in terms of which partner makes the most decisions in a relationship, but this approach has several drawbacks: It treats all decisions as if they are of equal weight, it fails to account for the authority to delegate decision-making responsibilities, and it overlooks the everyday division of labor within an intimate relationship. Another way to measure power is to look at resource differences between partners. The partner with greater resources—that is, more money, education, prestige, or status—is considered more powerful. Most studies that have examined the role of power in the etiology of intimate violence have operationalized the variable in one or both of these ways.

In studies of heterosexual partner abuse, researchers have usually found a strong association between the balance of power in the relationship and the incidence of battering (e.g., see Walker, 1989; Straus et al., 1980). Nevertheless, it is not always clear whether power is the independent or dependent variable. Does an imbalance of power between intimate partners increase the risk of intimate violence? Does violence simply serve to reinforce one partner's already greater power over the other? Or, does the abuse itself produce a power imbalance in the relationship that effectively puts one partner in a position of dominance over the other? Some studies of heterosexual couples (e.g., Gondolf, 1988; Finkelhor et al., 1983) indicate that the likelihood of intimate violence increases if the male partner perceives his power in the relationship to be waning; the violence is a means for him to reassert his dominance and control. Others (e.g., Straus, 1974), however, argue that the batterer in an abusive relationship is the partner with the most power; violence is just one manifestation or expression of that partner's greater power.

Interestingly, in studies of abusive homosexual couples, the association between power and violence has been less strong. For instance, Kelly and Warshafsky (1987) measured power in terms of both status differentials between partners and the division of household labor but found few significant correlations between these variables and the incidence of partner abuse among the gay and lesbian couples they surveyed. Differences in income, education, race, religion, and age were unrelated to the incidence of intimate violence in Kelly and Warshafsky's study. They did find, however, that there were significant positive correlations between three measures of the division of labor—responsibility for major expenses, minor expenses, and cooking—and the likelihood of victimization. In a study done by Bologna and others (1977), respondents' perceived lack of power in the relationship compared with their partner's was correlated with relationship violence, but in some cases this perceived lack of power increased the likelihood of perpetration, while in others it increased the likelihood of victimization.

In examining the role of power among battered lesbians, Renzetti (1992) measured power in terms of status differentials between partners, decision making, and the division of household labor. None of the division of labor variables correlated significantly with either frequency or severity of abuse. Two status differentials—differences in intelligence and social class—produced strong positive correlations with the most severe forms of abuse inflicted by batterers. However, other measures of economic inequality—including whether the victim earned more money than the batterer and the degree of the victim's economic dependence on the batterer—yielded contradictory findings. Batterers clearly had a greater say in decision making in these relationships. It was not clear from the data whether this arrangement was in place before the battering began or if it emerged subsequent to the battering as a further means for batterers to assert control in the relationship and as a way for their partners to appease them and try to stop the abuse.

Finally, in her study of lesbian couples, Coleman (1990), while not examining power per se, considered whether status incompatibility and status inconsistency might contribute to partner abuse. *Status incompatibility* refers to discrepancies of status between partners; whereas *status inconsistency* refers to a discrepancy between an individual's achieved status and what that individual would be expected to achieve given her (or his) background.[5] Interestingly, Coleman found no relationship between a couple's status incompatibility and partner abuse, but did find that the risk of violence increased with greater status inconsistency on the part of one of the partners. Her explanation of the latter finding is that status inconsistent individuals probably have lower self-esteem and experience increased stress; this, in turn, lowers their ability to cope and to relate to a partner in a healthy way.

---

[5]An example of status inconsistency would be an individual with a Ph.D. who is employed as a check-out clerk in a grocery store.

Unfortunately, Coleman (1990) did not compare the status inconsistency scores of women who batter with those who are victimized. She, therefore, was unable to test the hypothesis that status inconsistent individuals (or underachievers) are at increased risk of becoming abusive. Nevertheless, her research points in a useful direction because it highlights the fact that power in intimate relationships is a complex, multifaceted phenomenon. Her research is not incompatible with the feminist model of intimate violence, but rather enriches it by offering an answer to the question of why some individuals have a greater need than others to enhance their feelings of power. Another answer to this question that was suggested earlier in the chapter is that batterers are individuals who are highly dependent on their partners but feel ashamed of this dependency because they perceive it as weakness.

Dependency

Most readers would probably agree that a quality necessary to a loving intimate relationship is emotional interdependence between partners. Partners exercise mutual influence in the relationship, and each partner can rely on the other for emotional support (Lamanna and Riedman, 1994). Unfortunately, such a relationship is rather difficult to establish and sustain. Instead, most couples struggle throughout their relationships to balance the need for attachment or intimacy with their partner and the need for independence or autonomy from that partner (Peplau et al., 1978).

With respect to heterosexual relationships, it is commonly assumed that women are more attached to or dependent on their partners and the relationship than men are. Certainly, it is the case in our society that dependency has long been considered an acceptable feminine trait, and it has also been argued that women are more relationship-oriented than men (Cancian, 1985; Gilligan, 1982). It is not that men have no need for dependency or attachment in intimate relationships, but rather that cultural norms encourage them to repress these needs and to express them covertly rather than overtly (Cancian, 1985).

Given that overt dependency in men is devalued—indeed, it is viewed as deviant—a number of researchers have hypothesized that in heterosexual relationships in which the male partner has high dependency needs, there is a significant risk for intimate violence.[6] Walker (1989), for example, has described abusive husbands as being at least emotionally dependent on their wives, although some are financially and physically dependent as well. However, Byrne, Arias, and O'Leary (1992) report that those couples in which the husbands have high dependency (or affiliation) needs and the wives have high autonomy needs are at greatest risk for intimate violence.

---

[6]Research on elder abuse by Pillemer (1985) also shows that perpetrators of this type of interpersonal violence typically were adults who were still dependent on their elderly parents, usually for financial support. Pillemer relates the dependents' embarrassment about their situation to their abuse (see also Pillemer, 1993).

According to Byrne et al. (1992), the probability of violence increases in an intimate relationship in which a highly dependent husband attempts to control his wife, and she resists this control.

At the present time, it is difficult to point to any research that has examined empirically the role of relative dependency among partners in abusive gay male relationships. In contrast, research examining abusive lesbian relationships (Renzetti, 1992) found a significant positive correlation between the batterer's dependency on her partner and the frequency and severity of abuse inflicted. Moreover, the findings are similar to those of Byrne et al. (1992): The greater the batterer's dependency and the greater the victim's desire to be independent, the more likely the batterer is to inflict more types of abuse with greater frequency.

Studies of lesbian relationships have found exceptionally high levels of attachment between partners (Lewis et al., 1981; Peplau et al., 1978). This may be due to several factors. First, as already noted, the socialization and identity development of females in American society tends to attune them to the needs and wishes of others and predicates their sense of self on connectedness to others and others' views of them (Pearlman, 1989; Vargo, 1987). Second, the high level of attachment between lesbian partners is also likely a response to the relative lack of social validation and support that lesbian relationships receive outside the lesbian and gay communities. In response to the negativism and hostility of heterosexual society, lesbian couples may try to insulate themselves by nurturing their relationships as relatively "closed systems" (Krestan and Bepko, 1980). This fosters emotional intensity and closeness in the relationship and, thus, may make a significant contribution to lesbian partners' social and psychological well-being (Lewis et al., 1981). At the same time, though, this intensity and closeness may generate insecurity by disallowing separateness or autonomy for the partners (Lindenbaum, 1985). One partner may fuse or merge her identity with the other, so any attempt by the other to have separate friends, be emotionally distant, or even have a different point of view may be taken as rejection by the fused or merged partner (Pearlman, 1989; Lindenbaum, 1985).

When fusion or merging occurs, conflict is a likely outcome. The partner who is depended on often feels responsible for her partner's well-being, but also experiences increasing resentment toward her partner as well as increasing depression (Pearlman, 1989; Kaufman, Harrison, and Hyde, 1984). The dependent partner is likely to feel weak and ashamed, especially since dependency on a partner, as noted previously, is a trait associated with traditional femininity. Feminism, and in particular lesbian feminism, encourages independence, personal autonomy, and self-actualization for women. Consequently, dependency may be feared or despised because of its association with traditional heterosexual femininity (Burch, 1987).

As discussed earlier, several researchers have suggested that self-destructive behavior, such as alcohol abuse, may be one way that some lesbians cope with their fear of or shame about dependency. My own research (Renzetti, 1992) also indicates that partner abuse may be another means by which some lesbians try to compensate for high dependency needs. Other researchers, however, have not found such strong support for the association between dependency and partner abuse in lesbian relationships. Coleman (1990), for instance, measured the level of cohesion (which could be taken as an indicator of partner dependency) in lesbian relationships and found no correlation with violence in those relationships. Obviously, additional research is needed to clarify the connection between dependency and partner abuse. It will also be important to determine whether this association holds for gay male relationships in which the overall level of dyadic attachment has been found to be lower than that in lesbian relationships (see Lewis et al., 1981).

Internalized Homophobia

Up to now, those factors examined as potential contributors to partner abuse in same-sex relationships have also been found to contribute, more or less, to partner abuse in heterosexual relationships. One variable unique to homosexuals that has been hypothesized as a potential contributor to gay and lesbian partner abuse is internalized homophobia. Shattuck (1992) states this hypothesis as a question: How might the experience of being gay or lesbian (that is, oppressed and alienated by heterosexual society, being forced to "live outside the rules") affect one's relational abilities with an intimate partner?

Internalized homophobia occurs when gay men and women accept heterosexual society's negative attitudes toward them. In their discussion of internalized homophobia, Margolies, Becker, and Jackson-Brewer (1987) apply Allport's (1958) classic analysis of the negative effects on racial minority group members when they accept white people's prejudices against them. These include lowered self-esteem, perceived powerlessness, obsessive concern with group stigma, denial of group membership, withdrawal and passivity, identification with the dominant group, and aggression against members of one's own group. Margolies et al. (1987) and others (Nicoloff and Stiglitz, 1987; Vargo, 1987; Riddle and Sang, 1978) argue that in addition to lowered self-esteem and perceived powerlessness, these effects may manifest themselves among homosexuals in the forms of obsessive closeting of sexual preference, denial of difference between themselves and heterosexuals, failure to make a commitment in their intimate relationships, and self-destructive behavior such as substance abuse. Shattuck (1992) adds partner abuse (i.e., aggression against members of one's own group in Allport's analysis) to this list.

Unfortunately, to date there have been no empirical tests of the hypothesized relationship between internalized homophobia and homosexual partner abuse. Although developing a reliable and valid measure of internalized homophobia may prove daunting, this hypothesis is provocative and worthy of further exploration. Such research should also investigate what factors give rise to internalized homophobia. Why does it appear to have such a severe impact on some gay men and lesbians and not others, given that all homosexuals live in a heterosexist, homophobic society? Perhaps low self-esteem and perceived powerlessness are antecedents rather than consequences of internalized homophobia, putting individuals with such characteristics at greater risk of developing internalized homophobia, and becoming abusive toward their intimate partners.

Personality Disorders

It might be argued that many of the factors discussed so far—for instance, substance abuse, perceived powerlessness, the need to feel powerful, overdependency, and internalized homophobia—are simply symptoms of a more serious personality disorder in individuals who batter. In a careful review of the extant research on personality disorders and battering, O'Leary (1993) found that as the level of physical aggression against an intimate partner escalates, there is a greater likelihood that the abuser has a particular personality trait, style, or disorder that contributes to the abusive behavior. Thus, O'Leary (1993) attributes most incidents of aggression against an intimate partner to learned attitudes that support the use of physical force to right a perceived wrong or to get what one wants. Gender inequality, he also argues, is a critical but not a sufficient risk factor in the emergence of partner abuse (at least in heterosexual relationships). However, in studies that use clinical samples of men who are in treatment for having abused their female partners, a significant number typically are diagnosed as having specific personality disorders (Hamberger and Hastings, 1986, 1988; Murphy et al., 1992).

With respect to same-sex couples, research on personality traits or disorders and abusiveness or aggression is very limited. This may be due, at least in part, to reluctance among some researchers in this area to begin labeling particular interactions in gay and lesbian relationships, even abusive ones, as "sick" or "abnormal," given the negative way homosexuality itself has historically been viewed by the mainstream psychiatric and psychology professions. This reluctance, however, clearly is not shared by Island and Letellier (1991: 40) who argue forcefully that although batterers are not insane, they suffer from "a learned, progressive, diagnosable, and curable mental disorder. There is no other way to view these men. No well-functioning, mentally healthy man engages in domestic violence." Unfortunately, these researchers offer no empirical data from studies of gay men, abusive or otherwise, to support their assertions. Instead, they draw on research done on samples of heterosexual male batterers as well as anecdotes and personal narratives.

Coleman (1992) argues that intimate violence, homosexual as well as heterosexual, may best be understood through a multidimensional perspective that incorporates sociocultural and intergenerational factors but also takes into account the batterer's personality. Drawing on clinical data she has collected while treating lesbian batterers and their partners, Coleman concludes that batterers often have personality disorders, the most prevalent of which are borderline and narcissistic disorders.

Many of the characteristics symptomatic of borderline and narcissistic disorders—including an unclear sense of self, a need for power, and a sense of entitlement—are those previously found to be highly associated with partner abuse in both same-sex and opposite-sex relationships. But while Coleman's (1992) data are more systematic, and her analysis more rigorous than that of Island and Letellier (1991), they fall far short of establishing a causal or direct link between personality disorders and partner abuse among same-sex couples. Considerably more empirical research—especially studies using groups of carefully matched controls—is needed.

Meanwhile, O'Leary (1993) reports that in the fourth revision of the American Psychiatric Association's Diagnostic and Statistical Manual of Mental Disorders (DSM-IV), diagnoses of "partner relational problems with physical abuse" and "partner relational problems with sexual abuse" will be included, although they will not appear in the section of disorders attributable to a mental condition. O'Leary (1993) welcomes these DSM additions on the grounds that mental health and hospital personnel will become more accepting of the problems of abuse and more perpetrators and victims will be treated by private practitioners because the DSM is used by insurers to determine diagnoses eligible for treatment reimbursement. While Island and Letellier (1991) share O'Leary's (1993) enthusiasm, serious reservations must be raised, especially since some of the most methodologically sound research has indicated that personality disorders are apparent in only a small percentage of heterosexual male batterers. Is it really beneficial for either perpetrators or victims to medicalize partner abuse in same-sex or opposite-sex relationships? Couldn't clinical labeling have deleterious consequences by, for example, implying that perpetrators are not really responsible for their actions, that only certain "types" of individuals batter, or that victims share responsibility for the abuse? To answer these questions, future research must evaluate the impact of these DSM additions and the treatment communities' responses to perpetrators and victims in light of them.

Summary

Space limitations preclude the possibility of discussing current responses of the legal, medical, and counseling communities to same-sex partner abuse, as well as families' and friends' reactions to both perpetrators and victims (see Renzetti, 1992; Renzetti, forthcoming). Suffice it to say that the lack of attention to this problem—the failure to take it seriously, the outright denial of its existence in some quarters, and the reluctance to call the violence battering—has made it extremely difficult for victims to get the help they need both to escape an abusive relationship and to heal; and it has left batterers unaccountable and free to victimize others. Fortunately, this attitude is beginning to change. The inclusion in this book of a chapter on partner abuse in same-sex relationships is evidence of this change, as is the recent inclusion of papers on the topic at national conferences (e.g., the National Gay and Lesbian Health Conference) and the convening of a national conference that focused solely on violence in same-sex relationships in St. Paul, Minnesota, in 1992. At the same time, however, few states offer the same legal protections to gay and lesbian abuse victims as they do to heterosexual abuse victims, and widespread homophobia in shelters, domestic violence agencies, police departments, and the courts continues to mean that avenues of help and support available to heterosexual victims of intimate violence usually are closed (or are perceived to be closed) to homosexual victims (Witzer, 1993; Renzetti, forthcoming). To paraphrase Elliott (1990), before one can acknowledge homosexual partner abuse, one must first acknowledge homosexual relationships. In a homophobic society such as ours, is it any wonder that current research and theorizing on same-sex partner abuse is at about the same stage as research and theorizing on opposite-sex partner abuse was twenty years ago?

5

Intimate Violence: Does Socioeconomic Status Matter?

National Institute of Justice

Despite an incredible growth of research and commentary dealing with intimate violence, particularly wife battering, the issue of whether some women because of their socioeconomic status (SES) are more vulnerable to being victimized than others continues to be controversial (Okun, 1986; Schwartz, 1988; Straus and Smith, 1990; Fagan, 1993; Zawitz, 1994). In fact, much research on intimate violence has led many to conclude that the likelihood of victimization is little effected by socioeconomic status (Straus et al., 1980; Gelles and Cornell, 1985; Hotaling and Sugarman, 1990). This chapter will show the misleading nature of this premise. As with other forms of interpersonal violence, there are major differences in the probability of being victimized by intimate violence when socioeconomic status is taken into account. In fact, there is growing evidence that the likelihood of intimate violence is greater for those on the lower end of the socioeconomic scale.

This chapter examines evidence that bears on the question: "Are some women more at risk of being victimized by intimate violence than others?" Attention will be given to factors associated with variations in assault for persons in different economic levels of the class structure. Some of the limitations of "universal risk" arguments will also be discussed. This chapter will conclude with an overview of some strategies for developing a harm reduction approach for dealing with intimate violence across the social structure.

90

Intimate Violence: A Problem for All Classes

Methodological Issues

Historically, the view that violence among intimates (spouses, boyfriends, or nonmarital cohabitants) was confined to the poor was widespread. Much of the reasoning for this opinion stemmed from research conducted during the 1960s and 1970s, most of which relied on official data from police and medical records, precisely those agencies in which economically deprived individuals are likely to be overrepresented because of official actions. In contrast, individuals and families at the upper levels of the social class structure are better able to insulate themselves from the scrutiny of public officials charged with the task of dealing with social problems. Families on the higher end of the socioeconomic scale, who often live in detached homes, have greater privacy than the large numbers of individuals with lower socioeconomic status who often reside in dwellings with multiple residences. In addition, affluent families more often utilize private medical and legal agencies to deal with their problems, further concealing incidents of intimate violence.

But even studies that relied upon self-report surveys of representative samples yielded similar results to those that relied on official data (Straus, 1979; Straus et al., 1980). Research conducted during the 1960s and 1970s supported the view that women on the lower end of the economic scale were more likely to be victims of intimate violence. As a result, the claim that social factors were not related to acts of abuse within the family was challenged (Gelles, 1974; Levinger, 1966; Gayford, 1975; Maden and Wrench, 1977; Elmer, 1967; Gil, 1970; Parke and Collmer, 1975; Straus et al., 1980).

Much of the challenge was based on methodological issues; the most common of these took sampling bias into account. Studies that utilized police, shelter, social service agency, or court records over-sampled the poor, who are more likely to use such services (Okun, 1986); therefore, these studies lacked generalizability. In addition, research based on national samples was also criticized because of inconsistent measures of socioeconomic status across studies. Depending on which indicators of socioeconomic status were utilized—education, income, employment or occupational prestige—findings varied from one study to another.

Complicating this issue was the finding that studies on the social correlates of intimate violence suggested that the observed relationship between socioeconomic status and intimate violence might be a function of outcome measures. In their national study of family violence, Straus and others (1980) found the rate of violence between husbands and wives to be 500 percent greater for families living at or below the poverty level, compared with the rate of spousal violence in high-income (over $20,000) families. In addition, the results also indicated that rates of spousal violence were higher for men with blue-collar jobs and men who were either unemployed or employed part-time. When education was used as an indicator of socioeconomic status, the findings differed. Contrary to expectations, individuals with the least amount of education were not most likely to engage in intimate violence: In some cases they were even less likely to do so than the most highly educated. The disparity between the results of these studies suggested that evidence of socioeconomic influences on intimate violence may reflect measurement decisions more than actual differences in violent behavior (Fagan, 1993).

General population studies showing higher rates of spouse assault among women from lower socioeconomic status groups have also been challenged not only because such estimates are rarely based on sound statistical data, but also because of wide variations in the way in which socioeconomic status is measured across studies (Fagan, 1993). Reporting the magnitude of differences in intimate assault rates for women with low and high socioeconomic status may lead to the conclusion that the relationship between socioeconomic status and intimate violence is weak or nonexistent. Schulman (1979) found only a 3 percent difference between spousal assault rates for low-income women and women whose family incomes were $25,000 or above (11 percent versus 8 percent). In a secondary analysis of the Straus and others data (1980), Hotaling and Sugarman (1990) found no statistically significant differences in reports of verbal aggression and minor violence for women with low or high socioeconomic status, but significant differences in the likelihood of severe assault. Stark and Flitcraft (1988) also found that the effects of male unemployment on spouse-assault rates were negligible when controlling for race, income, and education.

Coupled with the methodological critiques used in early family violence research, there also was evidence that abusive behavior existed in all social strata (Straus et al., 1980; Steinmetz, 1978a). Because violence was found in all social classes, across all occupational types, and in all racial and ethnic groups, some researchers concluded that social factors, in particular income and employment, were not relevant in explaining intimate violence. Rather than consider social factors as an explanation for intimate violence, much research shifted the focus to the role of cultural factors or individual pathologies as causes of intimate violence (Fagan and Browne, 1994).

Shifting Explanatory Paradigms

The shift from socioeconomic status as a causal factor for intimate violence to alternative explanations is shown in the literature on intimate assault. In *Physical Violence and American Families,* Straus and Gelles (1990) devote little attention to the impact of socioeconomic status on intimate violence, despite the fact that much of their research has demonstrated this critical relationship. Although various measures of socioeconomic status are included in the research reported in several chapters of the book, only a cursory discussion of the relevance of social status to violence among intimates is provided. When we consider the importance of this relationship not only to understanding the problem but also to any type of intervention, it is surprising that greater discussion is not devoted to it.

In *Feminist Perspectives on Wife Abuse* (Yllö and Bograd, 1988), the relationship between intimate violence and socioeconomic status is not considered. Most of the contributions to this anthology focus on the dimension of gender with men seen as wielding power over women in all areas of the social system, and that male dominance within the family derives from this wider system of male power. Throughout the materials, intimate violence is viewed as a fundamental dimension of most families. Little consideration is, thus, given to the differential distribution of violence by race, class, and economic status. In contrast, Barnett and Laviolette (1993) examine the link between socioeconomic status and violence among intimates. Their research reports on studies that document this relationship, although the focus is primarily on the impact of battering on women's economic circumstances. Intimate assault, they argue, contributes to the economic dependence of women. Furthermore, Barnett and Laviolette contend that intimate violence aggravates the plight of poor women. Notwithstanding these views, the authors avoid discussing available research findings demonstrating that stressors associated with low socioeconomic status contribute to battering.

Given the major criticisms of intimate violence research, as well as the shift toward cultural factors and individual pathologies as explanatory perspectives, it seems to be an anomaly not to discuss the influence of socioeconomic status on violence among intimates. Not only is this anomaly evident in the empirical literature, but in theoretical models of intimate violence, as well. Rather than considering whether the experiences and exposure to intimate violence by women are differentiated by social status, many researchers, particularly feminists advance a "universal risk" perspective, whereby "all women are equally situated within a patriarchal society, and thus equally likely to be victimized by wife abuse" (Schwartz, 1988: 373).

Universal Risk Theory: Classless Intimate Violence

A theory of universal risk is appealing for several reasons. First, by contending that all women are equally likely to experience interpersonal violence, feminists are able to avoid the perceived classism and racism contained in other studies of abuse. Second, a theory of universal risk serves as a corrective to the pervasive myth that violence among intimates is confined to the lower classes (Gelles and Cornell, 1985). Finally, a universal risk theory provides a useful ideological base on which to mobilize women of diverse backgrounds to take a stand against a problem that is common to all women.

Feminists contend that violence against women can be linked to a patriarchal society, such as the United States and many other Western societies. Martin (1976: 15) contends that "The economic and social structure of our present society depend[s] on the degradation, subjugation, and exploitation of women." Moreover, most feminists argue that the family is the chief institution of patriarchy and that it is the family that encourages its members to conform to patriarchal ideologies and practices through sex-role socialization. As a result of this socialization process, men are viewed as possessing superiority and accordingly, are allocated public and private power (Messerschmidt, 1993). The power men possess in the public realm allows them to control women's labor and sexuality, while private power gives rise to marital rape and wife battering. Although the patriarchal perspective provides an explanation for why some men believe they have the authority to use violence against female partners, the role of socioeconomic status regarding intimate violence needs to be considered in the equation. The contribution of patriarchy to intimate violence may be a function of gender and economic inequality between and among women and men.

Universal risk theory also assumes that the likelihood of victimization is the same for all women, since they are confined to the same status under any patriarchal society. But even within a male-dominated society, a woman's social status will differ and, as a result, the likelihood of victimization will vary as well. In this regard, the life-style exposure approach lends support to the notion of disparity in risk for different types of individuals.

According to this perspective, variations in the probability of victimization can be attributed to life-style differences among victims (Meier and Miethe, 1993). *Life-style* is defined as "routine daily activities, both vocational activities (work, school, keeping house, etc.) and leisure activities" (Hindelang, et al., 1978: 241). Demographic characteristics (such as gender, income, and marital status) are associated with various role expectations, which in turn lead to differences in life-style, exposure to risk, and subsequently to differences in the likelihood of victimization (Hindelang, 1976). Research on factors associated with intimate violence demonstrates that abuse of women is more prevalent and frequent among those groups with lower socioeconomic status (e.g., Peterson, 1980; Gelles and Straus, 1988; Gelles, 1987; Straus and Smith, 1990), which suggest that the likelihood of victimization varies with social status.

A review of comparison group studies of men violent toward their wives (Hotaling and Sugarman, 1986) revealed a set of risk factors that distinguished these men from nonviolent husbands. Abusive husbands were found to have lower occupational status, lower income, and lower educational attainment than nonviolent husband comparison groups. According to Okun (1986: 48), "the most sophisticated studies do seem to establish a relationship between lower-class status and greater conjugal violence . . . even if one corrects for underreporting." In short, given the existing research on wife battering, it is not reasonable to conclude that all women are equally at risk for intimate assault.

If the argument that socioeconomic status is not significantly related to intimate violence is valid, then there is reason to believe that the etiologies and explanations for intimate violence may differ from those used to explain stranger assault. Furthermore, if the social factors that contribute to stranger violence are unrelated to intimate violence, then this would imply that the family itself is a causal factor in intimate violence (Fagan, 1993).

In contrast, the research presented previously demonstrates that intimate violence, similar to stranger assault, is mediated by social structural factors (see also Fagan, 1993). One of the risk factors that differentiates violent individuals from the nonviolent ones, is low socioeconomic status (Elliott and Ageton, 1980; Braithwaite, 1981). In addition, some researchers contend that intra-familial and extra-familial violence are not distinct phenomena (Fagan and Wexler, 1987), and that similar causal processes may account for both forms of interpersonal violence (Hotaling et al., 1990).

Since universal risk theory asserts that socioeconomic status and intimate violence are unrelated, it follows that social controls, and particularly arrest, should be equally effective, regardless of the social status of the abuser. This would imply that the family is the dominant influence in the control of intimate violence, and its impact is independent of formal and informal sanctioning of violent behavior (Fagan, 1993: 211). Recent evidence, however, suggests that, in fact, the effectiveness of social controls (formal and informal) are mediated by social status.

Four quasi-experimental studies of the impacts of arrest on repeat domestic violence (i.e., Berk et al., 1992; Dunford et al., 1990; Pate and Hamilton, 1992; Sherman and Smith, 1992) found that the deterrent effect of arrest varied with employment status. In Colorado Springs (Berk et al., 1992) and Metro-Dade (Pate, Hamilton, and Sampson, 1992), arrest was shown to have a deterrent effect for employed suspects, yet it increased the prevalence of domestic assault for unemployed suspects. Arrest served to deter future violence for employed suspects in Milwaukee (Sherman and Smith, 1992), yet arrest with short custody terms escalated the frequency of repeat violence for suspects who were unemployed. In Omaha (Dunford et al., 1990), the results were similar as in Milwaukee. The recidivism rate was reduced for employed suspects who were arrested, but arrest had a criminogenic effect for unemployed suspects.

Fagan and others (1984) also found that legal sanctions had the greatest deterrent effects for assailants who were highly educated, employed, and had no prior records. In interviews with women whose husbands had desisted their assaultive behavior, Bowker (1983) found legal interventions to be more effective in promoting desistance among men with white-collar jobs and less effective than social sanctions (e.g., relationship loss) for males with blue-collar jobs. Williams and Hawkins's (1992) study of perceptual deterrence suggests that legal and social sanctions interact to deter spouse assault. In their analysis of panel data, they found that the perceived costs of arrest, particularly loss of relationship, had a statistically significant negative effect on whether men would engage in wife assault.

These results not only indicate that social controls reflect the social structure of individuals, but that the effectiveness of formal and informal sanctioning, depends in part, on one's "stake in conformity." The "stakes in conformity" thesis, originally proposed by Toby (1957), lends itself to the suggestion that individuals subject to informal social control in employment and marriage are more likely to be deterred by arrest than those who are unmarried or unemployed. To the extent that an assailant has something to lose—employment with social and economic value and relationships with value—formal interventions become salient sanctions for controlling intimate violence.

Overall then, the findings of these research studies demonstrate the inadequacy of a universal risk theory for understanding the problem of violence among intimates (Schwartz, 1988). To argue that intimate violence is not distinguished by socioeconomic status is inconsistent with the extant literature. Moreover, the most recent research addressing this issue reveals that socioeconomic status is a critical element associated with intimate violence.

Current Research on Intimate Violence and Socioeconomic Status

Recent analysis of the National Crime Victimization Survey for the time period from 1987 to 1991 (Zawitz, 1994) indicates that women with family incomes under $10,000 have the highest rates of intimate violence, and those with family incomes over $30,000, the lowest. Furthermore, women with college degrees had the lowest rates of violence attributed to intimates compared with women with either a high-school degree or less. In addition, Zawitz reports that females are more likely than males to be victimized by intimates such as husbands or boyfriends. Compared to men, women experienced ten times as many incidents of violence by intimates.

The most recent analysis of the National Crime Victimization Survey substantiates Zawitz's findings. Bachman and Saltzman (1995) also found that women in families with incomes falling below $10,000 were more likely than women in higher economic status groups to be victims of intimate violence. Women age 19 to 29 were also more likely than women in other age categories to be victims of violence in intimate relationships. According to these estimates, women were approximately six times more likely than men to experience violence committed by intimates.

Additional research pertaining to legal intervention further demonstrates the influence of socioeconomic status on violence between intimates. Utilizing hotline data from the Milwaukee Domestic Violence Experiment (Sherman et al., 1992), Moore (1995) examined the relationship between victim attributes, legal sanctions, and revictimization and found that employment was significantly related to prevalence of revictimization. In addition, the presence of dependent children in the household also contributed significantly to repeat incidents of revictimization (see Table 5.1). However, educational attainment was not significantly associated with the proportion of revictimized individuals. In this respect, empirical evidence in both the Moore (1995) and Straus and others (1980) studies cautions the use of educational attainment as the sole measure of socioeconomic status.

Logistic regression analysis was used to estimate the likelihood of revictimization for the entire Milwaukee sample, which yielded similar results. Being employed significantly reduced the probability of future victimization (see Table 5.2). However, in the model, the presence of dependent children was not significantly related to the likelihood of subsequent violence. This lack of relationship suggests that future research should consider not only the presence of dependent children, but age and number of persons in the household as well.

The Need for a Different Approach

Throughout this chapter, it has been argued that violence among intimates varies according to socioeconomic status. Women on the lower end of the economic scale are at greater risk of victimization than their counterparts at the higher levels. Intimate violence is more prevalent and tends to be more frequent and severe among women

TABLE 5.1 Bivariate Relationships for Various Victim Attributes, Arrest, and Revictimization (n = 1,200)

VARIABLE		PROPORTION REVICTIMIZED	VARIABLE		PROPORTION REVICTIMIZED
All cases		0.302	Employed		
Arrest			No	(n = 854)	0.328[*]
No	(n = 398)	0.299	Yes	(n = 343)	0.230
Yes	(n = 802)	0.300	Cohabitating		
Race			No	(n = 136)	0.206
Black	(n = 854)	0.303	Yes	(n = 1058)	0.313[*]
White	(n = 296)	0.293	Victim's sex		
Marital status			Male	(n = 101)	0.089
Not married	(n = 769)	0.323[*]	Female	(n = 1094)	0.321[*]
Married	(n = 370)	0.284	Dependent children		
History of abuse			No	(n = 40)	0.250
No	(n = 198)	0.202	Yes	(n = 556)	0.350[*]
Yes	(n = 638)	0.331[*]	Education (high school grad)[+]		
Prior violence			No	(n = 304)	0.342
No	(n = 348)	0.273	Yes	(n = 396)	0.331
Yes	(n = 350)	0.391[*]			

[*]Indicates a significant difference at the 0.05 level in this outcome measure across categories of the independent variable.
[+]Data from initial interviews of victims in the Milwaukee Domestic Violence Experiment.

TABLE 5.2 Logistic Regression for Subsequent Revictimization Based on Various Victim Characteristics (Logit Coefficient, Standard Error, Significance of W)[a]

PREDICTOR VARIABLES

Constant	−7.61	(1.85)[***]
Arrest	−0.189	(0.413)
Black	0.151	(0.256)
Female	2.56	(1.03)[**]
Employed	−1.13	(0.290)[***]
High-School Education	0.046	(0.836)
Unmarried	0.098	(0.238)
Cohabitating	1.11	(0.452)[**]
Dependent Children in Household	0.263	(0.309)
History of Abuse	0.746	(0.299)[**]
Prior Acts of Violence	0.425	(0.221)[*]
Exposure Time	0.966	(0.461)[*]

[a]Significance of Wald: [*]p. 05; [**]p. 01; [***]p. 001

with lower socioeconomic status. Although socioeconomic status is not the only factor that contributes to intimate violence (community, cultural and individual influences are also important), the continued failure to consider its significance in the onset and persistence of intimate violence is a major oversight.

Given the disparity in risk of intimate violence, it is critical that interventions employed to address this serious problem be based on this information. Singular approaches, rooted in the assumption that intimate violence cuts across all economic classes uniformly, may yield unequal outcomes depending on the victim's socioeconomic status. For many women in lower socioeconomic status groups, strategies of this nature could exacerbate rather than alleviate the abusive behavior directed toward them. To adequately deal with these issues, a harm-reduction approach to violence among intimates is recommended.

Harm-Reduction Approach

The goal of a harm-reduction approach is not only to decrease the prevalence of intimate violence but to reduce its frequency and severity among those women in lower socioeconomic status. The adoption of this strategy acknowledges that intimate violence potentially affects all women but that the likelihood of occurrence varies across the social strata.

Since a primary goal of the harm-reduction model is to reduce the prevalence of intimate violence, it is necessary to communicate to victims and batterers the serious nature of this behavior. Widespread public awareness campaigns can be useful to this end. Through media attention, abused women learn that they are not alone and that other women are experiencing partner violence; they also are informed about where they may go for help in their community. Men learn that violent behavior is not only inappropriate, it's illegal. In addition, through public awareness programs, individuals not directly affected by intimate violence may become more sensitive to the issue and may be more willing to intervene to stop this problem. Furthermore, by educating young people about the problem of intimate violence, and counseling children who have witnessed it, partner violence can perhaps be reduced in future generations (Sorrells, 1977; Straus et al., 1980; Stark and Flitcraft, 1985; Fagan et al., 1993).

Directing widespread media attention to the problem of intimate violence can also be extremely beneficial in reaching individuals on the high end of the social strata. Because these women are more likely to rely on private agencies to handle incidents of intimate violence, media campaigns will need to focus on available resources and legal avenues if such incidents are to be reported to authorities.

In addition to increasing public awareness of violence among intimates, it is essential to address the needs of victims directly. Health care professionals should not only concern themselves with treating victims of intimate violence for their physical injuries but moreover, they should attempt to establish the level of seriousness and persistence if at all possible (Klingbeil and Boyd, 1984). This information could prove beneficial for subsequent legal proceedings.

Along with medical assistance, many victims of intimate abuse may require legal representation if a decision to file a complaint with the legal authorities is forthcoming. Moreover, legal assistance may enable an abused woman to extricate herself from the relationship whether or not she decides to press charges.

Employment and financial assistance are also important resources for victims of intimate abuse, particularly in light of research showing that education and employment (Gelles, 1976; Strube and Barbour, 1983, 1984) significantly influence the decision to remain in abusive relationships or seek outside help. Women who do not pursue outside intervention or leave the assaultive partner are more likely to be unemployed and less likely to have completed high school. Furthermore, Kalmuss and Straus (1982) found that higher rates of severe marital violence were associated with greater economic dependence (e.g., unemployment or the presence of small children in the home).

This chapter has attempted to demonstrate that intimate violence is more common, frequent, and severe among women at the lower end of the socioeconomic scale. Therefore, if society is serious about reducing the prevalence of intimate violence, battered women must be given the kinds of resources necessary for leaving abusive relationships or at least to control the violence directed toward them. Increasing the number of shelters for women who choose to leave assaultive partners will enable many abused women and their children to freely plan their futures in an atmosphere of security.

In the past, formal interventions for intimate violence have consisted primarily of advising couples about seeking outside help or providing some form of mediation. After the results of the Minneapolis Domestic Violence (Sherman and Berk, 1984) experiment were widely publicized, arrest became the preferred or mandatory response. Yet whether arrest actually serves to reduce subsequent violence is unclear. As noted previously, some studies indicate (e.g., Berk et al., 1992; Dunford et al., 1990; Pate, Hamilton, and Sampson, 1992; Sherman and Smith, 1992) that arrest interacts with social status, producing a deterrent effect for offenders with higher socioeconomic status but escalating violence for perpetrators with lower socioeconomic status. Unfortunately, few studies have considered the impact of arrest from the perspective of the victim.

The harm-reduction approach requires a coordinated, comprehensive legal response to intimate violence, namely, one that addresses the needs of both victims and offenders. Arrest in itself may not reduce subsequent violence, but arrest coupled with prosecution, conviction, and a jail-prison sentence may produce a strong deterrent effect. Thus, police agencies should make intimate violence a priority and require officers to document all reported incidents, establish arrest as a preferred response, make protection orders available, enforce protection orders, and maintain a current file of all valid protection orders in their jurisdiction. Prosecutors should organize specialized units to handle intimate violence cases and should neither require the victim to sign a formal complaint against the abuser nor to testify at preliminary hearings. Judges should consider a wide variety of dispositional alternatives based on the consequences of the harm done to the victim; they should also make protection orders available on an emergency basis, establish guidelines for handling intimate violence cases expeditiously, and impose conditions that limit dangerous defendants' access to victims. Formal interventions with batterers of intimate violence should not only include legal sanctions but also court-mandated treatment.

Summary

A review of recent research dealing with the correlates of wife battering indicates that social class and socioeconomic status are downplayed as significant causative factors in the onset and persistence of the violence. In contrast, both variables have been extensively considered in studies on testing bias in IQ tests, violent crime and delinquency, and early pregnancy and birth control. Yet, much evidence on the likelihood of victimization indicates that some women are more vulnerable than others to intimate assault. Research on this issue clearly demonstrates that violence among intimates varies according to the socioeconomic status of the victims. Based on these findings, it appears that the universal risk theory is inadequate for explaining the variations in assault among women at different economic levels of the class structure. Theory development must begin with an understanding that intimate violence is more prevalent in some socioeconomic arrangements than others.

Any strategies developed to address the problem of intimate violence must also be informed by the evidence presented in this chapter, if they are going to be beneficial. To disregard the impact of socioeconomic status decontextualizes intimate violence. Furthermore, non-context-specific interventions may yield dissimilar outcomes for women who are situated within different economic levels of the class structure. For women with lower socioeconomic status, these strategies could result in an escalation of violence rather than its reduction.

This chapter recommends a harm-reduction approach to the problem of intimate violence. Such a framework would focus on (1) decreasing the prevalence of intimate assault among all women and (2) reducing the frequency and severity of violence among lower socioeconomic status women. Different strategies may be employed to implement this approach—for example, educating individuals through the media, schools, and institutions of higher learning about the seriousness of violence among intimates; providing the kinds of social services that address the problem of intimate violence (e.g., shelters for women and children, counseling programs, or victim services agencies); increasing legal remedies available to victims of abuse; and providing women with the resources necessary to escape abusive relationships. These strategies are discussed in more depth in the later chapters of this volume. Whichever measures are adopted, they need to be congruent with the socioeconomic status of the victim.

PART II

Intimate Victimization: Strategies of Abuse and Survival

The chapters in this section focus on the interpersonal dynamics of intimate violence, especially the effects of victimization. While much research exists on victims of abuse, there is literally a dearth of in-depth research on abusive partners in terms of the motives and meanings associated with the use of force and violence against their intimate partners (Ptacek, 1988; Adams, 1988; Gelles et al., 1994; Stacey et al., 1994; Tolman and Bhosley, 1991; Vaselle-Augenstein and Ehrlich, 1992).

Yet, if integrated theories of intimate violence are to be established, it is all the more critical to understand the effects of the violence not only on the victim, but on the offender as well. Such data will increase our understanding of the factors that prevent victims from leaving abusive relationships; equally important, it will facilitate the development of appropriate strategies to eliminate the persistence and severity of intimate violence. In addition, the chapters that follow provide further evidence of the need for establishing categories of batterers and victims to account for the varied incidents of intimate violence that are generally lumped under the "domestic violence" umbrella.

The chapters by Ptacek and Ferraro provide insight into the effects of victimization and a glimpse of the meanings and motives behind the offenders' use of force and violence against intimate partners. Throughout the chapters, the authors focus on the process of domination that is achieved through the use of force and violence, the absence of reciprocity in terms of emotional involvement, the erosion of personal freedom and liberty, and the growing sense of terror that occupies the lives of victims.

In documenting the personal struggles that battered women undertake simply to survive, the authors demonstrate how violence is both integrated into and disassociated from the lives of victims and offenders. Through the words of the victims, the authors provide an insightful narrative on the terror that many women in abusive relationships experience. Although one-time offenders of intimate violence may inflict serious injury on their victims, they are not the focus of the chapters by Ferraro or Ptacek. These authors direct their concern to those batterers who persist in the use of violence even when public sanctions are threatened or administered. Given that it is these batterers and their victims who are more likely to become enmeshed in the social and criminal justice networks, the search for appropriate measures of deterrence is essential. In this regard, Ptacek, focuses on the motives of men who batter women, drawing on the personal accounts of the women these men battered. Given the recent "discovery" of intimate violence, the establishment of effective sanctions continues to evolve. Understanding the motives behind the infliction of intimate violence can only be beneficial to this process.

Using a random sample of requests for restraining orders, Ptacek profiles the women who seek these orders, as well as their reasons for doing so. He notes that most of the behavior on the part of the offenders is criminal in nature; 70 percent of it constitutes assault and battery under state criminal law. The seriousness of the violence, shown in Ptacek's analysis, places many women in continual fear of injury not only to themselves, but to their children because threats to injure the children are not uncommon by men faced with the potential dissolution of a relationship.

Ptacek shows that the use of violence and abuse is intended to achieve some objective on the part of the offender. For many batterers, the violence is a well-rehearsed tactic of social control that is available to men—one that destroys any level of negotiation essential to intimate partnerships. Although Ptacek's focus is on men who batter, the use of violence in any intimate partnership (including those involving same-sex partners) is an explicit expression of one partner's power and domination over another partner. When the violence becomes an integral part of the relationship, not only is the domination complete, but the partner's dominance is continually emphasized every time the violence is carried out or threatened for some alleged reason. To prevent and control intimate violence, we must understand why these relationships, so lacking in mutual levels of emotional reciprocity, persist.

As in the past when poverty was blamed on the willful behavior of those who found themselves in this condition (Katz, 1989), the persistence of intimate violence continues to be attributed to the victim's willingness to remain in the abusive relationship. Rather than focusing on the character of the victim to explain why victims remain, Ptacek and Ferraro provide an understanding of the kinds of barriers that prevent victims from leaving abusive relationships. Furthermore, both authors shatter the myth that battered women are largely passive or helpless victims, unable to confront or leave abusive partners. As Ferraro notes throughout her chapter, the continued reality of threats and retaliation for those victims who attempt to leave makes survival a significant part of their everyday routine activities.

The fear of retaliatory violence comes not only from actual incidents, but it is supported by the power men have within those institutions and organizations that use force and violence to attain their goals and objectives—for instance, law enforcement agencies, military groups, and sports teams (McBride, 1995). The privilege of force, largely held by men, establishes both a symbolic and a real sense of control within the private spheres of intimacy. Furthermore, the support for aggression within male peer groups, such as positive reinforcement for displays of exaggerated masculinity and toughness, are in direct contradiction to those supports necessary to establishing intimate relationships based on reciprocal trust and symmetry of power (Toby, 1974; Toch, 1992; Messerschmidt, 1993). There is, for example, growing evidence that some men may express violence in a variety of behavior patterns ranging from interpersonal behavior involving strangers to behavior within intimate relationships (Fagan et al., 1983; Fagan and Wexler, 1987; Kandel-Englander, 1992). In this context, violence or its potential threat can be an established technique of social and personal control whether it takes place within a group or within the intimate setting of dating, courtship, and marriage.

In recasting the image of the battered woman from that of victim to that of survivor, Ferraro elucidates the decision-making process in which women engage to eliminate violence in their relationships. Pointing to the intense physical and emotional involvement that develops in intimate relationships, Ferraro shows why most women perceive the first incident of intimate violence to be an aberrant event. If the battering persists, however, the level of emotional commitment between the partners is threatened. To protect this commitment, Ferraro argues that many victims engage in "techniques of neutralization," ranging from the denial of injury or its seriousness to appeals to the belief that the offender can be redirected to nonviolent behavior if the right conditions prevail. In addition, Ferraro demonstrates that these techniques cause victims to suffer diminished feelings of self-worth and bewilderment about their own behavior. Unfortunately, many women blame themselves for the persistence of violence and, in accommodating to the violence, relinquish their autonomy and support. Furthermore, because of the increased involvement of the public in private violence, the nature of the responses by institutions and organizations can either enhance or undermine the techniques of neutralization associated with the battered victim.

An additional barrier to leaving abusive relationships is the level of economic resources that battered women are able to garner. Women without job skills or work histories face exceedingly difficult obstacles in their quest for economic independence and security from abuse and violence. Those on welfare are especially vulnerable; not only do they have fewer resources, but many are socially isolated and distrustful of social service agencies. Under these conditions, violence and abuse may become more severe and persistent. Thus, just as the techniques of neutralization are influenced by the social and cultural context in which they occur, so too are the strategies of survival. Understanding how and under what conditions society condones the use of force in intimate partnerships is essential to the expansion of the preventive strategies aimed at ending violence between intimate partners.

6

The Tactics and Strategies of Men Who Batter

Testimony from Women Seeking Restraining Orders*

JAMES PTACEK

Tufts University

[T]he privilege, ancient though it be, to beat her with a stick, to
pull her hair, choke her, spit in her face or kick her about
the floor, or to inflict upon her like indignities,
is not now acknowledged by our law.
—*JUDGE CHARLES PELHAM, FULGHAM V. THE STATE,*
46 ALA. 146–147 (1871)

AFFIDAVIT: Describe in detail the most recent incidents of abuse.
State what happened, the dates,who did what to whom, and
describe any injuries. Also describe any history of abuse.
—*INSTRUCTIONS FOR OBTAINING A RESTRAINING ORDER*
IN MASSACHUSETTS COURTS (MGLC209A)

One of the first laws against wife battering was passed in the Massachusetts Bay Colony in 1641 (Pleck, 1987). More a symbolic act than the beginning of criminal prosecution of batterers, the law was rarely enforced and does not seem to have survived the Revolutionary War (Pleck, 1987, 1983). In the late 1800s, a period of active

*Department of Sociology and Anthropology, Tufts University. I am grateful to Bonnie Zimmer, Tina Nappi, Danielle London, Todd Crosset, Anne Richmond, Susan Ostrander, Shulamit Reinharz, Andrew Klein, Albert P. Cardarelli, and a host of feminist activists in the Boston area for their support and encouragement during this research. This chapter is part of a larger study of judicial demeanor and women's experience when they seek restraining orders. This research was supported in part by a Dissertation Fellowship from the Harry Frank Guggenheim Foundation.

political campaigns by women to increase the penalties for wife battering and rape, a series of state supreme court decisions, such as the one cited previously, established that the "privilege" of battering women no longer found legitimation in law (Pleck, 1983). In spite of these changes, another century would pass before laws against the battering of women began to be enforced with any regularity (Pleck, 1987; Lerman, 1981).

In the 1990s, after two decades of renewed feminist activism, violence by men against their intimate partners is more visible than ever before. Indeed, intimate violence has become bureaucratized; the complaint forms for restraining orders now contain the language shown in the epigraph, which indicates that while the "privilege" of men to abuse women is no longer acknowledged in the written law, the fact of its widespread occurrence is now openly conceded. In the glare of recent media attention to crimes against women, courts are now hearing the testimony of abused women in an unprecedented manner. Yet, there is already evidence of a backlash against the modest gains made by women in terms of recent legislation and much needed remedies within the criminal justice system for abused women. Ancient characterizations of women as liars and manipulators who exaggerate their suffering have assumed new forms in public discourse; some lawyers and judges claim that women are dishonestly seeking restraining orders to gain advantage in divorce cases, win child support settlements, or unfairly displace men from the marital home. Such misogynist allegations deny both the commonness and severity of violence against women in modern society (Mahoney, 1991; Ritmeester and Pence, 1992). At a 1993 forum on restraining orders sponsored by the Dorchester [Massachusetts] Bar Association, one defense attorney summed up this misogynist perspective bluntly: "Of the fifty to sixty thousand restraining orders issued, how many women get charged with perjury?"

Given the high levels of conflict inherent in the opposing views about why women seek restraining orders, it is increasingly important for researchers to understand the nature of the events that women are reporting to the courts. More specifically, both the means and the ends of intimate violence must be detailed. This chapter presents an analysis of the tactics and strategies employed by men, as reported by women in restraining order complaint forms. The term *tactics* refers to the types of violence and abuse men use against women. The term *strategies* refers to the goals of this violence and abusiveness—that is, what these men were trying to accomplish with their assaults. Essentially, this is an analysis of the motives of men who batter from the perspectives of battered women.

What can we learn about the motives of men who batter by listening to women's testimony? If by *motives* we mean "the goals of the violence," then it is essential that we understand how women explain and describe their violent experiences. Both feminist and criminological theories strongly emphasize the "social control" aspect of battering. For example, Barbara Hart (1988: 17) states that "Battering is the sum of all past acts of violence, and the promise of future violence, that achieves enhanced power and control for the batterer." In analyzing crime as social control, Donald Black (1983) discusses the ways in which battering is often a means of punishment or a way of violently enforcing a man's expectations of a woman. Battering is, therefore, a brutal form of communication; to the extent that a batterer is sending a message, an abused woman's perspective on the meaning of the violence is all-important to our understanding of intimate violence.

There is also evidence from studies of men who batter that their own accounts of the violence cannot be taken at face value. The treatment literature on batterers has emphasized the tendency of these men to minimize or deny the intentionality of their violence (Adams, 1988a; Dutton, 1988; Edleson and Tolman, 1992; Gondolf, 1985; Pence and Paymar, 1986). In interviews with men who batter (Ptacek, 1988), individuals would often switch back and forth between denying responsibility for their violent assaults and arguing that the women deserved it for failing to fulfill the obligations of a "good wife." Clearly, research on men who batter is needed in order to understand the self-perceptions of these men; the meanings that violence has for them; the social learning of violence; and the ways in which their violence can be stopped. In terms of the impact of violence and abuse on the social control of women, however, the perspectives of abused women will be more telling. Only women who have been battered can testify about both the physical suffering and the meanings that the violence has had in their lives.

This exploratory study of the motivations of violent and abusive men is based on court documents, which are notoriously incomplete; it offers evidence of only a limited range of men accused of violence. Nonetheless, a study of the types of violence and abuse reported to the courts is crucial to public policy debates on civil remedies for abused women and criminal sanctions for batterers. Affidavits by women in support of their requests for restraining orders are public record in Massachusetts. What these sworn statements lack in terms of depth and completeness is balanced by the immediacy of the women's accounts, their descriptions of the objectives behind their partners' violence, and the portraits they give of the dilemmas involved in separation.

This chapter is divided into three main sections. The first section presents a review of the research methods and a discussion of the status of the relationships between the women seeking protection and the men accused of violence. In the second section, reports of violent and abusive tactics by men are examined for the types of abuse that they depict, the levels of criminality that they contain, and the kinds of injuries and other consequences of the violence that they describe. The final section presents and interprets the strategies and ideologies that women report. It is hoped that this study will help anchor public policy debates over violence intervention in the everyday experiences of women who seek to free themselves from terror and fear.

Methodology

This section examines the testimony by women on the motivation of violent intimate partners, as contained in requests for restraining orders in two Massachusetts criminal courts: the Dorchester and Quincy district courts. The Dorchester District Court serves a working-class and poor population, predominantly Black and Latino; the Quincy District Court serves a middle- and working-class population, largely White. In 1992, these were two of the busiest lower criminal courts in Massachusetts; 2,251 restraining orders were filed in the Dorchester court; 1,695 restraining orders were filed in the Quincy court (Massachusetts Trial Court, 1993). In 1992, the Dorchester court was the second highest court statewide in restraining order filings; Quincy the sixth highest court. A record high of over 53,000 requests for restraining orders were filed in Massachusetts in 1992 (Massachusetts Office for Victim Assistance, 1993).

A random sample of 100 cases filed in 1992 were selected for study; 50 cases drawn from the Dorchester District Court and 50 cases from the Quincy District Court. Every fifth case selected involved a woman seeking an order against a husband, ex-husband, boyfriend, or ex-boyfriend, beginning on the same date in each court. In Massachusetts, court records on restraining orders are officially open to the public, in recognition of "the public's general right to examine and evaluate the quality of justice done in its courts" (Massachusetts Trial Court, 1990). Qualitative and quantitative data from the original complaint forms and the court orders issued by the judges were gathered in order to construct a profile of the relationships of the women to the defendants. The women's affidavits are also part of the court files. These affidavits are written statements, signed under penalty of perjury, which women file as part of the restraining order request. In their own words, written out in longhand, women detail the range of violence and abuse that prompted them to seek court protection.

Relationship status, in this analysis, incorporates four dimensions: marital status; residence status; parental status; and whether there is evidence that the relationship has been ended. Half of the women who sought orders at both courts were married to the men named as defendants. At the Dorchester District Court, 50 percent ($n = 25$) of the women were currently married at the time they sought a restraining order. At the Quincy District Court, 44 percent ($n = 22$) of the women were married to the men they identified as abusive. This proportion of women who were married is similar to the results from studies of restraining orders in Berks County, Pennsylvania (Gondolf, 1992), and Denver and Boulder, Colorado (Harrell, Smith, and Newmark, 1993). A recent study of restraining orders in New Haven, Connecticut (Chaudhuri and Daly, 1992), reported that 77 percent of the women were married to the defendants.

Only 35 percent ($n = 35$) of the women were living with the defendants when they applied for the restraining order. In the Dorchester court, of those women who were married, 44 percent were separated; another 8 percent of married women either left for a shelter or planned to leave home the next day. In Quincy, 45 percent of the married women listed different home addresses from their husbands. Most of the women in Berks County, Pennsylvania (Gondolf, 1992), and Denver and Boulder, Colorado (Harrell et al., 1993), were also living apart from the defendant when they filed restraining order petitions. This data is summarized in Table 6.1. There is also substantial evidence that a large proportion of the remaining women had either separated or had ended their relationships by the time they sought restraining orders. Women who were separated, divorced, had formerly cohabited, or who identified their defendants as ex-boyfriends constitute 44 percent ($n = 44$) of the cases. Since some women did not provide a detailed history, this must be seen as a low estimate; at least half of the relationships most likely had ended or, at the very least, had been drastically changed in status by the time the women reached the court.

TABLE 6.1 Relationship Status of Women in Random Sample of 100 Restraining Order Files

	DORCHESTER COURT	QUINCY COURT	COMBINED[*]
Married, living together	26%	24%	25%
Married, separated	24	20	22
Divorced	2	4	3
Cohabiting	6	14	10
Previously cohabited	16	10	13
Dating, no children in common	4	8	6
Ex-dating, no children in common	6	6	6
Children, unmarried, not cohabiting; residence history unclear	16	14	13
	100%	100%	98%

[*]Totals may not add up to 100 because of rounding.

Stereotypical images of battered women as passive or helpless are undermined by this evidence of resistance and refusal to tolerate abuse. This is further amplified when it becomes clear that these women are for the most part mothers of young children. In the Dorchester court, 82 percent ($n = 41$) of the women seeking orders were mothers; in the Quincy court, the figure was 70 percent ($n = 35$). This is consistent with other studies of restraining orders (Chaudhuri and Daly, 1992; Gondolf, 1992; Grau, Fagan, and Wexler, 1985; Harrell et al., 1993; Horton et al., 1987; and Simonidis, 1987). In the overwhelming majority of these cases, the men named by these women are the fathers of the children. This, of course, complicates everything these women set out to accomplish. Children not only increase the economic dependence of women on men; they make leaving, even for short periods, extremely difficult and hazardous. In addition, when children are involved, it is harder for a woman to keep a new location secret from a vengeful batterer.

Most of the women with children did not ask for child support as part of the restraining order, which they are entitled to do. In the Dorchester court, of the 16 mothers who requested child support, only two were awarded such support by the judge. In contrast, 8 of the 17 women in the Quincy court who made such requests were awarded child support. This difference reflects contrasting court policies toward battered mothers; the Quincy District Court has developed policies to empower battered women that have received national recognition (Diamant, 1992; National Council of Juvenile and Family Court Judges, 1992).

The Tactics of Men Who Batter

As might be expected, women who sought restraining orders describe a range of violence and abuse in their written testimony. When the kinds of abuse disclosed in these documents is compared with the criminal law in Massachusetts, it becomes evident that the majority of the incidents fall within the criminal code. Of course, to say that these acts fulfill the legal definition of *crimes* is quite different from saying that the acts are treated as crimes by the police and the courts. Since at least the last half of the nineteenth century, feminists have campaigned to change the laws that have trapped women in violent relationships and to increase the punishments for battering and other "crimes against women" (Pleck, 1983). Only in the past several decades, however, has substantial progress been achieved in treating battering as a violent crime; and even now this process is far from complete (Dobash and Dobash, 1992; Ferraro, 1993; Zorza, 1992).

Feminist approaches to the battering of women have also maintained that battering must be understood within the larger context of the oppression of women. Physical violence against women is part of a continuum of coercive control that includes sexual abuse, psychological abuse, and economic abuse (Adams, 1988b; Douglas, 1992; Ganley, 1981; Schechter and Gary, 1988; Pence and Paymar, 1986). Using these four categories, this chapter attempts to determine the various types of violence and abuse that women report to the courts.

Table 6.2 presents a breakdown of the physical violence reported by women. Seventy percent ($n = 70$) of the affidavits allege acts that constitute assault and battery

TABLE 6.2 Physical Abuse Reported by Women in Random Sample of 100 Restraining Order Files

	$n/\% = (n = 100)^*$
Assault/assault and battery with a dangerous weapon	24
Threatened with/used knife	7
Kicked, kneed, butted repeatedly with head	7
Threatened with hard objects (screwdriver, scissors, wooden board, beer bottle, ash tray, clock)	6
Threatened with/hit with/fired gun	2
Intentionally menacing driving of vehicle	2
Simple assault and battery	64
Punched	22
Pushed, thrown, dragged (including pushed into furniture wall, car, and onto floor)	19
Slapped, hit	14
"Physically abused" or "physically assaulted" or "caused me physical harm," no other description given	12
Strangle, choke, grab throat	11
Pulled hair, dragged by hair	8
Grabbed	4
Bit	2
Spit at	2

*n represents the number of women reporting the different *types* of physical abuse. This figure does not include the number of *occurrences* of these types of threats. The types of threats are *not* mutually exclusive. Since many women reported several different threats, the total number exceeds 100, the number of women's files examined.

according to Massachusetts law. Nine percent ($n = 9$) of the women said that the accused men had either threatened them with or had used knives or guns. A total of 24 percent ($n = 24$) of the women gave descriptions that fit the definition of assault and battery with a dangerous weapon. Eighteen percent ($n = 18$) of the women gave evidence of injuries, ranging from bruises and black eyes to broken bones, facial cuts, and swelling, miscarriage, and damaged eardrums.

Table 6.3 details the kinds of sexual violence and abuse, psychological abuse, and economic or resource abuse identified in the court documents. Six percent of the women indicated that their partners or ex-partners had either raped them or had attempted to force them to have sex. In addition, a number of descriptions seem to

TABLE 6.3 Sexual, Psychological, and Economic Abuse Reported by Women in Random Sample of 100 Restraining Order Files

	$n/\% = (n = 100)^*$
Sexual violence, sexualized violence	*11*
Rape/attempted rape	6
Punched in thighs, kneed between legs, hit in spanking manner, shoved on bed	5
Psychological abuse: threats	*44*
Threatened to kill woman	24
Threatened suicide	5
Threatened to kill child, boyfriend, neighbors	3
Threatened to harm woman physically	5
Threatened to harm daughter's boyfriend	1
Threatened to kidnap woman	1
Threatened to harm children	3
Threatened to take children	5
Unspecified threats, threatening phone calls	11
Psychological abuse: intimidation	*46*
Yelling, screaming, shouting obscenities, verbally abusive	39
Destroyed property (tv, bed, pictures, lights, doors, windows, car windshield, car tires, disabled car engine, phone)	14
Economic/resource abuse	*16*
Stole money, property	5
Threatened to make her lose job, make her mother lose job	3
Threw her out of home, locked her out of home, threatened to throw her out of home	3
Prevented her from access to transportation	3
Refuse to pay rent, child support	2
Prevented her use of joint bank account	1

*n represents the number of women reporting the different *types* of abuse. This figure does not include the number of *occurrences* of these types of abuse. The types of threats are *not* mutually exclusive. Since many women reported several different threats, the total number exceeds 100, the number of women's files examined.

represent other forms of sexualized violence. Five percent of the women described being punched in the thighs, kneed between the legs, assaulted in a spanking fashion, or being shoved onto the bed; several of the women who reported forced sex also described being punched or slapped.

Table 6.3 also lists the kinds of psychological and economic or resource abuse recounted in the affidavits of the women. Twenty-four percent of the women stated that the defendants had threatened to kill them. In a recent study of 355 restraining order complaint forms filed in Denver and Boulder, Colorado, 31 percent of the women reported a threat to kill (Harrell et al., 1993: 21). In all likelihood, both of these figures underreport the commonness of these threats. In Angela Browne's (1987: 65) study of 205 self-selected physically abused women, for example, 59 percent of the women said that their partners had threatened to kill them.

As shown in Table 6.3, 39 percent of the women reported that their partners or ex-partners screamed, yelled, or otherwise abused them verbally. Intimidation through the destruction of property was apparent in 14 percent of the complaint forms. The kinds of property destroyed were often symbols of the privacy and protective boundaries of the women; for example, doors were broken and windows were smashed. In a number of other cases, the men targeted the mobility of their partners by slashing car tires, breaking windshields, and disabling car engines. Efforts to isolate women by cutting the phone cord or ripping the phone out of the wall also appear in the women's statements.

Finally, Table 6.4 presents a breakdown of the violence and abuse that can be categorized as assault and battery; threat to commit bodily harm; malicious destruction of property; harassing phone calls; breaking and entering; stalking; and violations of an existing restraining order. Ninety-two percent ($n = 92$) of the complaint forms describe a recent or past action falling into one of these seven categories of criminal behavior. Seventy percent ($n = 70$) of the forms describe violence consistent with

TABLE 6.4 Criminal Behavior Reported by Women in Random Sample of 100 Restraining Order Files

CRIMINAL BEHAVIOR REPORTED BY WOMEN	$n/\% = (n = 100)$[*]
Assault and battery	70
Threat to do bodily harm	44
Annoying phone calls	16
Malicious destruction of property	14
Breaking and entering	4
Stalking	3
Violation of restraining order	3
No clear evidence of above criminal acts	8

[*]n represents the number of women reporting the different *types* of crimes. This figure does not include the number of *occurrences* of these types of criminal behavior. The types of crimes are *not* mutually exclusive. Since many women reported several types of criminal behavior, the total exceeds 100, the number of women's files examined.

assault and battery; this level of criminality is consistent with the findings from a study of 644 restraining orders issued in the Quincy court in 1990, in which 64 percent of the women provided evidence of assault or assault and battery (Klein, 1994). An additional study of 500 restraining orders issued by the Quincy court in 1992 found that 78 percent of the women who were granted orders presented facts sufficient to support criminal complaints for assault and battery, threats to do bodily harm, annoying phone calls, stalking, or breaking and entering (Kramer, 1992a).

The Strategies of Men Who Batter

One of the major objectives of the present research was to determine how women who seek restraining orders describe the logic of the violence and abuse used by their intimate partners. By interpreting violence in terms of strategies, this study draws from the sociology of emotions, as developed by Arlie Hochschild (1975, 1979, 1983, 1989, 1991). Two of her concepts are useful here: gender ideology and gender strategy. *Gender ideology* is a set of beliefs about men, women, and relationships—beliefs that have deep emotional anchors. As they emerge from adolescence, Hochschild claims, individuals come to embrace or identify with a set of cultural ideals about manhood and womanhood. A *gender strategy* is the attempt to implement this ideology in daily life, including the emotional preparations necessary to follow this plan of action (Hochschild, 1989). In their affidavits, women are often eloquent in their descriptions of the strategic goals of the batterers' abusiveness. While it would be necessary to talk with the men named as defendants to fully explore their gender ideologies, nevertheless these affidavits suggest outlines of the deeply held beliefs by men regarding what they are entitled to as husbands, fathers, boyfriends, and as ex-partners.

Out of the randomly selected sample of 100 cases, exactly one half of the women gave some indication of the objectives behind their partner's violence and abuse. The types of strategies described in these affidavits can be characterized as: (1) attacks on the women's attempt to leave the relationship; (2) punishment, coercion, and retaliation against the women's actions concerning children; (3) coercion or retaliation against the women's pursuit of court or police remedies; and (4) assaults upon the women's challenges to drinking behavior, to sexual entitlement, and to other dimensions of male authority. Each of these strategies is described here.

Attempts to Deny a Woman's Efforts to Separate

In a feminist critique of legal discourse on battered women, Martha R. Mahoney (1991) prescribes a new concept to describe the kinds of assaults men use to curb the autonomy of women, specifically those assaults designed to prevent women from leaving, force women to return, or retaliate against women after they have left. Discussions of "why does she stay?" focus less on the coercive actions of the batterer than on the failures of the battered woman, Mahoney states. What is needed is a way to alter our perceptions of battering to refocus public attention on the struggle for power and control that is implicated in battering, a struggle that is only intensified when women attempt to separate themselves from violent intimate partners. Drawing from her own experience and the stories of other women who have suffered violence in relationships, Mahoney coins the new term *separation assault.*

There is a significant difference, Mahoney insists, between stating that a woman's attempt to separate "triggered" a man's violence, and saying that his violence represents an assault "on separation itself" (Mahoney, 1991: 66). The latter view highlights the strategy behind the assault: to deny women their autonomy. *Separation assault* names the violence and abuse that keep women in destructive relationships and terrorize them after they leave. Mahoney's analysis parallels that of other researchers who have examined the subjectivity of women in violent relationships (Dobash and Dobash, 1984; Gordon, 1988; Kelly, 1988). Liz Kelly (1988: 23), for instance, states that "male violence arises out of men's power and women's resistance to it." In particular, a number of researchers have found that men are often violent when women attempt to leave the relationship (Dobash and Dobash, 1984; Gordon, 1988; Wilson and Daly, 1992). Desmond Ellis (1993) and Ellis and Walter S. DeKeseredy (1989) have, for example, given particular attention to violence against separated and divorced women. Using the term *post-separation woman abuse,* Ellis associates an increased risk of violence with a woman's assertion of independence. Mahoney is concerned, however, that this term neglects attacks on the very decision to leave; she argues that these attacks on autonomy occur while women are still in relationships with their batterers. In the previous description of the relationship status of the women seeking restraining orders at Dorchester and Quincy courts, it was noted that most of the relationships have either ended or, at the very least, have changed status dramatically. Mahoney's concept of "separation assault" finds substantial support in the present data. Fully 48 percent of the affidavits ($n = 24$) describe motivations that fit the kinds of attacks on the subjectivity of women that she identifies in her work. Violence and abuse aimed at *preventing women from separating* was reported by 18 percent of the women who identified the motives of their intimate partners. Women described being assaulted for attempts to get a divorce; being physically prevented from leaving abusive situations; and suffering violence and abuse for their efforts to get the batterers to leave. The following statements from court documents illustrate the kinds of testimony given by women who seek restraining orders.

> [He] has repeatedly threatened to kill me threatened to burn down my home threatened to wreck my car pushed shoved me thrown things at me, broken furniture and household items every time I have tried to discuss divorce/separation. He said he would not leave voluntarily. I would have to get a restraining order and if I did I wouldn't live to get to probate court.

> I have asked him many times to leave but every time I do he will punch me and physically abuse me.

> We are like a prisoner in the home. . . . My husband told the kids that I can't get him out of there. . . . By breaking the door he is proving to me that I can't do anything.

Violence and abuse are clearly part of the plan of action for these men; in each case, the men are repeatedly attacking any movement by the women toward independence. This stifling of subjectivity is also reported by women who have left; 8 percent of the women indicated that their former partners made threats or attempts at physically *forcing them to return to the relationship.*

When we got to his car he choked me when I asked him to please leave. He also said, "If you don't stay with me I will kill you."

The defendant has said in a telephone conversation, and in person, that he would be coming to my wedding. . . . he said he would like to kidnap me and take me away.

[My estranged husband] offered me a ride home in his car. After I got into the car he tried [to force] me to have sex with him.

In another 22 percent of the cases, women reported violence and abuse in *retaliation for leaving.*

[I] have tried to end the relationship, but fearful, intimidated . . . [once he] came to my office, cried and threatened suicide if I left him. Finally, I ended it . . . and since [then] . . . threats to use any means. . . . He has a gun permit.

[He] called me at my place of employment and threatened me. He told me that if he couldn't have me, no one will and also that he wanted to "cut my heart out."

[My ex-partner] found some jewelry from my male friend. He began questioning me then started calling me dirty names. Then I asked him to leave my home— he didn't. He argued with me and threatened me, then he started choking me pushing me on the bed.

These attempts to maintain a coercive connection with women reportedly occurred even years after the relationship had ended. The following examples describe incidents between intimate partners that occurred a year or more after the couples had been separated.

[He] called my house three times saying things like he was going to beat me up and also my boyfriend.

[He] came to the window and started to threaten [my male] companion. I went out of the building to try to intervene. . . . [He] threatened bodily harm with a [piece of lumber]. . . . police . . . arrived and arrested the defendant. I am now in fear of my life.

The sense that not only marriage, but even a past dating relationship entitles these men to possess or control the women is apparent throughout these accounts. Adrienne Rich describes this kind of gender ideology as follows:

> It would seem that a man experiences the violation of some profound "right" when a woman leaves him: the "right" to her services, however lacking in mutuality the relationship. Through patriarchal socialization, men learn to think in terms of their "rights" where rights are not actually the issue: in areas like sexual behavior, maternal behavior, which are seen, not as springing from a woman's choice and affections but as behavior to which a man is entitled *as a male.* (Rich, 1979: 220).

Rich identifies "father-right" and "husband-right" as forms of this entitlement. In the violent relationships encountered throughout the restraining order documents, this entitlement appears to have been extended to include both cohabiting and dating relationships. There now seems to be a belief in "boyfriend-right," even "ex-boyfriend-right" and "ex-husband-right."

Women who demonstrate independence or who are no longer willing to remain with these men are, according to the affidavits, verbally degraded: They are called "whores," "bitches," and other misogynist names. These sexually demeaning terms serve to transform and dehumanize women in the minds of these men. Such "transformations" are a common practice among men to avoid dealing with women as peers (Astrachan, 1986). Such verbal assaults also serve as emotional preparation for further attacks on women, just as the use of the term *gook* by U.S. troops in Vietnam facilitated violence against Vietnamese soldiers and civilians (Lifton, 1992).

Mahoney (1991: 68) argues that separation violence represents "the main reason women seek protective orders." Taken together, attacks and abuse aimed at preventing any separation by these women, forcing the women to return, or retaliating after they leave are described in nearly half (48 percent) of the affidavits that recount strategies on the part of the intimate partner. The evidence from this investigation supports Mahoney's assessment. While previous research on restraining orders has not identified the motives of violent men, the findings from the present study are consistent with research showing that many women face increased danger following separation (Browne, 1987; Ellis, 1992; Sonkin, Martin, and Walker, 1985).

Punishment, Coercion, and Retaliation Concerning Children

Motherhood profoundly affects the experiences of violence and abuse, Mahoney argues. Yet both the law and much feminist legal theory, she claims, assume "that women with children are individual actors" (Mahoney, 1991: 19). A mother's connections with her children are "existential, social and extremely practical," Mahoney states; "in many significant ways—our 'selves' simply are not single" (Mahoney, 1991: 20). Of the 100 randomly selected cases in the present study, over three quarters ($n = 76$) of the women were mothers. Underscoring the relevance of motherhood to violence and abuse, 7 percent of the women describe violence and abuse suffered while they were pregnant. One woman reported being assaulted while holding her baby in her arms. Eleven percent of the women detailed physical abuse, sexual abuse, or threats directed against children, while 5 percent were threatened with the potential kidnapping of their children. The situational circumstances of the abuse are also relevant to children, especially when women are not living with the fathers of their children. In 9 percent of the cases, women reported violence or abuse taking place during those times when they were either dropping the children off with their fathers or picking the children up from their fathers.

In the 22 percent ($n = 11$) of the affidavits in which goals were indicated, the women described the violence and abuse as centering on the parental authority or responsibilities of the abusive partner. Eight percent of the women described their abuse as *punishment for questioning men's authority over the children,* as shown in these accounts:

> He then became extremely abusive after I told him that I didn't like his language and how he was treating my daughter—with his language. . . . He then kicked her. . . . I was also physically abused.

> [He] called our [daughter] names. . . . I asked him to stop because she started to cry and got scared. . . . He then went into our bedroom and started to smash things. All our pictures of the children, lights. . . . When he was doing this all he was screaming. Terrible dirty dirty words to me.

From these descriptions, there seems to be an expectation on the part of the men that their authority as fathers should not have been questioned, regardless of how abusive they had become. These men seemed to be saying that women, whether as wives or unmarried partners, ought to defer to the rights of men as fathers.

Threats and violence aimed at *coercing custody and child care decisions* were reported in another 8 percent of the women's affidavits.

> He said he would get someone to kill me and make it look like an accident so he could get custody of our son.

> Threatened to kill me if I was going to try to take his daughter away from him. He also stated that if he was to go and take her from where ever she is, no one will be able to stop him even if he has to hurt them.

> He got furious and threatened to kill me if I send her to a day care [instead of having him baby sit the child]. . . . He said if I got a restraining order, the police won't be here all the time, and he can kill me then.

These threats against women and their children represent another kind of assault on the autonomy of women. From the perspectives of these three men, father-right is not incompatible with criminal threats and cruelty toward mothers and their own children.

Another dimension of father-right is expressed in the violence and threats by the men in *retaliation for women seeking child support.* This strategy was detailed in 6 percent of the women's statements.

> The defendant . . . and myself engaged in a very heated argument about financial support for our child. . . . As a result, he became very violent striking me in the head with his closed fist, also attempting to strangle me.

> [He] called to tell me he was sending court papers to _____ court regarding child support. [He] does not want to pay child support because he doesn't see my [child]. Then . . . he called back and told me I would be hurt very soon. . . . He then called [a third time] and told me he would be at my house [within minutes]. I called the police.

If unquestioned authority over children is one dimension of father-right, another expression of it is a refusal to accept material obligations toward one's children. This is a common means of expressing hostility toward women for separation. The severity of the threats and violence in these cases indicates the level of bitterness and desperation among some men at losing their relationships. Here again, separation is not really a solution for these women, but rather shifts the ground in a continuing power struggle to matters involving their children. Batterers' counseling programs have long understood that estranged fathers will often use children as weapons against their former wives or partners. This is a central theme of the Duluth Domestic Abuse Intervention Project's work with batterers (Pence and Paymar, 1986; Paymar, 1993). Emerge, the Boston area batterers' counseling and education program, has developed a checklist for their work with men that identifies thirty-four violent and controlling behaviors towards children (Emerge, n.d.).

Retaliation and Coercion Concerning Court and Police Actions

In 12 percent ($n = 6$) of the accounts of motives, women testified that the violence or abuse was related to legal actions that they had taken besides those involving custody and child support. These actions against which men retaliated included calling the police; being somehow responsible, in men's eyes, for convictions and sentences for rape; and taking out restraining orders that lead to convictions and sentences for violating the orders. Here are several examples of the women's testimony.

> Kicked me in my back. Hit me in the back of my head. Threatening to get a gun and shoot because I called the police.

He thought I called the police (I have called them in the past) and he grabbed me, dragged me by my hair into the kitchen and threatened to kill me. He has repeatedly threatened to kill me and threatened me with kitchen knives.

He was released [from prison four days ago] since then I have been receiving crank calls all times of the night. . . . stating that I will not get away with this he will pay me back.

[He] came into my home and physically abused me. . . . [He] just got out of jail [three days before] for violating a restraining order. . . . [He] told me several times [that night] that he's going to kill me.

This testimony frames the dilemma of legal intervention in the starkest terms: These are nightmare stories. They represent the terror that the legal system will only make matters worse. Among other goals of their violence, these men are seeking *vengeance against women for being held accountable to the law.* The men act as if the privacy of the home ought to protect their privileges, including the right to abuse women, and that any breach of this protective cloak represents a betrayal that merits retaliation.

Two other affidavits identified *retaliation and coercion regarding divorce* as strategies.

[He] has put me in fear and is behaving aggressively with abusive language over the phone [and] when he returns children to me. He is especially angry over the recent court orders for me to have exclusive use and occupancy of our marital home . . .

[He] told me he wants a divorce but he wasn't going to move out and if I don't get it . . . he'll make me wish I had. . . . My husband has threatened me and threatened to destroy my property and my job. . . . My husband believes in payback. Please help me.

This kind of disregard for the law and the courts produces extraordinary fear and despair in women. When Judge Albert Kramer, former presiding justice at Quincy District Court, testified at a public hearing about batterers' defiance of the law, he made the following observations about batterers who came before the bench:

[W]hen we are dealing with batterers and perpetrators of domestic violence, more than any other violent offender, they are the most dangerous and with them you have the most potential for harm. . . . There is no other group of perpetrators of violence that is more tenaciously resistant to court orders and court efforts to curb their violence and prevent their almost relentless pursuit of their victims (Kramer, 1992b).

The "ancient privileges" of husband-right and father-right—along with their modern equivalents as boyfriend-right and ex-partner-right—represent for many men a more compelling moral order than that symbolized by the courts. How well the courts are negating these patriarchal privileges is the focus of much recent research (Buzawa and Buzawa, 1992, 1993; Gondolf, 1992; Harrell et al., 1993; Hilton, 1993; Klein, 1994; Knudsen and Miller, 1991; Steinman, 1991; Viano, 1992).

Retaliation for Other Perceived Challenges to Male Authority

In 12 percent ($n = 6$) of the affidavits, women recount how the violence and abuse converged on two matters deemed essential by some men to the fulfillment of masculinity in the United States: drinking and sexuality. In one-quarter ($n = 25$) of the 100 restraining order complaint forms, women described their abusers as drinking, drunk, or involved with drugs and alcohol. But alcohol or drugs do not supply strategies in themselves, in the sense of the goals of violence and abuse by men. Rather, alcohol figures into these goals when the drinking behavior meets intolerance. In 6 percent of the complaint forms, women noted that they were abused after raising the issue of drinking behavior with their partners. The goal of this violence and abuse appears to be, at least in part, the men's *defense of their prerogative to get drunk at will,* regardless of the consequences.

> When I was five months pregnant we had an argument over how he's an alcoholic and how he's treated me. I was trying to tell him that he needs help. He got real angry and started pushing me. . . . He grabbed me and pushed me down hard into the [furniture]. . . . I spent the night in the hospital. . . . he knows he hurts me, he knows I suffer. He does it deliberately.

> [I] questioned the defendant about his drinking because he's not supposed to be drinking, he's on probation. The defendant got angry and gestured with a beer bottle. . . . The police came because someone had called-he had been yelling and punching.

The guiding premises of this kind of violence would seem to be that men have the inviolable right to drink, along with the license to act irresponsibly, which drinking provides. Notions that battering is mostly drunken, "impulsive" violence, however, do not account for the routinized, repetitious nature of a man's drinking behavior, nor for the defense of this behavior when the perpetrator knows the consequences of his behavior for others.

The sexual entitlement and possessiveness of men has already been addressed with respect to separation assault. Beyond these assaults on women who attempt to separate from violent partners, there are additional strategies related to the men's belief in nonreciprocal sexual "rights." Two affidavits recount *assaults on a woman's questioning of a man's affairs.*

> [My husband] was drunk and I caught him talking on the phone with his girl-friend that he has. And I started yelling at him so he hit me and I left. . . . I'm afraid he'll kill me.

> [My husband] is and has been having extra marital affairs with another woman. This morning he threatened to hit me when I notified him that I knew about his affair.

The familiar double standard appears to be operating in these cases: Not only are men entitled to nonreciprocated sexual latitude, but women are not even allowed to bring it up.

Another woman reported her husband's *jealous verbal attacks and extreme possessiveness.*

> [H]e accused me of sleeping with my daughter's boyfriend. . . . I was called a whore and a bitch and the angry hurtful words just kept on [for the past five months]. . . . I am a grown woman and I am not allowed to speak to a male or even say hello unless it's someone he associates with.

Accusations that a woman is secretly sleeping around represent more than a feeling of jealousy; such accusations represent the abusive man's strategy, based on deeply felt entitlements, to circumscribe a woman's social life and make her negotiate the world outside the family household only through him.

Lastly, there is a residual group of affidavits in which women named revenge as a goal without further specification.

> [He called and said] he is sick of the way things are going and that he was going to meet me on my job and take care of me. . . . [Later] He grabbed me and, putting his hand on his gun, told me that he would "blow my goddamn brains out." . . . [I] phoned the police.

> [He] began calling my home making threats against my life "I will kill you." . . . [The next day] he came to my door. I did not open it, he started screaming that he would get me one way or the other. He also screamed many vulgar statements and then drove away.

Neither of these were isolated incidents, according to the accounts; they were part of a pattern of similarly threatening acts by these men.

Threats to kill a woman, made repeatedly over a period of weeks or months, are a form of psychological torture (Herman, 1992; Romero, 1985; Russell, 1990; Tifft, 1993). Again, threats to kill were reported in 24 percent of the sample of 100 cases. The parallels between the tactics used against battered women and the means of torture

TABLE 6.5 Men's Strategies Reported in Affidavits of 50 Women

	n	%
Separation assault	24	48%
Punishment, coercion, and retaliation concerning children	11	22
Retaliation or coercion regarding women's legal action	6	12
Retaliation against other perceived challenges to men's authority		
In response to challenges to his drinking behavior	3	6
In response to questions regarding his relationship with other women	2	4
In response to actions arousing his jealousy	1	2
Unspecified vengeance	3	6
	50	100%

used against political prisoners have prompted some feminist researchers and activists to call woman battering a violation of international human rights (Schuler, 1992; Bunch and Carrillo, 1991; Carrillo, 1992; Chapman, 1990).

Table 6.5 summarizes the types of strategies described in the sworn statements by women. The gender ideologies of many of the men depicted in these accounts appear to be held with extraordinary tenacity, self-righteousness, and depth of feeling. There is additional evidence that as a group, the men appearing in these restraining order files have histories of being violent and of being charged with both violent and nonviolent crimes. While criminal records of the men named as defendants in these orders were not obtained, a recent study of 644 restraining orders at Quincy District Court (Klein, 1994) found that 78 percent of the men named as defendants had a previous record of criminal complaints; 43 percent had records of violent crimes against persons. The average number of prior criminal complaints was 13. On a statewide basis, a study found that nearly 80 percent of the first 8,500 men identified in restraining orders had prior criminal records (Cochran, 1992).

There are two important implications of these findings. First, a large number of these men have what Cardarelli (personal communication, 1994) calls a "proficiency" at being violent. In comparison to the women who are or were their wives or partners, violence is a well-rehearsed tactic of control, rehearsed both physically and also in terms of the emotional preparation for acting violently. If a man has been arrested for assault and battery on another man, his partner likely knows this. This colors the negotiations between them, whether or not they live together. A threat by this man that he will kill her has credibility. Even when a man's criminal record is for nonviolent offenses, such as drunk driving or drug possession, threats to physically harm a woman may draw power from this other evidence of lawlessness. While the incompleteness of these court documents must be kept in mind, both the testimony of the women and the research associated with restraining orders in Massachusetts provide ample reason for high levels of fear on the part of women who seek restraining orders.

Summary

Violence against women by intimate partners persists as a widespread social phenomenon, despite the development of new resources, the creation of laws prohibiting it, and the remedies available to women from the courts. Sylvia Walby (1989, 1990) states that the patterning of violence against women represents a distinct social structure. She makes her argument based on the ritualized forms that this violence assumes; the common availability of violence as a resource for men; the routine consequences violence has on women's lives; and the traditional reluctance of the state to intervene.

The personal accounts of women seeking restraining orders in two of the busiest courts in Massachusetts provide a unique sketch of the kinds of violence and abuse to which these women are subjected by their intimate partners. Contradicting the popular image of battered women who seek restraining orders, the present research found the number of women living apart from their abusive partners to far outnumber those living with such partners. An examination of the affidavits of these women reveals a variety of physical, sexual, psychological, and economic tactics used by abusive men, most of which are criminal in nature. The women's testimony in these affidavits gives rise to four main themes derived from the kinds of strategies that motivated their partner's violence and abuse. First, nearly half of the incidents correspond to the definition of separation assault previously discussed where violence is used either to prevent separation, to coerce a return, or to retaliate for departure (Mahoney, 1991). The remaining themes revolve around strategies aimed at asserting their rights as fathers; reacting to legal actions pursued by the women; and finally, violence directed to any perceived challenge to male authority.

The consequences of battering identified in these documents include not only physical injuries to both women and their children, but also the terror of being threatened with murder, destruction of property, economic losses, and the disruption of being forced to leave home. Violence also colors what Dobash and Dobash (1978, 1979: 127–133) call the "negotiation of daily life," the discussion and allocation of money, time, and other resources in family households. These are resources over which men generally have greater control. Given the inferior position of women in the paid labor force and their greater responsibility for their children, women must negotiate for these resources from a subordinate position. What the affidavits used in the present research show is that after separation or even divorce, women are often still forced to negotiate child support, child custody decisions, and visitation under threats of violence. The term *domestic violence*, therefore, loses meaning when the web of fear and terror is spread this widely.

The evidence from these 100 restraining order case files challenges claims that the increase in restraining orders is the result of attempts by women to gain leverage in divorce settlements, win battles over child support, or claim the marital home. Half of the women seeking restraining orders in the present study were not married to their defendants; thus, they were unable to seek any advantages associated with divorce. In addition, the majority of women with children did not request child support as part of the restraining order, and most who did request such support, did not receive it. Advocates for battered women volunteering at these courts report that women with children are often too afraid to ask for child support. Furthermore, since most women seeking orders are not living with the defendants, most are not even seeking to have a man removed from their home.

What women are asking for is an end to violence, terror, and harassment aimed at limiting their autonomy. More than 120 years after Judge Pelham condemned the practice of men beating women with objects, pulling women by the hair, choking them, spitting in their faces, and kicking them, these identical practices were found in a random sample of 100 restraining order files. The testimony of the women in these affidavits frames the question "What are the best ways to support the moves by women toward independence and break the ancient, yet modern, control that batterers exercise over their lives?"

7

Battered Women:
Strategies for Survival

KATHLEEN J. FERRARO
Arizona State University

Women in violent intimate relationships often continue to live with abusers for many years or until the death of one partner. Over the past decade, scholarship on the battering of women has been critical of analyses that focus on the reasons women remain in violent relationships (Jones, 1994; Loseke and Cahill, 1984; Tifft, 1993; Radford and Russell, 1992). The question, "Why do battered women stay?" is misinformed and misdirected. Most women not only eventually leave their abusive partners, but they are more likely to be battered in the process of leaving or after they leave than while living with an abusive partner (Schwartz, 1988; Harlow, 1991; Barnett and LaViolette, 1993). More fundamentally, the question of why women stay implies that the battered women's behavior is problematic, rather than that of their abusive partners. The more relevant questions are "Why do men batter?" and "Why do they stay when women tell them to go?" (see Marano, 1993).

Over the past five years, scholars have begun recasting the image of battered women from "victim" to "survivor" (Gondolf, 1990; Hoff, 1990; Kelly, 1988; Campbell et al., 1994). This shift emphasizes the competent decision making women perform to end intimate violence. The obstacles to escape are daunting, and some women may never lead lives free of male violence. Still, many women are able, over time, to eliminate violence either through divorce or through other help-seeking efforts. Campbell and others (1994: 105) found that after two and a half years, 43 percent of battered women had left their abusers and two-thirds of the women were living in nonviolent situations. The researchers' interviews with women who had escaped do not suggest a simple solution to violence, but complex and persistent strategies for survival.

Although focusing on women's behavior may be a form of "victim blaming," most of our understanding of battering has come from listening to women. From women, we know that it is extremely difficult to escape from intimate violence. The contextual nature of woman battering differentiates it from other forms of interpersonal violence. One goal of this chapter is to discuss some of the many dimensions of the context within which women who are battered develop strategies for survival. Both the context of the violence and the process women go through in their responses to battering are important issues for those concerned with women's well-being. By examining these issues, we hope to develop and implement policies that effectively respond to women's needs and desires. Battering is not a simple phenomenon, but a complex experience involving relational, institutional, and cultural contexts. Each of these contexts will be explored in this chapter with an emphasis on the process by which women develop strategies for survival.

The analysis and examples are drawn from empirical work with women who have lived in battering relationships with husbands or lovers. Thus, the focus is on heterosexual battering, which (as Renzetti notes in chapter 4) is not always identical in nature to same-sex battering. The cases are drawn from research in shelters, on police ride-alongs, with women who called the police, with battered women who killed their abusers, and with women who came to talk to me about their problems. While the interviews were conducted for separate purposes, they illuminate different aspects of the context and processes addressed here.

The chapter outlines the stages of engagement and disengagement with the intimate relationship in which battered women participate, including ardor, accommodation, ambivalence, and terror. The factors that influence the engagement process (relational, situational, institutional, and cultural) will be examined as they support or discourage women's safety. Individual-, relational-, and institutional-level strategies will be presented for each stage, emphasizing the successful and detrimental aspects of strategies and institutional responses. The chapter concludes with recommendations for understanding the contextual and process-oriented nature of women's responses to battering and their strategies for survival.

Stages of Engagement

Ardor

Intimacy neither begins nor ends instantaneously, but follows an emotional career. Retrospective interpretations by women often identify clues that could have predicted their partners' future violence. However, the early stages of courtship are characterized by physical and emotional attractions that overshadow negative characteristics and forewarnings of danger. It is in this stage of *ardor* that individuals become bonded to the relationship and the positive feelings it generates. Most women report no experiences of physical violence during the first six months of their relationships. As described by Dobash and Dobash (1979), Walker (1979), and Kelly (1987), the first stage of a battering relationship often involves increasing isolation of the woman from her friends and family. In this stage of ardor, she usually enjoys the time alone with her partner and does not perceive his desire for social exclusivity as oppressive or abusive, but as an expression of their mutual affection. The isolation that begins to occur in this early phase, however, may establish conditions that facilitate the batterer's efforts to control his partner at a later time.

Observers, both official agents and the general public, often express surprise and sometimes disdain for women who say they love the men who have assaulted them. But this love is the dominant theme of contemporary culture, in children's films (e.g., *Beauty and the Beast*); adult literature, film, and theater; and all kinds of music and advertising. Because of the glorification of heterosexual romantic love, a high value is placed on intimate relationships; this value is socially reinforced through elaborate and expensive engagement and marital rituals. It should not be surprising that women "love" the men they live with.

At the relational level, the intense physical attraction and emotional involvement that usually are part of new intimate relationships builds ardor. Women who have been battered often discuss the deep feelings of kinship that they share with their partners; often women say that their partners are the only ones who really know and understand them. Women describe their partners as "charismatic" or "charming" and uniquely suited to meet their needs. As one woman said:

> He's all I've got. My dad's gone, and my mother disowned me when I married him. And he's really special. He understands me, and I understand him. Nobody could take his place (Ferraro and Johnson, 1983: 330).

Recently, Goldner and Walker have examined battered women's and their partners' perceptions that "the other knows them more profoundly and accepts them better than anyone before" (Marano, 1993: 49). These feelings contribute to a context in which initial violence is perceived as a profound violation of trust and intimacy, but rarely as a justification for the outright rejection of the violent man who, until then, represented her soul mate.

Accommodation

The first act of physical violence marks the beginning of the transition from ardor to the next stage of engagement—that is, *accommodation*. It is extremely unusual for a woman to leave an abusive man after the first incidence of violence. Physical violence is so inconsistent with expectations of an intimate partner that most women perceive the first instance as an exceptional aberration. A tremendous emotional commitment is threatened by recognition of battering, and most women protect that commitment through techniques of rationalization. These techniques draw on cultural scripts, excuses by abusers, and reactions of acquaintances and institutional actors to provide these women with accounts of the battering that preserve the image of intimacy between the partners (Ferraro and Johnson, 1983). Specific techniques include appeals to the salvation ethic; denials of injury; denials of victimization; denials of who the victimizer is; denials that there are options; and appeals to higher loyalties. At the relational level, the denials related to the injury, victimization, victimizer, and options represent an internalization by the women of some of the excuses and justifications offered by batterers (Ptacek, 1988). The denial of victimization, for example, reflects the batterer's attempt to reject responsibility for his violence by focusing on the woman's behavior, which he defines as provocative or deficient. As one woman told me, "I just can't learn to keep my mouth shut. I shouldn't have asked him. I don't know why I had to ask him." These statements describe her feelings of responsibility for an incident in which her partner shattered the door of their apartment and threw her against the wall because she had asked him if he wanted to take a piece of his birthday cake to work.

The strategies of denial become intertwined with the women's diminishing sense of self-worth, which results from physical and emotional battering. Men who continually denigrate their partners, particularly when the women are isolated from other sources of nurturance, establish a definition of the situation that encourages self-blame. Women usually express feelings of bewilderment (e.g., "What did I do wrong?"), but simultaneously they believe they must have done *something* to provoke the violence. For example, one woman commented on her feelings of responsibility for her husband's violence to others as well as to herself in the following manner:

> I blamed me, and I still feel sometimes like it was my fault that he did things to other people. What was it about me that made him want to hit me? I don't think I was the terrible person he said I was. Someone would call and get the wrong number, and just hang up, and I cannot tell you how many times I was thrown against walls for that.

This viewpoint exemplifies part of the confusion many women experience when they try to understand how they can control a batterer's violence with their own behavior, yet simultaneously see that accusations against them are not justified. It is particularly obvious to women that they are *not* having affairs with men walking down the street, at the grocery store, on the other end of a wrong telephone number, or anywhere else. When their partners beat them for these imagined infidelities, the women know they are not at fault. Still, many of these same women try to analyze why their abusers have such bizarre fantasies and what they could do to prevent future violence. They know at one level that they are not "that terrible person" their partner accuses them of being but, at the same time, believe there must be *something* wrong with them to evoke such rage.

Discussions with women who are trying to cope with battering reveal two forms of self-blame: behavioral and characterological (Manley, 1982; Barnett and LaViolette, 1993). Behavioral blame focuses on "specific controllable actions that led to the occurrence of the negative events," while characterological blame "is the identification of an enduring quality or trait that caused the hurtful events" (Barnett and LaViolette, 1993:

79). Behavioral blame encourages women to identify and eliminate behaviors, and it may contribute to a sense of control over their lives. While the women's behavior usually has nothing to do with their partner's violence, the perception that controlling behaviors will diminish his violence helps to maintain a sense of "internal locus of control"; that is, women maintain a sense of human dignity in which their actions matter. This may explain why Walker (1984) found that battered women were much more likely to have an internal locus of control than the general population of women. They may believe that by "walking on eggshells" they can maintain a safe environment.

Characterological blame, on the other hand, represents an internalization of the batterer's denigration of the woman's core sense of self. She begins to accept her partner's definitions, namely, that she is "a bad person," "a whore," "ugly," and undesirable to anyone but him. Characterological blame is debilitating, and it leads to depression, because there is nothing a woman can do to change. It is this form of self-blame that accompanies the feelings of "learned helplessness" described by Walker (1979). Through repeated experiences of noncontingency, a woman learns that there is nothing she can do to control the abusive context; thus, she begins to lose the ability to perceive alternatives to terror.

At the extreme end of the continuum of battering, abuse may be inflicted without any immediate prior interaction or even during a woman's sleep. The same woman quoted previously, who was beaten because of wrong telephone numbers, also said:

> He very much believed that a home is a man's castle, and he can do anything he wants there. I just found it easier not to argue. I knew there was just so far I could go, and I couldn't cross that line. Sometimes it wouldn't even matter, I wouldn't cross that line. He would wake me up in my sleep and start beatin' on me.

Batterings that occur "out of the blue" contradict the notion that men become violent when women resist their domination (see Wesson, 1994: 3). Once violence becomes an established pattern, there is not much a woman can do to prevent its occurrence. Nevertheless, most women try.

At the relational level, women try to control their own behavior based on their historical knowledge of their partners' violence. At the accommodation stage, women try to eliminate those conditions that have preceded violent incidents in the past, knowing that it is impossible to predict which specific behaviors will become an excuse for violence. Thus, large categories of behavior, such as talking to people or looking at strangers, are excluded from a woman's repertoire of actions. For example, one woman described how she learned not to speak or look at anyone while driving.

> It just got to the point where I don't say anything, if you say anything, he just starts yellin' at you. So I just let it be, and I just let a lot of things go . . . And then you can't even look at somebody walkin' down the street or road, and he'll get mad at you, tell you "Get your _____ eyeballs back in your eyes," you know, stuff like that, so, wherever I used to go, I used to just go to sleep . . . or just pretend to sleep, half the time until we get to where we're going.

Another woman explained how she learned not to express her own opinions.

> There's been times when we'd be sitting there having a conversation about any-thing, and maybe I didn't agree with him, and he'd haul off and smack me one. I got so I didn't express my opinion, I found out how he felt about it, and that's what I'd say. It was just easier.

In accommodating violence, or trying to do what is "easier" because it might diminish the violence, women relinquish both autonomy and support. Learning not to talk or express opinions may work as a temporary strategy, but it also lessens the women's sense of self-sufficiency, as well as any sense of intimacy. Similarly, eliminat-ing contact with friends and family as a strategy for controlling the jealous partner also eliminates important sources of support and validation. In this respect, most women describe how their friends and relatives were scared away from them, and how the women themselves stopped trying to interact with others to avoid accusations of infi-delity. One woman explained that her husband beat her after a visit to her family.

> When I used to go see my brothers and my family, and I used to come back and he used to accuse me.

> He accused you of being with your brothers?

> And my father, and stuff like that. And he gave me certain time to go over there, and if I was so many minutes late, he would start beating up on me, hitting me around. And that was one of the reasons why I didn't go see my relatives or my family, because of the way he used to act. I just started ignoring my friends, my relatives, my family. He didn't do anything when they were there, but when we get home, he would just start hitting me, cussin' at me, and start beating me up.

Some women tell of their efforts to "do everything right," which suggests that all of their actions are oriented toward pleasing the batterer and preventing future vio-lence. This strategy is all-consuming, and encourages women to abandon their own standards and judgments to meet those set by the batterer. In extreme cases, it is pos-sible for the ethical perceptions of a woman to be deformed or distorted by attempts to adhere to a violent partner's criteria. One woman indicated how her efforts never really succeeded in improving the ways in which her husband treated her.

> He used to wake up in the mornings grouchy, and I used to have everything done before he gets up, so he won't start with me, start beating me and cussing me, I always wanted everything to be clean and ready for him so that he would appre-ciate me at least that one day. But I never got that.

The relational strategies that women develop for controlling male violence are also accompanied by institutional and cultural components. At the institutional level, responses by law enforcement agencies, courts, social service agencies, and religious institutions all cooperate with or undermine techniques of rationalization. Denial of victimization, for example, is enhanced when police, under mandatory arrest policies, arrest women who have fought back, even verbally, against their batterer. In Phoenix, Arizona, in 1993, 18 percent of domestic violence arrests were of women. Norris (1994) in interviewing ten of these women, found that all had been battered women. In terms of the effectiveness of mandatory arrest laws, one woman incarcerated for killing her abuser said:

> I've seen women in jail taken in because of defending themselves from their hus-
> bands. I wouldn't call the police, no, uh huh, who's gonna' protect me when he gets
> out? No one. And its gonna' be worse, I know, I been there. I think that law is
> crazy. They say, well, "Why didn't you call the police?" Well, what was I supposed
> to do, say, excuse me a minute while I go use the phone? In [country], he was so
> mad at me, he locked me in a trunk and left for the day. When he got back, I was
> so glad to get out of there, calling the police was the furthest thing from my mind.

Even when arrests of batterers do occur, unless the physical damage is severe, punishment will usually consist of a night in jail and probation. At the felony level of aggravated assault, Ferraro and Boychuk (1992) found that 16 percent of cases involving intimate partners were dismissed against the wishes of the victim. Furthermore, the vast majority of successfully prosecuted cases resulted in minor sanctions; only 11 percent of all defendants received prison sentences for violent offenses including homicide and rape. Among those cases involving violent assault by an intimate partner, severe sentences were even less common. Only in those instances involving separated couples in which severe physical injury was inflicted on the woman was a prison sentence likely to be imposed, and when administered, was usually less than two years in length (Ferraro and Boychuk, 1992). While the evidence that the incarceration of batterers is an effective deterrent of such behavior has not been convincingly demonstrated, the release of these offenders with little or no consequences is likely to send battered women the message that their abuse is not only unimportant, but that there are few options for achieving a safe haven.

Although the development of temporary restraining orders (TROs) and orders of protection was intended to provide potential victims with greater legal means for protection, the orders appear to be effective only in certain types of battering relationships. Those men who are in the early stages of battering and who are less likely to be influenced by alcohol or drugs are more likely to be deterred from harassment or stalking behavior by a court order. On the other hand, those men with long histories of dangerous and persistent violence are unlikely to be deterred from such behavior by a court order (Chaudhuri and Daly, 1992; Klein, 1996).

In addition, some women who do obtain court orders are often themselves held to be in violation of the intent of the court order by their own behavior. Thus, women who show a positive response to visits or contact by partners, when the court order required them to refrain from such behavior, are usually informed by police that they have violated the court order by allowing these individuals on their property, thereby precluding any further enforcement of the order (Ferraro, 1989). In these instances, women are given a message that it is *their* responsibility to control the violence of their partners, and *their* fault if their partners fail to do so.

Social service agencies, especially child welfare agencies, may also contribute to a woman's sense of self-blame. One woman had her children placed in foster care after she was hospitalized for three weeks because of a brutal beating; after nine months, she was unable to regain custody of her children, and may only visit them under supervised conditions. Furthermore, she has been categorized as "emotionally unstable," certainly an understandable reaction to a beating from her husband that resulted in a coma, but dubious grounds for removing children from her custody. Another woman was told by a shelter counselor during couple counseling that she had to promise not to do anything to make her partner hit her. Even when institutions intend to help, through mandatory arrest policies, laws, and the like, they often serve to reinforce the mechanisms that define the violence as appropriate and inevitable and the woman as responsible for controlling the men's behavior.

The best-trained criminal justice personnel and most sensitive legal policies depend on women who are convinced that invoking external parties is the best course of action for their families. The current cultural context is not, however, conducive to such a decision. During the administrations of Ronald Reagan and George Bush, "family values" became a focus for resolving the social problems that plagued the United States. The simplistic media portrayal of "broken families" suggested that poverty, drug abuse, teen pregnancy, HIV, and gangs were direct consequences of the breakdown in the patriarchal nuclear family. Women were bombarded with media images that inform them of the shortage of men, the perils of delayed childbearing, and the misery of choosing careers over marriage (Faludi, 1991). In *Mrs. Doubtfire,* one of the most successful 1993 films, a professional woman becomes the source of her family's downfall when she seeks divorce. Her husband, who is sympathetically portrayed as her victim, resorts to transvestism in order to be hired as his children's nanny. *Mrs. Doubtfire* reinforces the myth that divorce is disastrous to children and that women who divorce unsatisfactory men betray themselves and their children.

Battered women who are trying to survive in violent marriages at the accommodation stage must negotiate these cultural messages as they evaluate their own alternatives. Within the context of husbands' or boyfriends' accounts of victim provocation, isolation from supportive friends and family, and lack of effective intervention by criminal justice and social service agencies, these cultural scripts reinforce a woman's belief that it is her responsibility to control her partner's violence and to make the best of a bad situation.

Ambivalence

Despite the weight of forces colluding to support women's accommodation to violence, behaviors that challenge commitment may lead to the stage of *ambivalence.* The transitions in individual women's lives are impossible to predict, and some women may never move past the stage of accommodation to their partners' violence and abuse. For others, however, ambivalence about continued engagement in the relationship may be instigated by actions that are clearly at odds with intimacy and caring. These catalysts may be physical, such as a sudden increase in the severity of violence, or emotional, such as partners' flagrant affairs with other women. Sudden increases in the severity of violence may break through a woman's prior efforts at minimization and may shock a woman into realizing the potential lethality of her partner's actions. While slaps, kicks, and even beatings may be rationalized as confusing, regrettable aspects of a relationship, stabbings and threats with loaded guns are significantly more blatant violations of personal safety. As one woman said:

> It was like a pendulum. He'd swing to the extremes both ways. He'd get drunk and beat me up, then he'd get sober and treat me like a queen. One day he put a gun to my head and pulled the trigger. It wasn't loaded. But that's when I decided I'd had it. I sued for separation of property. I knew what was coming again, so I got out. I didn't want to. I still loved the guy, but I knew I had to for my own sanity (Ferraro and Johnson, 1983: 331).

At the emotional level, bonding to an abuser is sometimes facilitated when periods of love and contrition are interspersed with phases of tension building and battering (Walker, 1979). Dutton and Painter (1981) refer to the traumatic bonding that can occur as a consequence of intermittent violence followed by kindness. Living with "a pendulum" perpetuates hope for many women. When episodes of kindness and affection diminish or disappear, women may begin to question the nature of their relationships. The disappearance of any outward signs of emotional commitment from their partners, combined with an awareness of their partners' sexual infidelities, may lead women to reevaluate their strategies of accommodation. One woman who left her abuser to stay in a shelter said:

> At first, you know, we used to have so much fun together. He has kind've, you know, a magnetic personality; he can be really charming. But it isn't fun anymore. Since the baby came, it's changed completely. He just wants me to stay at home, while he goes out with his friends. He doesn't even talk to me, most of the time . . . No, I don't really love him anymore, not like I did.

In the stage of ambivalence, prior efforts to control behavior may give way to strategies of controlling the violence that focus less on self-blame and more on protection. One such strategy is selective fighting back. Women's violence against men has been a controversial topic in the literature, with a small group of researchers claiming parity or even greater violence by women against men (Straus and Gelles, 1990). The few detailed examinations of violence by women that do exist demonstrate that women usually use physical violence as an episodic defensive tactic, rather than a habitual offensive strategy of domination (Berke et al., 1983; Saunders, 1988; Norris,

1994; Dobash et al., 1992; Campbell et al., 1994). Selective fighting back may be used to demonstrate resistance and lack of acceptance of abuse. It is not usually effective in stopping male violence, and it may even escalate abuse.

Occasionally, however, fighting back is an effective strategy in deterring violence by male partners. One woman, in describing her perception of the police response to her call, recounted her successful use of defensive violence as follows:

> He had his arms around me and . . . and I didn't want him to get the loaded gun. So I shot him to get him to let me go and leave me alone . . . I just looked at them [the police] and I said, "I was tired of being hit. I wasn't going to be hit anymore" . . . I told him that I wasn't going to be hit again because I had been married to two other abusive husbands and I'm just, I'm tired of it.

And how is your relationship now?

> It's very, very good; quite stable. We have plans you know, going on ahead and staying married and being together . . . You couldn't ask for a happier, more content couple.

The use of defensive violence in this instance is unusual both in terms of its effectiveness and in terms of the absence of any punitive response by the criminal justice system. Both the women and her husband received alcohol counseling and stopped drinking after the shooting incident, which had occurred after two years of wife abuse and heavy drinking by both partners.

The vast majority of women who employ defensive violence are less fortunate, however. When their response to abuse involves minor property damage or assault without injury, they are usually arrested for misdemeanor violence. When the women's response becomes lethal, they are almost always charged with homicide and later sentenced to prison.

Another strategy in the ambivalence stage is to leave the relationship. In contrast to popular views of battering, more women are battered *after* they leave a relationship than during it. According to National Crime Survey data, most victims of battering are divorced or separated from their assailants (Lehnen and Skogan, 1981). Attempts to leave a violent man are dangerous; women are more likely to be killed while trying to leave a relationship than by trying to remain in it.

While most women in violent relationships eventually attempt to leave, the first attempts do not usually result in permanent separation. Shelters for battered women report that about half their residents return to the relationships they have fled (Pagelow, 1984). Women return for a variety of reasons, including fear, continuing emotional involvement, desire to keep the family together, and lack of viable alternatives. Generally, the process of leaving begins after accommodation strategies have begun to break down. Women usually make between five and seven attempts to leave before they leave for good.

A violent man's pleas and promises are commonly cited by women as reasons for returning. Such promises are almost always never kept, however. As one woman explained:

> Every time I tried to take my kids home with me, get away from him, either he would drink and be there with my parents, he would come with his mother, and they would say, "come home" he would cry, and say he would never do it again, and I'd go home, and two days later, my other black eye would be goin' away, and he would say, "why did you tell them? why did you go to your mom, why did you have to tell them, they have nothing to do with our problems," and it just continued.

Other women try to get their abusers to leave but find that the abusers keep returning and that they beg to come back and threaten those women who refuse to take them back.

> Sometimes, you know, [it] gets so bad sometimes, I just take him to [town], and tell him to go home, and go, you know, and he won't get out until you leave him. And he'll come back, you know, bother you, call us, or he'll threaten that he's gonna' burn the house down, or lay there and shoot everybody that comes in the house, and stuff like that.

A significant factor in determining a woman's ability to leave is her economic independence. Battering crosses all classes, races, occupations, and nationalities. While celebrity status and seven-digit incomes do not protect women from battering, economic independence is an essential factor in the ability to terminate a violent relationship. In Johnson's (1992) study of 426 battered women, income and employment were found to be more important to decisions to leave violent men than psychological characteristics, such as self-esteem. Of the 85 women in her sample who were unemployed, severely abused, and whose husbands earned over $10,000, 88 percent returned to their abusers after leaving a shelter (Johnson, 1992: 173). As Johnson notes:

> A battered woman with few or no marketable skills or access to employment may perceive her alternatives inside the marriage as being more rewarding than alternatives outside the relationship, even though she is subjected to severe abuse. No abuser is violent 24 hours a day, and the victim may evaluate her costs and benefits and decide that it would be less costly to stay with an abuser who is financially capable of supporting her and her dependents. In such cases, the woman's economic needs may take precedence over her physical and emotional need to be free from abuse (1992: 175).

Women's decision making reflects relational as well as individual needs (Ferraro and Pope, 1994). When a woman's abuser is unemployed, leaving the relationship will probably not decrease her children's economic well-being. An abuser who provides a high level of income to a woman who does not work outside the home, however, poses the threat of deprivation if she tries to leave. Such men also have the means to challenge maternal custody and, according to Chesler's research (1986), usually succeed. Women who have been most obedient to traditional sex-role ideology, devoting their lives to mothering and homemaking, thus face the most difficult obstacles in achieving economic independence and freedom from abusive partners.

Many women discover that although *they* reach a point at which they no longer desire to go on with the relationship, their partners will not let them go. Beyond crying or threatening, some men employ severe violence or psychological torture when women try to leave. It is at this point that some women move beyond ambivalence to the stage of terror.

Terror

At the *terror* stage, women perceive their abusers as possessing superhuman power to control and destroy them. Constant surveillance, threats, and punishments convince these women that the men they live with pose an omnipotent and omnipresent danger. It is important to note that this terror is not mere fantasy on the women's part. It is based on experiences that would be categorized as terrorism if they involved military opponents. The perception that there is no escape from this terror is based on concrete encounters intended to demonstrate the woman's lack of alternatives. One woman who told her husband that she was going to leave him was given the following "lesson."

> He made me get in the car and drove me way out in the middle of nowhere, out in the desert, and made me get out of the car and kneel on the ground. He put the gun at the back of my head and cocked it and said, "if you ever try to leave me, I'll kill you."

Other women are exposed to the murder of pets and death threats against their children. One woman who recanted her courtroom testimony regarding her assault informed me that her partner had said that he would cut out her son's liver if she persisted with the prosecution. Prior to this threat, the husband had driven her to a remote location and bragged to her about committing a similar murder. Another woman was threatened as follows:

> "If you try to leave me, first I'll take [their daughter] and make you watch me kill her, and then I'll kill you." I didn't know it at the time, but he was saying the same thing to her.

These terrorist tactics convince most women that leaving an abuser is more dangerous for them and their children than staying. It is at this point that women enter a period of despair, characterized by use of prescription and illegal drugs and alcohol and thoughts of suicide. Physicians and psychiatrists who are untrained in the phenomenon of battering often prescribe psychotropic medication to hide the symptoms of depression and posttraumatic stress syndrome (Kurz and Stark, 1988). Many women begin to view suicide as their only alternative.

> There was one time I thought about shootin' myself, and in fact I had the gun in my mouth, and I was gonna' pull the trigger, and then I thought about [daughter] having to be raised by him, without me there, and it stopped me. Several times, I came close to doin' it, but every time, I thought about her. I thought about doin' a lot of different things. I thought about taking medication, but somethin' stopped me every time. One time in [country] I thought about driving off a mountain, but I think I just chickened out. I thought about it several times. To me, it was the only solution. But I think [daughter] would've really gotten it bad, because I wasn't there to protect her.

At this point of despair, women find that external, decisive intervention, such as police arrest, is most desired and most to be mistrusted. The distrust stems from the women's perception that such arrests will not only lead to more violence, but that the arrests will increase their vulnerability to such violence. As one woman said, "I don't think anything can help."

Homicide

Homicide is not a "strategy for survival," because it is not consciously planned. Women who resort to lethality in their struggle for survival are not strategically calculating the best method to ensure their safety. It is relevant to discuss homicide, however, since it is increasingly the outcome when other survival strategies fail. Overwhelmingly, it is an outcome that does not benefit the battered woman, whether she is sentenced to prison or remains free. Homicide is not a solution that leads to peace and happiness.

As noted by Browne in chapter 3, most homicides committed by battered women occur in the context of an immediate confrontation. These confrontations often do not meet the legal criteria for self-defense, but they exceed the battered woman's definition of "imminent danger" based on her past experiences. Over the course of a long-term battering relationship, women become adept at reading the cues that predict violent assaults. As one woman, who is currently in prison for killing her abuser, told me:

> I *lived* it, that's how I knew, I'm not ESP, not psychic. I just didn't want him to hurt me anymore. How did I know he was gonna' hurt me? I had been through it so many times [Italics added].

Some women when told by their partners that they are going to be severely beaten or killed react in defensive violence that leads to death. In one such case, a woman walked in her door to find her drunk husband lying on the couch pointing a gun at her and saying, "You're gonna' die bitch." He threw the gun at her, and she shot him.

She later was charged with second-degree murder. The prosecutor said that since she had the gun, she should have walked back out the door. Another woman awoke in the middle of the night to find her estranged husband pointing a gun at her. She alleged that he turned the gun around, put her hand on the trigger, and shot himself. She also was charged with second-degree murder.

The same cultural context that encourages women to remain married and denies adequate protection from abuse reacts punitively when battered women kill. When death of the abuser is the final outcome of a battering relationship, most women are sent to prison. There are approximately 2,000 women serving prison time in the United States for defending themselves against a batterer (MCTFADA, 1994: 4). Since the late 1970s, efforts have been initiated to educate criminal justice personnel about the impact of battering. Now a few states have laws that require judges to admit testimony about battering when it is relevant to the defense of women who kill. The National Clearinghouse on Battered Women's Self-Defense keeps records and literature on efforts to provide alternatives to incarceration. Currently, there are efforts under way in many states to require review of such cases for consideration of clemency. Most of these women pose no threat to society, and they are often separated from their children who have already lost one parent.

Even women who are not sentenced to prison for homicide continue to suffer after the death of their abusers. If they blamed themselves for being battered, they torture themselves for killing their abuser. Both their love and their fear survive the physical death of the partner. Three women who killed their abusers described their feelings as follows.

> I was screaming for help, someone to call the ambulance. It took almost an hour. They pulled me away from him. It was just like a nightmare . . . I never did hurt him, I never did try to fight back or anything, I loved him so much. . . . and when I think about it, I think to myself, I didn't do that, I didn't do that. No, at times I still do love him, sometimes I think I'm crazy, after all the things that I went through, all the pain.

> Sometimes I don't even know if I'm comin' or goin'. I try not to cry in front of the kids, it's mostly at night that I have to go through all this. Sometimes, I just get to the point that—I miss him, I miss him a lot. No matter what he put me through, I miss him. There are days where I wonder, why am I alive, stuff like that.

> Even when he's dead, he got me . . . he still has this control over me, I still catch myself saying, "Oh, I can't do that, [husband] won't let me do that." I feel like he's watching me still, I catch myself looking.

For these women, the scars of being battered and the grief of losing a partner to whom they were bonded will last for many years. They escaped with their lives, but they remain lonely, fearful, and guilt-ridden. Their stories, however, may be helpful to women in the earlier stages of battering relationships who are looking for support.

Successful Survival Strategies

Given the overwhelming barriers to escape, it is amazing that women do survive battering relationships. Factors that facilitate survival depend on the available resources, the current context of the relationship, and the women's stage of engagement. The most important aspect of the context is the batterer's level of dependency. Men who are extremely dependent emotionally on their partners are difficult to change or to leave. They will not accept a woman's decision to end the relationship, often responding with "If I can't have you, no one else will." They stalk, harass, threaten, and often assault or kill the women for whom they proclaim undying love. This drastic response requires drastic survival strategies, which disrupt women's lives. It is, of course, true that battered women should not be the ones to leave their homes, friends, and jobs. However, they cannot depend on their partner's fear of arrest for protection. When it is clear that men will continue to prey on their partners, regardless of the expressed wishes and efforts by women to separate, the most realistic strategy, under current law, is for women to leave and begin new lives. In fact, during the course of my research, several women with children left their communities and assumed new identities in new locations. The shelter network operates like a modern version of the Underground Railroad acting as a referral and support system for women who need to take radical steps to escape from abusers who are determined to own and control them, and who need to protect themselves and their children (Ferraro and Johnson, 1985).

In terms of social policy, a more desirable approach would be to require repetitive batterers and stalkers to leave the state in which their partner resides. Such men could be banished from the state, logged onto FBI data files, similar to those kept on federal fugitives, and arrested if they set foot in the prohibited state. Violation of banishment orders could result in lengthy prison terms. The danger of this approach is that women in other states would be unaware of the violent pasts of these men. Banishment is also inconsistent with current criminal justice policies, which prohibit punishments that infringe on an individual's right to serve a specified sentence length and then continue life as a free person. Because banishment is an unlikely prospect, women will continue to bear the burden of escape from persistently violent men.

For women involved with violent men who are not intent on keeping or killing their abusive partners, strategies that focus on the development of emotional and practical resources seem to offer the best hope of escape. Several studies, for example, have found that the major reason cited by women who leave shelters to return to abusive partners is the lack of alternative housing and income (Roy, 1977; Schechter, 1982; Johnson, 1992). Furthermore, because many women need legal assistance in obtaining child support and spousal maintenance and because attorneys usually request retainers of between $1,500 and $3,000 for contested divorce cases, many women are effectively prohibited from obtaining the legal help needed to permanently escape from an abusive relationship. Legal aid services not only are limited and involve lengthy waiting periods, but qualification for such aid is often based on family income. One result is that battered women who are married to men with above-poverty-level incomes are disqualified from receiving such assistance. Battered women who are not legally married to their abusers are usually not able to obtain any court-ordered financial assistance when they leave.

The amount of low-income housing, especially for women with children, is far from adequate. One source estimates that 50 percent of homeless women are escaping violent relationships (Schneider, 1994). Because shelters provide only temporary refuge, they cannot accommodate the large numbers of women seeking assistance. To establish a societal commitment to battered women would necessitate increasing the availability of low-income housing.

The list of resources required for survival outside of a battering relationship is lengthy. Women need day care, health care, transportation, housing, clothing, food, utility assistance, and employment. Many women need job training after having devoted themselves to bearing and rearing children and maintaining the household. In the current economic environment, women, especially older women, who have nontechnical or entry-level job skills will be noncompetitive in the job market. A basic level of income maintenance will be required for many women who are unable to obtain steady employment (Albelda et al., 1988).

While the idea that battered women need therapy has been rejected by most advocates and analysts (Dobash and Dobash, 1990; Martin, 1976; Jones, 1994), women do need advocacy, information, and support. Because of the obtuse character of the legal processes involved in filing criminal charges, obtaining orders of protection, and maintaining child custody, it is difficult to obtain the necessary information that women need for effective advocacy. Women need advocates familiar with the legal system to help make phone calls and fill out appropriate forms. While individual therapy focusing on the woman's psychological issues may not be appropriate, it is important to recognize that women who have been battered have experienced both trauma and loss. These experiences create depression, confusion, and grief, so the women need emotional support in order to successfully return to a violence-free life. For some of these women therapy may be entirely appropriate.

Summary

Realistically, with all the practical and emotional resources provided, some women will continue to live with violent men. For an outsider to the relationship, it is difficult to know how to be most helpful in these situations. It is important to recognize that every woman has her own complex understanding of her situation and needs that is not accessible to outsiders. The most beneficial form of assistance will depend on the woman's level of engagement with the relationship. If she is still in the stages of ardor or accommodation, any demands that she recognize and act on the danger of her situation will only increase her sense of alienation. It is especially important that agency representatives, such as law enforcement officers and social workers, respect the ability of women to interpret their situation and make choices that are best for them.

The best survival strategies for women in violent relationships cannot be divorced from the social and cultural context that supports intimate violence and the subordination of women. In this respect, it is essential that any discussion of women's experiences not overshadow the macro-level forces that encourage male violence against women and limit the practical and emotional options available to them.

PART III

Toward a Proactive Response to Intimate Violence

Given the historical division of labor between men and women in both the private and public realms of Western culture, it follows that men have played the crucial role in defining the meanings and responses to violence. The penalties for assault and battery as well as rape have traditionally been viewed as less serious when they are perpetrated by spousal partners as opposed to strangers, and accordingly have resulted in lesser sanctions by the criminal justice system. As noted in the introduction, for decades the official response to domestic violence has been a widespread "hands-off" policy, even when there were little differences in the consequences to the victims when compared to stranger violence.

In her chapter on how the criminal justice system has responded to intimate violence, Caringella-MacDonald examines the ways in which prevailing historic myths in American culture have influenced the direction and development of policy toward intimate violence. Among the myths discussed by Caringella-MacDonald are the myth that women provoke their own victimization and the myth that women falsely accuse men of sexual and nonsexual violence for ulterior motives unrelated to the violence itself.

In bringing together data and research that disprove these beliefs, Caringella-MacDonald shows how myths not only underlie many of our traditional legal statutes, but how they prejudice the legal processing of intimate violence by the criminal justice system. In effect, many women are not only victims of violence and abuse by intimate partners, but are further victimized by a system of criminal justice that has, until recently, been reluctant to enforce the laws against domestic offenders of intimate violence (Davis and Smith, 1995).

In an overview of changes in the criminal justice system response to intimate violence, Caringella-MacDonald examines some of the major reforms in the criminal justice system since the 1970s (including legislation), ways in which intimate violence is processed from arrest to prosecution, and the growing demands placed on abusers by the courts in regard to child and spousal support. These changes have not come easily, however, and Caringella-MacDonald notes that serious obstacles still remain for women victimized by intimate violence.

Female victims of intimate violence, she argues, continue to be treated unjustly in many jurisdictions, especially when women are victims of sexual violence within the domestic realm. Furthermore, the unwillingness of many police officers to arrest alleged perpetrators in cases of intimate violence, coupled with the serious lack of services for victims, has played a part in the discriminatory treatment that victims of intimate violence receive within the criminal justice system. To eliminate this discrimination and maltreatment, those within the judicial system must realize that, if battered women are not provided with appropriate protection by the police and courts, they are more likely to be abused further and they are less likely to seek assistance. In these circumstances, there will be little, if any, deterrence evident.

Because the criminal justice system cannot be expected, by itself, to both prevent and control intimate violence, the community response to battered women is becoming increasingly important. Sullivan's chapter provides a critical overview of the ways in which the community at large has responded to intimate violence. Sullivan points out that although one in four women who seek emergency medical care are victims of intimate abuse, there is continued reluctance among many physicians and hospitals to treat intimate violence as an important health issue either in terms of health care received or in terms of its consequences for the victims' families. Not only are the health care professions in need of improved policy responses to the continued presence of domestic and intimate violence, the same holds true for the social work professions and the clergy from whom many battered women seek assistance.

In examining essential strategies for improving the response to victims of intimate violence, Sullivan shows that in spite of the continued growth and importance of shelters for battered women, major problems remain. Some groups, especially lesbians and women of color are hesitant to use shelters, because they believe they will receive less-than-equal treatment because of their sexual orientation or color.

Sullivan also notes the growing importance of having trained advocates within the social service delivery system to ensure that victims of intimate violence receive the kinds of service appropriate to their needs. Such proactive strategies, Sullivan contends, are critical if social service providers are (1) to supply effective and coordinated services to the victims of intimate violence and (2) to educate the public about the everyday realities of terror and violence that many victims endure for lack of these services. In the long run, it will become increasingly important for communities to establish multiple levels of intervention in reference to intimate violence, including immediate protection, support, and treatment services for the victim and children if they are involved and the establishment of policies outlining specific arrest, prosecution, and treatment procedures for those partners who use force and violence in their relationships.

The arguments by Caringella-MacDonald and Sullivan for systemwide reform and expansion of services do not, of course, preclude the development of individual treatment programs. Despite legal and social changes directed to family and intimate violence, victims still suffer physical and psychological trauma that must be dealt with at the individual level as well. Because of the debilitating psychological effects of violence for many victims, especially those with long histories of abuse, treatment programs are a necessary part of the healing process for victims who are making the transition from violent to nonviolent relationships.

Hansen and Harway make an important contribution in elucidating how one form of clinical practice, based on feminist theory, functions with abused women. The chapter gives an overview of the feminist perspective on intimate violence. In relating theory to practice, the authors demonstrate the process by which therapists incorporate feminist ideals and perspectives into the therapeutic practice. In their analysis of the connections between feminist theory and therapy, Hansen and Harway argue that feminist therapy is a direct challenge to the male-centered theories of psychology and human development that have dominated traditional therapeutic approaches. Rejecting the value-free perspective that is historically associated with psychology, the authors reveal ways in which the social and political contexts affect the social reality of the therapeutic experience.

Responding to the existing social context that devalues women, feminist therapists recognize battering as a gender-specific process that promotes the privileges of men. In acknowledging the power differential that derives from gender difference, feminist therapists actively work to expand the options available to battered women, including those germane to the economic environment.

In working with women who suffer spouse abuse, feminist therapists attempt to integrate feminist therapeutic theory with standards of good clinical care. Adhering to the crisis-intervention model of treatment, the therapists believe that client safety is a major component of the therapeutic process. In addition, feminist therapists make major efforts to reduce the self-blame ideology that exists among many battered women. In so doing, these therapists hope to empower their clients so that the women can actively take charge of their lives, thereby reducing or eliminating the abuse and violence that brought them to therapy in the first place.

Taken as a whole, the following chapters demonstrate that any intervention strategies to prevent and control intimate violence must not only involve a coordinated response among legal, social and health agencies, but they must be capable of responding to the varied patterns of intimate violence discussed throughout the present volume.

8

Women Victimized by Private Violence

A Long Way to Justice

SUSAN CARINGELLA-MacDONALD

Western Michigan University

This chapter examines the criminal justice system's level of acknowledgment and response to incidents of intimate violence. In this analysis, several historic myths relating to violence between intimate partners are examined in order to inform the discussion of policy changes that have taken place in relation to the violence itself. In addition reform measures and the implemented outcomes concomitant with these changes are critically assessed. The chapter interprets various patterns of intimate violence in terms of the myths and discriminatory treatment that continue to prevail within the criminal justice system. It discusses how both myth and discrimination operate to undermine reform measures that attempt to deal with the nature and extent of violence between intimate partners.

Women victimized at the hands of men have historically been revictimized when they attempt to use the justice system to redress their victimization. Women have been punished for being victims of men's violence since antiquity—from the first laws that allowed rape victims to be stoned, drowned, and killed along with their attackers (Brownmiller, 1975; Dean and DeBruyn-Kops, 1982) to the laws that transformed a marriage license into a hitting, beating, punching, and killing license (Martin, 1981; Walker, 1984). Even today, women continue to be victimized by laws that fail to recognize that rape in marriage is not a contradiction in terms, and by laws that punish women and discriminate against them through unique evidentiary requirements and exacting legal standards. Similarly, nonsexual violence by intimate partners continues to be viewed by many people as less serious than assaults and violence inflicted by strangers. This view of intimate violence has negative consequences for its victims in that it creates "a special category (of domestic abuse crimes) with a higher standard for intervention" (Micklow, 1988: 416).

The lack of appropriate remedies on the part of the criminal justice system for protecting victims of intimate violence, especially when prosecution is pending, is acknowledged by most observers as being a serious detriment to the rights of women to remain free from bodily harm and threats of violence and abuse (Davis and Smith, 1995). Intimate victimizations vary widely, but in most cases, they are not considered to be criminal or at best are viewed as minor transgressions in comparison to stranger crimes and victimization. Susan Estrich (1987) uses the term *real rape* to refer to rapes by strangers as opposed to rapes by intimate partners. Her distinction leads to the conclusion that all other victimizations, such as those between parties who know one another are not really criminal in nature or, at least, are less serious kinds of victimizations. Some people take a less serious view of intimate violence because it takes place mostly within the private, as opposed to the public, sphere of interaction; because the violence is directed against women as a subordinate group, it has a diminished status within the criminal justice system. Many law enforcement jurisdictions throughout the country routinely classify domestic assaults as misdemeanor crimes, even though the conduct involves serious bodily injury (Langan and Innes, 1986).

The Role of Myth in the Victimization of Women

Erroneous beliefs, or myths, about the private victimization of women serve to doubly victimize women (Holmstrom and Burgess, 1978). Myths about rape, sexual assault, woman battering, and marital rape are in many ways parallel. Misguided beliefs about victimized women always blame females for being "illegitimate" victims (Elias, 1986), while they simultaneously exculpate male perpetrators. Although such attitudes vary, some level of culpability is usually attributed to the female victims of male violence. This skewed perspective is characteristic of beliefs about stranger rape and stranger assault; it is even more pronounced and exaggerated in relation to private, intimate violence.

One characteristic myth posits, for example, that women ask for, bring about, or deserve to be victims (Adler, 1987; Bart and Moran, 1993; Gordon and Riger, 1989; Hanmer, Radford, and Stanko, 1989; Kelly, 1988; Sanday, 1990; Schwendinger and Schwendinger, 1983; Scully, 1990; and Tifft, 1993). The premise underlying this myth is that women precipitate or provoke their own victimization. Victims are often blamed for drinking or being out alone at night (in cases of rape), for jealousy or not satisfying the partner's general needs (in cases of courtship or spousal assault), or for withholding sexual access (in cases of marital rape). Tifft's list of such attributions in the case of intimate violence epitomizes such blaming. His descriptions of victims range from "provocateurs" and "man-haters" to "whores, drunks, failures, enablers, or codependent partners" (Tifft, 1993: 5).

Another kind of victim-blaming myth posits that women falsely accuse men of sexual and nonsexual violence, that is, that they exaggerate and lie about victimization (Adler, 1987; Freedman, 1985; Gordon and Riger, 1989; Herman and Hirschman, 1993; Kelly, 1988; Sanday, 1990; Schwendinger and Schwendinger, 1983; and Tifft, 1993). This myth is founded on the premise that women desire, or at least ultimately consent to, sexual and nonsexual violent domination. In reference to wife abuse, the myth is supported in circumstances in which the abused woman fails to (or is unable to) leave (or must return to) the abusive relationship. This myth, particularly when applied to rape, often entails the corollary belief that women consent to sexual activity and then "cry 'rape'" for ulterior motives, for example, to hide the origin of pregnancy or disease. In addition to these myths, there is a widely-held misconception that judges and juries are inclined to be overly sympathetic to victimized women and that they are, therefore, all too eager to convict men who may be viewed as blameless and innocent.

Debunking Myths and False Beliefs

The misguided nature of the myths discussed so far can be convincingly demonstrated from any variety of perspectives. Pragmatically, a woman may for a whole host of reasons need to put herself in vulnerable situations, such as walking alone at night. In these instances, it is ridiculous to suggest that she "was asking for it" and sheer meanness to suggest she "deserved it" or "had it coming." Similarly, it is impossible to support the view that some otherwise normal women enjoy or at least secretly desire the terror and brutality resulting from sexual and nonsexual violence.

Statistical data on violence provide further evidence to disprove such beliefs. Crimes of violence against women traditionally have been the most underreported offenses in the country (U.S. Department of Justice, 1990). For example, when rape cases do come to official attention only an incredibly small percentage (less than 5 percent) are declared to be false ("unfounded") or "victim-precipitated," even by official judgments (FBI, 1985; *University of Pennsylvania Law Review,* 1968). The few isolated cases of intimate versus stranger violence that make it as far as criminal proceedings are typically those cases most obvious in terms of serious, external signs of injury. Of these cases, few result in successful prosecution, fewer yet in conviction, and fewer yet in incarceration (Caringella-MacDonald, 1985; Fain, 1981; Lerman, Landis, and Gosozweig, 1983; Martin, 1981; Walker, 1984). While cases of violence against women do not come to the attention of the justice system very often (in relation to the incidence of such violence), the cases that do often result in little justice or appropriate redress for female victims.

The negative impact of these myths can be discussed in still another fashion. Many legal safeguards and protections exist for all accused persons, including men accused of sexual and nonsexual violence in general and those who victimize their wives, dates, and partners. The additional obstacles constructed around private

male–female violence cases are highly prejudicial in addition to being simply unjus-
tifiable. The maltreatment of women as victims and the protection of men as offenders by the justice system not only punishes victims who come forward, but leaves little
incentive for other women to report, charge, or go forward with their "legitimate"
complaints. Significant disincentives to call the police for help or to press charges
result in revictimization among many intimate violence victims; moreover, attackers
often promise or threaten to retaliate if victims pursue such a course of action. Threats
about future, escalated levels of violence loom especially large in intimate violence
cases, because victim and offender live together or have regular contact. Like other
victims of violent crimes, battered women have a justifiable fear of retaliatory violence
by their intimate partners. A significant proportion of battered women are revictimized within six months of the initial incident that resulted in intervention by the criminal justice system.

The Role of Myth in the Legal Process

Myths about battered women not only underlie traditional legal statutes and requirements, but they operate to prejudice the legal processing of intimate violence cases by
criminal justice personnel; therefore, the myths serve to doubly victimize women. The
maltreatment of many female victims, instead of appropriate prosecution of male
offenders is evident in the typical sequence of events that victims experience once they
enter the judicial system. Typically, they must endure the intrusion of official authorities into their private lives; tell their accounts of the violent victimization to unfamiliar
and often unsympathetic men; and repeatedly answer intimate questions posed by
skeptical authorities, often in public places where others can listen and observe their
sense of shame and humiliation. This scene is repeated at each stage of the judicial
journey from the police station to the prosecutor's office, if the police decide to take the
case forward (by making an arrest). If the case is taken seriously by the initial prosecutor assigned to the case and if prosecution is sought and the case goes to trial, the
victim will be challenged by the defense attorney. Furthermore, many victims are continually interrogated about the behavior associated with their relationships, for example, about their decision to stay in a violent partnership, their provocation, their general
blameworthiness, and their overall contribution to the victimization. Meanwhile, victims must relive and retell their victimization publicly, sometimes over a period of
months or years, while having to confront and accuse their assailants directly in close
courtroom quarters. This extended process commonly heightens victims' fears about
previous threats or promised retaliation. Finally, this public stigmatization, even in the
best of cases, is likely to result in a dismissal or acquittal (Caringella-MacDonald, 1985;
Fain, 1981; Lerman et al., 1983; Martin, 1981; Walker, 1984).

Female victims of intimate violence by males have fared little better when it
comes to injunctive and civil relief. In intimate violence cases, the police rarely arrest
male attackers because of the historic provision that required officers to witness misdemeanor crimes, like spousal assault, before an arrest could be made. Likewise, victims of spousal violence have traditionally been denied the alleged protection of

emergency or temporary restraining, protection, or injunctive orders unless a divorce was pending at the time of the assault (Finn, 1991; Taub, 1983). Moreover, even if the victim is lucky enough to secure an order that prohibits the offender's repeated violence or contact with the victim, these judicial decrees have been described as "not worth the paper they are written on" (Martin, 1981). Put differently, in the past, there has been little, if any, enforcement of restraints and little, if any, protection against subsequent attacks for domestic victims of intimate violence.

Civil suits for damages and injuries have, in like fashion, been denied to marital victims of spousal assault and rape. These two types of offenses are treated alike because of the "unity doctrine" that views a married couple as a single legal entity (Martin, 1981; Walker, 1984). This provision secures male dominance and entitles a man to treat his wife in virtually any way he pleases. As with married women, sexual assault victims have the same lack of redress in civil litigation. Overall, successful civil litigation claims levied to collect for physical or psychological damages or injuries are still very infrequent.

Justice Reforms

Legislative Initiatives

Since the mid-1970s, there has been a flurry of changes in legislation regarding the violent victimization of women. Reforms across the country have attempted to rectify a range of problems, such as those previously described, through changes in criminal and civil statutes and procedures aimed at enhancing the treatment of women victimized by men in general, as well as those victimized by men they know in particular. Changes have sought to encourage reporting, arrest, prosecution, and conviction of male assailants and to, thereby, render the processing of intimate violence cases more comparable, that is, less discriminatory, in relation to other case processing (Davis and Smith, 1995; Buzawa and Buzawa, 1996).

Specific changes in rape legislation have altered the language of statutes to reflect the continuum of sexual violence inflicted on women. Broader definitions that encompass the full range of acts and a wider range of victims have been attempted, and degree structures for sexual violence charges have been provided. Such reforms have specifically encompassed acquaintance, date, and even marital rape, in addition to "real," (Estrich, 1987) or stranger, sexual assaults. Graduated degree structures have delineated specific crime circumstances, such as victim–offender relationships (focusing on positions of power-authority), the presence of weapons, visible additional injuries, and other factors that allow one to "objectively" determine the seriousness or level of the crime to be charged. Furthermore, these changes endeavor to eradicate traditional reliance by decision makers on unique and discriminatory standards, such as the corroboration and resistance requirements that have historically attended rape prosecutions. These requirements have traditionally levied nearly insurmountable obstacles to the successful prosecution of rape cases. The difficulty in meeting such biased requirements and standards is easily described. Rape, for example, is most typically committed in private residences between people who know one another when there are no witnesses to corroborate any charges by the victim. Furthermore, there is likely to be little, if any, corroborative evidence if the victim washes, decides not to seek medical assistance, does not sustain visible injuries, and so on. In addition, rape victims are subject under law to existing resistance standards. Many victims are paralyzed by threats and fear, and consequently unable to resist, or are simply overpowered by the men who attack them. Perhaps the most frequent reform affecting the crime of rape is commonly referred to as rape shield legislation (Field and Bienen, 1980). The unique prejudicial practices once common in cases of rape have been redressed by legislative reforms that disallow past sexual character evidence from being introduced into the courtroom. The stipulation that victim–plaintiffs cannot be interrogated about their reputation or about all of their past sexual activities has aimed simultaneously to restrict defense attorneys from badgering plaintiffs about their credibility, and to officially acknowledge the irrelevance of at least some past sexual behavior. Similarly, the placing of restrictions on the open (public) court questioning of victims recognizes (at least implicitly) the "real" nature of intimate sexual violence, or acquaintance, date, and marital rape.

Another reform measure pertaining to sexual assault that deserves separate treatment concerns the particular crime of marital rape. Most of the states have specifically delineated marital rape as a criminal offense (Finklehor and Yllö, 1985), hence, repealing the spousal exemption in rape prosecution. The extent to which these reforms address the sexual victimization of married women by their husbands, however, varies widely. Some legal stipulations protect only divorced women from their husbands, while others protect wives who have filed for divorce-separate maintenance or married wives who simply live together with their husbands.

Reforming the Processing of Intimate Violence

Changes surrounding nonsexual intimate violence also target both criminal and civil definitions and procedures. By the early 1980s, for example, "wife beating was a criminal offense in every jurisdiction in this country" (Walker, 1984: 137). Perhaps the most salient reform in the criminal realm is the provision that empowers police to make an arrest on the basis of probable cause in domestic violence cases. Such cases have typically been treated as misdemeanors, requiring the officer to witness the crime or to secure a warrant in order to effect an official arrest. In this respect, many states have begun to look more closely at the requirements for arrest in domestic abuse cases. Currently forty or more states have mandatory arrest statutes of some type for reducing domestic violence. Some states have taken these changes a step further by defining spousal abuse as a new and separate crime, distinct from the traditional assault and battery misdemeanors (Lerman, Landis, and Gosozweig, 1983). In addition, many states now require police officers to (1) provide victims with information on domestic violence case processing and community services and (2) to stay at the residence until danger has passed or to transport victims to shelters, hospitals, and so forth (Ferraro, 1989a). New policies have also been instituted that require legal and law enforcement personnel to receive special training, to treat domestic- and stranger-violence cases in the same way, and to arrest or prosecute in particular types of intimate violence cases (Bureau of Justice Assistance, 1993; Cahn and Lerman, 1991; Goolkasian, 1986; and Myers, Tikosh, and Paxson, 1992). An additional and important feature of some office policy directs prosecutors to be responsible for pursuing cases through court, without further burdening victims by relying on victim decisions concerning proceeding (Cahn and Lerman, 1991; Friedman and Schulman, 1990; Lerman, 1986).

Perhaps the most frequent kinds of intimate assault reforms are those that remove the "unity doctrine" (or spousal exemption) in civil courts (Fain, 1981). Such reforms have empowered courts to issue temporary or emergency restriction and protection orders if couples are simply living together, but are not married, or are already filing for divorce or have completed divorce proceedings (Makepeace, 1989). These restraining orders typically specify conditions for pre-trial release or mandate that the accused refrain from violence, or that the accused refrain from contact with the victimized party, or that the offender vacate the premises all together (Lerman et al., 1983; Myers, Tikosh, and Paxson, 1992). Restraining orders for injunctive relief have also been changed so that they are now issued to the victim without the usual requirement that the offender also be present; this latter process is referred to as an *ex parte* hearing (Bureau of Justice Assistance, 1993; Fain, 1981). Moreover, lower court magistrates have been enabled to issue such orders and to open up court sessions in the evenings and on weekends—in order to be able to function when the need is at its peak level (Lerman et al., 1983). Finally, many jurisdictions have enacted reforms that now delineate contempt of court or misdemeanor offense charges as corollary to the violation of any such orders, in which case fines and incarceration are available as sanctioning mechanisms (Bureau of Justice Assistance, 1993; Commission on Civil Rights, 1982; Finn, 1991; Goolkasian, 1986; Lerman et al., 1983).

Although court orders requiring offenders to cease and desist their violent behavior and to leave the premises of their victims along with the specification of law enforcement duties constitute the predominant reform measures overall, a variety of other changes have also been a part of reforms. Myers, Tikosh, and Paxson (1992) list over eighty different elements that are found in reform statutes. Sundry types of changes have, for instance, allowed bail to be denied in domestic violence cases and have required that police not discourage complaints when responding to domestic violence calls. Other changes require abusers to pay medical costs, lost wages, child support and spousal support, while still other reforms allow judges to order offenders to undergo counseling.

Persisting Injustice for Intimate Violence Victims

Such broad reform measures herald success, but the road to justice is still beyond the reach of many women who are victimized by the violent men with whom they are acquainted. This is not to say that some degree of progress and improvement for victims has not been realized, but that serious obstacles for privately victimized women still remain, in spite of even the best of efforts aimed at their amelioration.

The sheer amount of reform activity can be viewed in the most positive fashion. The widespread increases in shelters for battered women, the strengthening of police arrest powers, and the growing use of injunctive relief measures in the domestic violence area provide more easily available remedies to battered women. In addition, research in at least some jurisdictions has shown that intimate violence is now taken more seriously; that victims have higher levels of satisfaction with the criminal justice system (Bowker, 1983; Ferraro, 1989a); and that suits have been successfully levied against criminal justice personnel for non-enforcement of laws (Ferraro, 1989a; NOW, 1987). Progress has also been made with cases involving sexual violence. Although there have been very few prosecutions, the crime of marital rape has been increasingly recognized across U.S. jurisdictions. Enhanced levels of prosecution in acquaintance and date rape have, in a similar way, been found to obtain in some jurisdictions (Deming, 1983; Polk, 1985). Improvements in the experiences of victims are also noted in sexual assault case processing (Spohn and Horney, 1992; Marsh, Geist, and Caplan, 1982). Finally, past sexual history evidence associated with the victim is seen as less relevant in many jurisdictions that have enacted reform measures (Spohn and Horney, 1992; Marsh et al., 1982).

Despite all the changes and positive results just stated, progress has, in reality, been quite limited. Female victims of intimate violence continue to be treated unjustly in many jurisdictions. In many instances, historic patterns reassert themselves: violence is not taken seriously, disbelief and blame are attributed to the woman for her victimization, and criminal justice processing revictimizes the victim (Attorney General's Task Force on Violence, 1984; Bannister, 1993; Bureau of Justice Assistance, 1993; Buzawa and Buzawa, 1990; Cahn and Lerman, 1991; Finn, 1991; Goolkasian, 1986; Guberman and Wolfe, 1985; Hanmer et al., 1989; Hatty, 1989; Horne, 1993; Miller, 1993; Muraskin and Alleman, 1993; Yllö and Bograd, 1988).

The sequence of events previously depicted, from the initial complaint to the acquittal-dismissal of a case, constitute a pattern that still exists in too many cases. Victims continue to be scrutinized and questioned by cynical male personnel, and are ultimately discredited by many police officers, prosecutors, defense attorneys, judges, and juries. Victim credibility and blame continue to be a more pivotal focus in the processing of sexual and domestic violence cases than in other types of criminal offenses (Maidment, 1985; Quarm and Schwartz, 1985; Walker, 1984). Because of factors such as these and because of the vast discretion residing in criminal justice decision making, attrition in the handling of intimate crimes of violence against women remains seriously problematic (Caringella-MacDonald, 1985; Maidment, 1985; Quarm and Schwartz, 1985; Walker, 1984).

Many police still avoid arresting in cases of intimate violence, even in jurisdictions that have presumptive arrest laws and policies (Ferraro, 1989a). In addition, arrest may not be the cure-all it has been made out to be. Although some earlier research identified that arrests in domestic violence cases deterred future violence (Sherman and Berk, 1984), more recent research has identified differential outcomes and raises more questions than answers (Dunford, Huizinga, and Elliott, 1983; Steinman, 1988; Sherman and Smith, 1992). Miller (1993), for example, discusses how arrests may lead to more serious violence and how mandatory arrest policies may operate in contradiction to the best interests of lower-class and minority women. Further problems result when police officers do not consistently follow the policies of staying in the home with the victim or informing victims of advocacy agencies or community services (Stanko, 1985b). Moreover, criminal justice personnel often proceed on misdemeanor assault charges, rather than on the felonies that would otherwise be charged in nonmarital situations (Barak, 1985; Bowker, 1983; Dobash and Dobash, 1979; Ferraro, 1989b; Maidment, 1985; Stanko, 1985a; Walker, 1984). Furthermore, the violation of protection or restraining orders in domestic violence cases results, at the very best, in misdemeanor charges that the victim herself must initiate and pursue with the court (Fain, 1981; Maidment, 1985; Taub, 1983).

Civil suits are at least equally problematic in domestic abuse cases. Civil litigation generally neglects the issues of further/future violence; neglects the consideration of the availability of orders at immediate times of crisis; and finally, ignores emotional and psychological damages (Fain, 1981; Lerman et al., 1983; Taub, 1983).

Two additional, but different, types of problems for victims of intimate violence have been identified by researchers or practitioners alike. First, the remedy of litigating against police or prosecutors for negligence (Ferraro, 1989a) or for non-enforcement of woman battering under the equal protection clause (Tong, 1984) has not been widely available as a tactic because this strategy requires money, time, attorneys, and so on. Second, money continues to be a serious problem in the provision of services for victims. Indeed, the situation has worsened, as difficult fiscal times and changing political climates have eroded the limited monies for domestic violence organizations, shelters, and services (see Ferraro, 1989a). With fewer dollars, it is hard to maintain staff for hot-line and crisis center assistance, to provide services like medical care, counseling, and skills/job training, and to provide a sufficient number of beds in shelters for women and children in times of need.

In parallel fashion, marital rape charges are only infrequently sustained. Prosecution and conviction are incredibly rare occurrences in those states that have either repealed the marital rape exemption or have otherwise provided for the crime of rape in marriage. More commonly, only the most brutal and sensational marital rape cases ever come forward for prosecution (compare the Greta Rideout and Lorena Bobbitt cases). Marital rape victims continue to be blamed even when they are able to substantiate charges with physical evidence of gross injury (Bienen, 1983; Finklehor and Yllö, 1985). A significant problem has occurred in jurisdictions that maintain the spousal exemption for rape. Not only have some jurisdictions failed to repeal this exemption, but in some jurisdictions it has been extended to non-married couples who cohabit (Finklehor and Yllö, 1985; Micklow, 1988).

The persistence of unique requirements, standards, and practices for private violence committed against women presents yet a further source of injustice for those violently victimized at the hands of their partners. Corroborative evidence has been found, for example, to be required in a de facto manner in the legal processing of intimate violence cases (Caringella-MacDonald, 1985; Spohn and Horney, 1992; Stanko, 1985a; Taub, 1983). This is tied to official doubts about the validity of victim claims. Because of this, the crimes of intimate violence against women continue to be treated differently than more public violent criminal offenses. This means that the discriminatory treatment of private sexual and nonsexual violence against women endures well beyond reforms.

Summary

In few crimes are victims so suspicioned, or treated so unfairly as those involving intimate partners. The strength of the aforementioned myths in relation to intimate violence figures strongly into reform failures. Erroneous beliefs about battered women not only preclude the realization of justice reforms, but they serve to perpetuate the double victimization of those victims who come forward with charges of intimate violence. The myths that promulgate the beliefs that women provoke and ask for their victimization, that they lie and falsely accuse men they know of violence, that they, at least subconsciously, desire or enjoy the domination by the men they know, all serve to buttress the justice system's continued prejudicial and discriminatory treatment of privately victimized women.

Because of these persisting myths as well as the continued maltreatment of women victimized by private violence, women who are violently victimized by men continue to face a prospect that can only be described as a catch-22. If a woman comes forward and attempts to pursue her case of victimization, she is likely to encounter additional hardship because of the differential beliefs and practices that continue to define so much of the case processing in this realm. If the victim instead remains silent and does not move forward to pursue her victimization, her pain remains private, her victimization unaddressed, and her assailant free to revictimize her, or move on to victimize others. In this way, recourse for the intimate violence against women remains inordinately problematic. While some progress has been made to help victims of intimate violence, the road is long and hard. The similarities between private sexual and nonsexual assaults lie in the continued difference between the responses to these crimes and all others. Tenacious prejudices about battered women thwart the potential effectiveness of reform measures.

Public and official attitudes and beliefs must be targeted in subsequent efforts to diminish the plight of victimized women. We must renew efforts to educate the public and law enforcement and legal personnel through, for example, mass media campaigns, special school programs, and in-service training programs in order to continue the fight against violence directed privately against women. Furthermore, to reduce the incidence of revictimization now so common, both the police and courts must begin to establish appropriate safeguards for those victims who seek to prosecute the batterer. Continued monitoring of offenders who have a history of violence against the victim-plaintiff should be mandatory. In addition, and perhaps more importantly, the structured inequalities that make men superordinate and women subordinate in marriage and other partner relationships must be taken to task if future progress is to be made in changing the face of private violence against women.

9

Societal Collusion and Culpability in Intimate Male Violence

The Impact of Community Response toward Women with Abusive Partners

CRIS M. SULLIVAN

Michigan State University

W omen who have been physically, emotionally, or sexually abused by their intimate male partners generally turn to a variety of sources for help in order to end their victimization. Unfortunately, society often colludes in woman battering by tacitly allowing and, in some ways encouraging, men to maintain power over their female partners (Adams and Penn, 1981; Breines and Gordon, 1983; Goodman, Koss, Fitzgerald, Russo, and Keita, 1993; United Nations, 1989). This collusion takes form through the social customs and mores that expect women to provide more direct care of children and to put the needs of the family above their own, while expecting men to be "heads of households"; prevalent religious doctrine that upholds and preaches traditional, patriarchal values; and legislation that discriminates against women. Cross-cultural studies have suggested a direct correlation between the status of women within society and the prevalence of intimate male violence against women (Counts, Brown, and Campbell, 1992; Lester, 1980). In those cultures in which women have low status (i.e., less power) in relation to men, wife beating is very common. Conversely, in those few societies in which male dominance is not accepted or condoned, wife beating is absent or negligible (Mitchell, 1992; Nash, 1992). This supports the contention that intimate male violence is simply one form of male dominance over women in general (DeKeserady, 1990) and that societal mores, customs, religions, and laws have a tremendous impact upon this phenomenon. The patriarchal values of society as a whole permeate the medical, legal, and social systems to which battered women turn for help. This chapter describes the societal response to battered women, primarily in the United States, in order to understand how the society-at-large colludes with and is culpable for intimate male violence.

The magnitude of intimate male violence against women has been detailed elsewhere in this volume. This chapter focuses on the aftermath of intimate male violence. Specifically, how do women attempt to end the violence they have experienced, and how do various societal agencies help or hinder their efforts?

Women's Help-Seeking Efforts

The decision whether and from whom to seek help is a complex one for women with abusive male partners. Women are often threatened by their assailants with more serious abuse should they make any attempts to leave (Browne, 1987; Schutte, Malouff, and Doyle, 1988). As earlier chapters have shown, these threats are far from idle. There is now ample evidence that abuse often escalates, sometimes to the point of homicide, after women attempt to separate from their assailants (Harlow, 1991; Lehnen and Skogan, 1981; Mahoney, 1991; U.S. Department of Justice, 1983). Not only do many women fear for their lives and the lives of their loved ones should they leave, but they are also often held captive by economic realities. Women in general, regardless of level of abuse in their relationships, can expect their standard of living to decrease after divorce (Corcoran, Duncan, and Hill, 1984). The jobs women can expect to get continue to be overwhelmingly low-status jobs that offer low pay (Blau, 1984; Faludi, 1991); two thirds of adults living in poverty are women (U.S. Bureau of the Census, 1989). Added to this, abusive men often use economics as a leverage in which to continue to harass and torment their partners (Barnett and LaViolette, 1993; Schutte et al., 1988). They wage custody battles, draining women of their resources, or they fail to pay child support or alimony (U.S. Bureau of the Census, 1989). Stalking women at their places of employment until they lose their jobs is also a common tactic (Shepard and Pence, 1988). Many battered women have also been isolated from their friends and family, or they receive strong messages from their loved ones that they must make the relationship work (Mitchell and Hodson, 1983). Given these realities facing women with abusive partners, it is surprising that so many people ask, "Why does she stay?" It appears more appropriate to wonder, "Given everything against them, how is it that any women leave abusive men at all?"

Despite the fear of retaliation and continued economic and physical abuse, many women do seek help to end their partners' violence. A nationally representative sample of 3,665 women reported that 68 percent of those battered had sought help at least once (Wauchope, 1988). One comprehensive study of more than 6,000 women from fifty different shelters found that the women had made an average of six help-seeking efforts before entering the shelter (Gondolf, 1988). Other studies have reported on the high rate of women's help-seeking efforts as well (Binney, Harkell, and Nixon, 1981; Bowker, 1983; Horton, Simonidis, and Simonidis, 1987; Schulman, 1979). Dobash, Dobash, and Cavanagh (1985) found that the longer the duration of the violence, the greater the number of agencies women contacted to escape it. Unfortunately, women are often unsuccessful in receiving adequate help from those agencies and institutions designed to provide it (Binney, Harkell, and Nixon, 1981; Dobash et al., 1985; Gondolf, 1988; Reidy and Von Korff, 1991).

Community Response to Battered Women

With the exception of domestic violence shelters, the most common institutions to come into contact with battered women are police officers and the legal system, the health care system, the social service system, therapists, and the clergy. This chapter describes the typical responses of institutions other than the criminal justice system to whom battered women often turn. Domestic violence shelters will be explored in the following section, as they were established in response to the ineffective assistance survivors received from the other systems.

The Health Care System

Straus (1986) has estimated that approximately 1.5 million women seek medical treatment for injuries sustained from abusive partners each year. A study of randomly sampled emergency room patients found that nearly 1 out of 4 of the women (24 percent) were identified as intimate abuse victims (Goldberg and Tomlanovich, 1984). Similar statistics were found in studies of other health care settings as well (Hamberger, Saunders, and Hovey, 1992; Helton, 1986). One study concluded that virtually all women's multiple injuries, excluding those received from car accidents, are the result of intimate abuse (Stark and Flitcraft, 1982).

Unfortunately, many physicians and nurses are unlikely to recognize symptoms and signs of abuse unless they are directly informed by the victims (Stark and Flitcraft, 1988; Warshaw, 1993), and women are not likely to offer such information unless asked. Many doctors continue to overmedicate battered women, generally in the form of tranquilizers and antidepressants (Easteal and Easteal, 1992; Johnson, 1985). Physicians are also more likely to label battered women as having neurotic, hypochondriacal, or psychosomatic disorders and to refer them to psychiatric treatment (Kurz and Stark, 1988; Stark and Flitcraft, 1988).

Some hospitals and clinics have begun to address intimate violence as a health issue and have initiated special trainings and standard protocol to provide more effective services to battered women. The one study that has evaluated such changes, however, reported less than encouraging results. Warshaw (1993) examined all emergency room files at one hospital, over a two-week period, in which women had been deliberately injured by another person. The emergency room had a formal protocol for dealing with such instances, which included indicating the probability of abuse on the discharge form, providing shelter information to the victim, and referring the patient to a psychiatric or social work consultation. Results indicated, however, that 90 percent of the doctors failed to obtain a psychosocial history or history of intimate violence, and 92 percent of the discharge diagnoses did not indicate abuse. Shelter information was provided in only 2 percent of the cases, and referrals to psychiatric and social work consultations were rarely made (4 percent and 8 percent, respectively). These findings suggest that even in those hospitals with improved policies regarding woman abuse, survivors are still receiving less than adequate care and assistance.

The Social Service System

One might expect social workers to be the most empathic and helpful of all the service providers to whom battered women turn, given the very nature of their occupations. This unfortunately does not generally appear to be the case. Social workers have been found to underestimate the number of cases that involve intimate violence and to view women primarily in their roles of wives or mothers (Johnson, 1985). One study randomly sampled social casework files and found that one-third contained direct reference to woman battering. Notes within the files indicated that overall, social workers were apathetic or blamed the victim, sometimes encouraging women to stay with assailants "for the sake of the children" (Maynard, 1985). Similar findings by Dobash and others (1985: 160), concluded that "Although some social workers did attempt to confront the men and/or actively pursue assistance for the woman, they acted primarily upon individual initiative and not because of priorities or policies set by the agency."

The Therapeutic Community

Two studies have examined the responses of therapists/counselors to women with abusive partners. In one study providing vignettes of wife battering to therapists, only 22 percent correctly labeled the problem "violence/battering," and 17 percent viewed the relationship as abusive. Only 10 percent of the therapists addressed the woman's need for protection, while 60 percent called for work on a nonviolent marriage problem (Hansen, Harway, and Cervantes, 1991). The other study, involving 232 volunteer counselors, led the authors to conclude that battered women will receive the most appropriate help from women age 20 to 29 who have master's degrees and a good deal of experience working with battered women. Abused women will receive the least appropriate help from male psychiatrists over age 60 who work in mental health settings (Hall-Apicella, 1983).

Response from the Clergy

Many women turn to religious leaders for assistance in coping with abusive partners. One study found that women were more likely to contact the clergy over every other source of help except the police (Bowker and Maurer, 1986), and in Pagelow's (1981) sample, the clergy was the most common institution turned to by women. The response by clergy to women with abusive partners, however, continues to be problematic and, in some cases, even dangerous to their safety. Alsdurf's (1985) study of Protestant ministers in the United States and Canada revealed that 26 percent believed that women should submit to their abusive husbands and trust that God would reward them by ending the abuse or giving them the skills to endure it. One-third stated that the abuse would have to be quite severe to justify a wife ending the marriage, and 1 out of 5 (21 percent) believed that no amount of violence justified a woman leaving. Another study of religious leaders, both Christian and Jewish, found that many refused to believe that abuse had happened in their parish or synagogue or that it was their place to intervene (Martin, 1989). It is clear that not only is it unlikely for women to receive helpful assistance from their clergy (Bowker, 1982; Thompson, 1989), but that some responses by religious leaders may in fact put women in more danger. For a spiritual leader to tell a woman that she should not leave an abusive man no matter how violent he may become gives a strong message to the abuser that he can increase his abuse with no consequences.

There is strong evidence to support the argument that male battering of intimate female partners is more than a dyadic relationship gone awry. The high prevalence of woman battering, coupled with community unwillingness to protect victims or hold batterers accountable for their violence, suggests a high degree of societal collusion and culpability in this area. Men are clearly given the message, not only through our laws, but through institutionalized community systems and organized religions, that they are the dominant sex and, as such, may use force against women to maintain that dominance. It seems logical that, were women respected more in our society, intimate violence would be infrequent, if not nonexistent. If we are to eliminate intimate male violence against women, we must design and implement strategies that affect and influence the various components of society that currently collude with men in the degradation and battery of women. The following section delineates current strategies to improve the community response to women with abusive partners. Included are descriptions of domestic violence shelters, advocacy interventions, and public education campaigns.

Strategies to Improve Community Response

Domestic Violence Shelters

Shelters for women with abusive partners were virtually nonexistent before 1976. Most developed out of the feminist movement of the 1970s, during which time consciousness-raising groups led to women talking, often for the first time, about the abuse they were experiencing in their homes. The first shelters were often no more than women opening their homes to battered women and their children, and none initially relied on governmental funding (Schechter, 1982). Within the last eighteen years, however, the Battered Women's Shelter Movement has been successful in educating the public and demanding an increase in services for women with abusive partners. Today there are more than 2,000 domestic violence programs (primarily shelters) across the United States. Most of these programs provide emergency shelter, 24-hour crisis lines, and numerous support services. Some are beginning to provide second-stage housing as well (Scyner and McGregor, 1988). Unfortunately, the number of programs available is still much lower than the need. Shelters are less likely to be available to women in rural areas, and most struggle continually for enough money to stay open. The National Coalition Against Domestic Violence estimates that for every woman who receives shelter, three are turned away for lack of space (Rita Smith, personal communication, 1993).

Shelters have been found to be one of the most supportive and effective resources for women with abusive partners, according to the residents themselves (Bowker and Maurer, 1985; Sedlak, 1988; Straus, Gelles, and Steinmetz, 1980). Most programs provide all services free of charge and were created to empower and respect women (Ridington, 1977–78; Schechter, 1982). Berk, Newton, and Berk (1986) reported that for women who were actively attempting other strategies at the same time, a shelter stay dramatically reduced the likelihood of further violence.

Although shelters receive high "effectiveness" ratings in general by their residents, not all women feel that shelters are options for them, and some are distrustful of the experiences they might have there. Lesbian women, for example, are much more likely to have negative shelter experiences or to believe that shelters are for heterosexual women only (Irvine, 1990; Renzetti, 1992). This is due to a number of factors. Some lesbians perceive that they will be discriminated against in shelters, while others fear that shelters would be unsafe because their abusers, also being women, could gain entry into the shelters more easily than could male batterers. Some lesbians are even battered by women who work within the shelter movement or who know women who work within the shelter. While these issues of safety and discrimination are beginning to be dealt with in many shelters, the complexity of the problems makes it difficult to guarantee safety for lesbian women at the present time.

Some women of color, regardless of sexual orientation, also hesitate to use shelters for various reasons. Many shelters are staffed primarily by white women, who may be insensitive to the unique needs and issues within diverse cultures. For instance, some African American women are more hesitant to call the police because they fear the racist treatment their assailants might receive from the predominantly white system (Williams, 1981). Language barriers prevent other women from seeking shelter, as do shelter policies that are more likely to be comfortable to women who are both white and middle-class (Davidson and Jenkins, 1989). Obviously, many white women need to educate themselves about the different needs of all shelter residents and work to respect those differences.

Another group of people underserved by shelters are those women under age 20 or over age 60 (e.g., see Berk et al., 1986; Gondolf, 1988; Hilbert and Hilbert, 1984; Okun, 1986; Schutte et al., 1988; Sullivan et al., 1992). A study of all Florida shelters found that, although 27 percent of all Florida residents are senior citizens, fewer than

1 percent of shelter residents were over age 60 (Vinton, 1992). Given the potential effectiveness of shelters, more outreach to younger women, older women, women of color, working-class women, and lesbians appears important and necessary.

Community-Based Advocacy Services

Most, if not all, shelters include some form of assistance that they would call advocacy among the various services they offer. This form of assistance ranges from helping a woman move her belongings out of her residence to accompanying her through the varied stages within the criminal justice system. However, agencies and individuals differ in their definition of *advocacy*. Jeffrey Edleson and Einat Peled (cited in Edleson, 1993) recently conducted a national survey of 379 battered women's advocacy programs in order to better understand how advocacy is being defined in the field. For the majority of the programs surveyed (87 percent), *advocacy* meant "direct services to women." Approximately one-third worked with public housing, private landlords, or health care systems, although it was not specified whether this work involved direct service to the woman or attempts to create systems change. While direct assistance can be quite valuable for a woman coping with an abusive partner, such assistance is not the same as advocacy. As Knitzer (1976) outlined in her historical piece on child advocacy, there are six principles common to all forms of advocacy:

- Advocacy assumes that people have, or ought to have, certain basic rights.
- Advocacy assumes that rights are enforceable by statutory, administrative, or judicial procedures.
- Advocacy efforts are focused on institutional failures that produce or aggravate individual problems.
- Advocacy is inherently political.
- Advocacy is most effective when it is focused on specific issues.
- Advocacy is different from the provision of direct services.

To this list, Herbert and Mould (1992: 117) add the following: "[A]dvocacy is not primarily concerned with providing a service, but rather with assuring the availability and relevance of the service that is provided. It implies a *proactive step* beyond the mandated delivery of service" (italics added). Given this definition, it would appear that some agencies may be confusing advocacy with the provision of direct service. That notwithstanding, some groups and agencies have provided true advocacy intervention as a means of improving community response to the issue of intimate violence.

Sullivan and colleagues (Sullivan, 1991; Sullivan, Basta et al., 1992; Sullivan, Tan et al., 1992; Sullivan, Campbell et al., 1994) have attempted to increase the effectiveness of social service providers by providing trained advocates to women after they have resided at shelters for battered women. Their research has substantiated that women are in need of numerous resources when they leave a shelter and that working with advocates increases a woman's effectiveness in obtaining those resources from the community. Thus women who worked with advocates reported higher satisfaction with their social support systems and an overall higher quality of life, but they were no more or less likely to be revictimized by their assailants than were the women who did not work with advocates. While advocacy can be a helpful intervention for women with abusive partners, it is not generally enough in and of itself to end their intimate partners' violence.

Changing Societal Attitudes

A great deal of the work invested in changing societal attitudes has centered around education within the school system and educating the public through mass media. Education programs within schools have had mixed results. One study provided a film on intimate violence to high school boys but found no attitudinal changes immediately after or one month later (Walther, 1986). A more intensive program for high school students, however, lasting either half a day or a full day, resulted in significant positive changes, which remained at the five-week follow-up. For a small percentage of the boys, negative results were found. These results led the authors to hypothesize that these same boys were already predisposed to being abusive and that they may require secondary, rather than primary, prevention efforts (Jaffe, Sudermann, Reitzel, and Killip, 1992). It makes sense to begin education in the schools, given the prevalence of intimate male violence against young girls (Levy, 1991), but more work appears necessary to develop a program that will benefit students over time.

The media has begun presenting more realistic portrayals of woman battering in movies (e.g., *Sleeping with the Enemy*), made-for television movies (e.g., *The Burning Bed* and *The Tracy Thurman Story*), and even prime-time television shows (e.g., episodes of "Roseanne"). Public service announcements and documentaries have also been successful in giving a societal message that intimate male violence will not be tolerated (Kaci, 1990). Still, most media portrayals of women continue to be stereotypical and one dimensional. Women in movies and on television are still often victims of stranger violence who need men in their lives to protect and save them; most likeable main characters and heroes continue to be men. Community education efforts, in the media as well as in neighborhoods and legislatures, are crucial to reducing intimate male violence. Politicians, judges, police officers, and social workers are simply people who have been exposed to the same false images of women that the media have portrayed and who have accepted these stereotypes, myths, and beliefs as true. It is at the most basic level of community education that the most change is likely to occur.

While shelters, advocacy programs, and public education campaigns have been and continue to be developed to prevent and eradicate intimate violence against women, the aforementioned programs and endeavors are by no means an exhaustive list of current efforts. In the medical field, educational programs are being developed for primary health care providers (Campbell, 1986; McFarlane, Anderson, and Helton, 1987). Batterer intervention programs have begun to be developed and evaluated in a number of communities (Edelson and Tolman, 1994; Shepard, 1992). In summary, practically all communities are developing at least some types of intervention strategies to deal with the problem of intimate violence. That these efforts are often fragmented, disconnected, or unavailable to many of the people who need them remains a problem that will need to be addressed in the future.

Summary

Researchers, activists, and survivors of intimate male violence have been calling for a more coordinated community response to the problem of woman battering. There are four broad areas in which work must be done to eradicate intimate male violence: the criminal justice system, legislation, community service providers, and general societal attitudes.

The Criminal Justice System

Given the criminal nature of intimate male violence, an obvious arena in which to create change is the criminal justice system. Work has already begun in this area, with more police forces mandating arrest and overnight incarceration of batterers. While this change in and of itself sends a stronger message to women and their assailants, there is still a great deal more to be done. Policies are only as effective as the officers who implement them, and many police are still leery of pro-arrest policies, even when they have been found to be effective (Jaffe et al., 1986). Therefore, specific domestic violence training should be instituted in all police academies, along with in-services for trained officers. Research has found that such training does improve the attitudes of police, especially if battered women are involved in the design or as public speakers (Buchanan and Perry, 1985; Stubbing, 1990). It is also crucial to follow arrest with some type of punishment for batterers. One random sample of abusive and non-abusive men found that while the men tended to perceive arrest as an extremely severe disincentive to abuse, over half also believed that there was no likelihood of being arrested if they beat their wives (Carmody and Williams, 1987).

One example of a successful criminal justice intervention is the Minnesota Intervention Project. This is a large-scale program that coordinates the local criminal justice system response with those social service agencies that serve batterers and their victims. This coordination involves arresting and detaining batterers overnight whenever possible, offering support and advice to victims, and encouraging prosecutors to aggressively pursue intimate violence cases. Advocates also assist women with temporary restraining orders (TROs), custody and visitation issues, and other community resources. A separate component within the project offers group treatment to batterers, reserving space for court-mandated offenders. Syers and Edleson (1992) have concluded from their longitudinal research on the Minnesota Intervention Project that the entire system (police, prosecutors, judges, and batterer programs) must be coordinated to adequately fight intimate male violence.

Albuquerque, New Mexico, and Newport News, Virginia, have also reduced their family homicide rate by (1) implementing pro-arrest policies, training officers and supervisors, and evaluating their efforts; (2) implementing court-mandated programs for batterers; and (3) initiating family violence task forces (Stubbing, 1990). Clearly, these two programs should be models for other cities and states that are serious in their efforts to eliminate intimate male violence.

Legislation

While all states now have legislation specifically dealing with intimate male violence (Kalmuss and Straus, 1983), they differ in the level of protection provided to battered women. Not only are orders for protection more comprehensive in some states than others (Lerman and Livingston, 1983), but in many states, intimate male violence is not taken into consideration when deciding child visitation or custody, and sometimes mediation is mandated when couples divorce, regardless of whether abuse has occurred (Kinports and Fischer, 1993). Many laws currently ignore the realities of women's lives, and must be modified if the police are to be effective in protecting victims of intimate violence (Browne, 1993). For instance, many states do not have laws recognizing the battered-woman syndrome, which can be essential in the defense of women who have murdered their assailants. Efforts are currently being made, not only to strengthen existing laws (Biden, 1993), but to convince state governors to grant clemency to women wrongly imprisoned for murdering their abusers in self-defense (Osthoff, 1992). As the laws of any society are indicative of its people's values and customs, legislatures throughout the country must recognize and condemn women's experiences of violence within the home. Until this is an accepted policy, laws will continue to tacitly support intimate male violence.

Community Service Providers

Currently, the community services that battered women seek are too often inaccessible, disjointed, and eager to blame the victim. Stark and Flitcraft's (1988: 313) research led them to conclude that "changing the behavior and attitudes of service professionals and removing the structural incentives for them to neglect abuse are important first steps to early identification and prevention." Others have concurred that services need to be more accessible and effective if we are to stop life-threatening abuse in the home (Reidy and VonKorff, 1991; United Nations, 1989).

Some researchers have even made specific recommendations toward increasing the effectiveness of social service providers. Shepard and Pence (1988), for example, suggest that social workers need to examine how abuse contributes to employment problems for women. McDonald (1989) recommends that therapists focus less on intrapsychic therapy and more on providing women with practical assistance in their communities. Goodman and others (1993) urge psychologists to focus on the social institutions that support male violence against women, and Martin (1989) has applauded the few religious organizations that have started shelters or programs within the religious community. Clearly, efforts need to be continued, expanded, and improved to hold service providers accountable for providing effective services to women who are escaping intimate male violence.

In summary, future strategies, designed not only to assist battered women but to eradicate intimate male violence altogether, must focus on raising the status of women within society by improving our laws and law enforcement, demanding that social service providers supply effective and coordinated services to survivors, and educating the general public about the realities of women's experiences. To the extent that this is not occurring, our communities will continue to collude with and be culpable for intimate male violence against women.

10

Theory and Therapy

A Feminist Perspective
on Intimate Violence

MARSALI HANSEN

Pennsylvania Child and Adolescent Service System

MICHELLE HARWAY

California Family Study Center

The present chapter explores feminist contributions to understanding intimate violence and abuse with special emphasis on the societal context in which abusive relationships exist. In particular, societal rather than intrapersonal factors are considered when trying to explain male violence against women. New directions consistent with the feminist formulation are subsequently developed. Special emphasis will be given to the ways in which society supports male aggression; the manner in which gender-role socialization prepares men to expect control over their domestic partners and women to accept abusive interactions; some of the theoretical perspectives that attempt to explain the battered woman's behavior; and the ways some institutions continue to support and foster battering. The latter part of the chapter focuses on the contributions of feminist therapists and feminist family therapists to the feminist conceptualization of battering and clinical examples of feminist therapists' formulations. The chapter concludes with a presentation of feminist goals for social change and change within the context of therapeutic treatment.

Societal Support of Male Aggression

A growing body of literature suggests that much of the increase in violence and aggression in the United States can be attributed to social causes. Furthermore, the National Academy of Science's Panel on the Understanding and Control of Violent Behavior notes that the United States is now more violent than other countries (National Research Council, 1993). As noted in the early chapters of the present volume, intimate violence is not the only form of violence that is increasing in American society. Incidence figures for rape, sexual abuse, and sexual harassment also reflect the general increases. While early studies of abuse, but especially of battering, focused on identifying the characteristics of the perpetrators, most experts on batterers (Gondolf, 1993; Hotaling and Sugarman, 1986; Hamberger and Hastings, 1991) agree that there is no single uniform profile to describe those men who engage in intimate violence. Feminists, for example, argue that the very prevalence of these violent crimes suggests that the problem has its root causes in American society's view of women. In this respect, some writers have concluded that theories of individual pathology do not provide an adequate explanation of battering, and that the appropriate focus should be on the structural and cultural factors (McHugh, 1993). Much of the research conducted on battering, moreover, has focused on the characteristics of the battered woman, painting her as a helpless victim (see Harway, 1993, for a discussion of these findings). Some of the more recent publications, especially those with a feminist orientation, have begun to look toward the strengths of survivors of abusive relationships. Only recently have professionals begun to look for "common causal pathways" of male violence (Koss, 1993: vii). In 1991, for example, the American Psychological Association's Committee on Women in Psychology established a Task Force on Male Violence against Women. The task force was charged with reviewing "current research on the prevalence, causes, and impact of several different forms of violence against women. . . . This . . . is a call to psychologists to address the crisis of violence against women in a comprehensive and systematic way" (Goodman, Koss, Fitzgerald, Russo, and Keita, 1993: 1054).

Understanding why American society is more violent than others may be related to the dynamics of power: Many forms of violence (rape, child sexual abuse, spousal abuse, and sexual harassment) share predominantly female victims and male perpetrators, exhibit some form of aggression by men against women, and occur in the context of relationships that involve power differentials. Examining the power dynamics that describe most male–female relationships may help us understand the prevalence statistics (Connors and Harway, 1993), for it is the use and abuse of power that is at the heart of much of today's violence. With spousal violence as with other forms of intimate violence between males and females, the socialization of the two genders serves to teach men and women behaviors that enforce and maintain gender status differences. Connors and Harway (1993) note that the forms of abuse just cited are precipitated by situations in which women threaten existing power relationships and, therefore, abuse becomes a means for keeping women in subordinate positions.

Battering, in particular, is often described by some writers as a strategy to control one's spouse: "Men who assault their wives are actually living up to cultural prescriptions that are cherished in Western Society—aggressiveness, male dominance and female subordination—and they are using physical force as a means to enforce that dominance," report Dobash and Dobash (1979: 24). These cultural prescriptions are important in trying to explain not only why men batter the women they purport to love, but why many women remain in these abusive relationships (see Ferraro, chapter 7 of this volume; Harway, 1993). Feminist writers, for instance, argue that it is also important to understand the emotional bond that forms between the battered woman and batterer, a condition Painter and Dutton (1985) have described as "traumatic bonding." In their analysis, the authors point to the similarity to other conditions in which strong emotional ties are developed under conditions of maltreatment, for example, situations in which hostages develop positive feelings for their captors and abused children are strongly bonded to abusive parents. The term *traumatic bonding* refers to the "strong emotional ties that develop between two people when one person intermittently harasses, beats, threatens, abuses, or intimidates the other" (Painter and Dutton, 1985: 364). Other writers in describing the bond between the battered and batterer (Hilberman, 1980; Symonds, 1979; Follingstad, Neckerman, and Vormbrock, 1988) view it as being related to the "Stockholm Syndrome," (Ochberg, 1966) an emotional bond that develops between captor and hostage. The two features that battered-batterer, hostage-captor, and abused child-perpetrator all have in common, then, are the power imbalance and the intermittent nature of the abuse (Painter and Dutton, 1985).

Painter and Dutton (1985) describe how the person in the subordinate position becomes more negative in self-appraisal, less capable of existing independently, and more in need of the dominating person. The superordinate person, on the other hand, is described as one who develops a need to maintain the relationship, thereby embroiling the two individuals in a mutually interlocking relationship involving intermittent patterns of abuse and violence; cycles of abuse involve (1) the tension building phase, (2) the acute battering phase, and (3) the loving contrite phase (Walker, 1984). It is, as noted in earlier chapters, the loving and kind behavior of the batterer during the third phase that appears to provide reinforcement for the cycle, allowing the battered woman to convince herself that her batterer is capable of change. The cycle then begins all over again, with the violence usually escalating in frequency and severity. In this respect, Painter and Dutton (1985) conclude that the repetition of the buildup, the trauma during the battering, and the reconciliation that follows serve to traumatically bond the battered woman to her batterer and decrease the likelihood that the woman will leave the relationship. Their conclusions are supported by others such as Rounsaville (1978) who speculated that the intermittent nature of the battering followed by a loving reconciliation leads the battered woman to ignore the problem or distort its meaning to that of an aberration in the relationship.

Gender-Role Socialization

In addition to the use of physical force to maintain dominance, gender-role socialization teaches and reinforces the ways in which males and females handle power in personal and social settings. Thus, several studies of gender-role socialization help to explain how women are more likely to accept control by men and men more likely to impose control on women. Belle (1987) and Hobfoll (1986) report that women are more likely than men to aid in the well-being of others, while Aukett, Richie and Mill (1988) report that women consider relationships to have more importance in their lives. According to these studies, the relationship maintenance behaviors set women up to cooperate when faced with abusive behavior or with behavior that aims to control them because of the female orientation to value the relationship over their own opinion, rights, or advancement. Similarly, Eagly's (1987) meta-analyses of data on gender differences in adults found that men are significantly more aggressive than women, that they are more assertive and much more willing to use hostility or force to get their way, and that they are less concerned than women with the needs and rights of others. Eagly concludes that these data show that social roles reinforce the continuation of gender differences. She also indicates that the power that men are given for being born male not only trains the male child to be aggressive, but further reinforces this behavior by giving him easy access to rewards. At the same time, females not only are denied access to rewards, but are socially trained not to behave in powerful ways, thereby, setting the groundwork for tolerating abuse.

Studies of male–female interactions further help to explain the genesis of interactions between batterer and battered. Maccoby's research of same-sex and cross-sex dyads (1984) indicates that among children as young as age 3, girls will play cooperatively with other girls. When boys were present, however, the girls became somewhat passive, allowing the boys to do what they wanted. The aggressiveness of the boys themselves was one reason for this change in behavior. By middle childhood, the interactional styles of boys are significantly more win-oriented and restrictive, and girls are less able to influence their behavior. Research in the communication area parallels these findings. Studies of gender differences in communication indicate that men tend to be more assertive, loud, dominant, interrupting, and influential, while women tend to be more hesitant, personal, encouraging, and less listened to (Lott, 1981; Sandler, 1986; Tannen, 1990). Lott (1990), in studying task-related behaviors, found that men made more negative comments to female partners, ignored women's advice, and physically turned away from them. In organizational studies, women were as highly involved as men in work flow and social interactions in organizations, but they had less access to power interactions (Brass, 1985). In those same settings, women tended to use more indirect and passive tactics to influence (Fairhurst, 1985), and they tended to emerge less often than men as the recognized leaders of groups in small-group studies (Eagly, 1983). These studies suggest that gender-role socialization may play a significant part in the expectations among men and women to interact with unequal power. Male aggressiveness and female relationship orientation may further translate into family roles in which women are controlled by men's aggressiveness even as they struggle to maintain a family bond.

The Challenge of Feminist Psychotherapy

Feminist psychotherapy essentially developed within a social–political context in response to the dominance of male-created theories of psychology and human development (Weiner and Boss, 1985). Feminist therapists, having experiencing direct contact with victims of intimate violence, challenged traditional therapeutic approaches for being gender biased and formulated more gender-sensitive models. Traditionally, women were diagnosed and treated by therapists trained in male models of psychotherapy. Early feminist research (Broverman et al., 1972) suggested that conformity to female roles was the same as emotional unhealthiness. Early formulations of interpersonal relations conceptualized development from the perspective of the child's relationship to his mother; all problematic characteristics that resulted were attributed to the mother's inability to provide appropriate parenting (Caplin and Hall-McCorquodale, 1985). Alternative perspectives began to be developed as the number of women in the field increased, and they began to critique male-centered models. These authors, self-proclaimed feminist therapists, formulated new tenets for the practice of psychotherapy. These generally agreed on tenets provide a focus for the approach feminist therapists take toward the treatment of intimate violence and toward the conceptualization of battering. Feminist therapy "reflects certain values and therapist's attitudes regarding women and their role in society" (Riche, 1984).

In essence, a major theme of the feminist therapeutic perspective is the view that all people function within a social context that devalues women. No views, either the views of the therapist to the client or the client's interaction with peers, are regarded as "value free." The social context dictates the social reality of the therapist and, therefore, the manner in which the therapist views the client. Thus, the social reality dictates the theories that the therapist utilizes in understanding the client's functioning, or pathology, and in formulating appropriate treatment (Hamilton and Jensvold, 1992). Furthermore, the social reality also dictates the therapist's view of effective interventions, the client's response to the interventions, and the reality of the client before, during, and after completion of treatment. Within this social context, psychotherapy has historically blamed mothers and idealized fathers for the problems the clients experience (Hansen, 1993). Therapists trained in traditional approaches learn to diagnose and treat clients within a context that devalues the positive contributions of mothers to child development (Hare-Mustin, 1978).

Feminist therapists also recognize gender as a fundamental category that dictates clinical conceptualization, observation, and theorizing (Goldner, 1985; Avis, 1988). Not only are gender-based distinctions a cultural universal present in all societies, but gender provides the context for the social experience and for development from birth to senescence (Goldner, 1985). Feminist therapists believe that the different experiences of males and females are dictated by a society that is structured along the dimension of gender. Recent writers have begun to stress the interaction of cultural variability and ethnicity with the gender-based experience of women (Espin and Gawelek, 1992). Thus, for example, the oppression of white women is viewed as a fundamentally different experience from the oppression of women of color. Feminist theorists, in stressing the importance of cultural context in the formulation of a theory of therapy, are now beginning to explore multicultural and variable experiences of women.

Feminist therapists further focus on both the "oppressiveness of traditional roles" (Hare-Mustin, 1978) and the relegation of women to positions of lower status. For feminist therapists, recognizing the inequity between men and women is a critical component of empowering clients to formulate alternatives in treatment. Inequity is seen as a contributing factor in the batterer's perception of privilege in relation to the ways in which he treats his partner; this viewpoint is consistent with research that has shown spouse abuse to be more frequent in relationships in which the woman has a higher status outside the home than the man.

Not only are personal values and subjective experiences incorporated by feminist therapists into their clinical work, but efforts are made to avoid reinforcing traditional roles and values that limit the options of women and devalue their contributions (Avis, 1988). Feminist therapists "assert the value of women and women's experience" (Wheeler, 1985). With this view, therapists question and examine their own experiences, recognizing that these experiences occur within a social context that devalues women. As noted, the focus of this assertion is currently becoming expanded to include the complex interaction of gender and culture (Espin and Gawelek, 1992).

Feminist therapists also recognize gender-biased language and have been working toward a level of communication that does not devalue or demean women (Hare-Mustin, 1978). For feminists, communication is not gender free; the language used by the therapist formulates the perspective used in therapy. Viewing a mother's sensitivity to her child's feelings as "enmeshment" or referring to "family violence" rather than "battering," for example, creates a very different focus in treatment. In the former instance of "enmeshment," the focus of treatment would be to reduce a negatively perceived characteristic of the relationship rather than acknowledge the importance of sensitivity in the relationship between a mother and child. In the latter case of "family violence," the responsibility and direction of the abuse are diffused by the terminology.

Lastly, feminist therapists recognize that all therapy takes place within a social and political context. Rather than attempt to approach therapy "apolitically," an awareness of gender-based inequality is introduced into the therapeutic milieu. Efforts to empower clients to function with this awareness are viewed as critical components of treatment. Specifically, crucial elements in the treatment of intimate violence include both the recognition of the limitations of the legal system in protecting victims of intimate violence and the economic limitations of women, particularly women with children, to support themselves without the economic assistance from the batterer (Hart, 1993; Liss and Sahly, 1993).

The Practice of Feminist Therapy

For feminist therapists, the therapeutic premises previously described are applied to the conceptualizations of intimate violence and interventions with women who are victims of this abuse. In this respect, battering is recognized as occurring within the social context that devalues women while promoting the privileges of men. Among these privileges are the ancient views of women as property and a man's home as his castle. Within this context, social rules that govern behavior toward other men do not apply; that is, spouse abuse is viewed and responded to differently than aggression directed toward other men. Men are allowed primary prerogatives in how they choose to "address their wives." Homes are respected as private, and what occurs within the home is given far greater tolerance than behavior occurring outside the home (Mugford et al., 1989).

The Goals of Feminist Therapy

Feminist therapy further recognizes that battering is gender specific, not a function of the relationship between equal partners, and most often seeks not only to separate a woman from her abusive partner, but to focus on the concerns of the woman that are socially influenced by her gender role. While safety is a foremost consideration in treatment, therapists also recognize the potential danger in separating women from those men who threaten harm and violence if they try to leave. In these circumstances, whenever feasible, men who batter are referred to group therapy (Register, 1993). Unlike earlier approaches, feminist therapy gives appropriate attention to the statistical realities regarding the effectiveness of treatment for batterers. For feminists therapists, potential reconciliation is often regarded with skepticism and viewed as potentially dangerous for the victim (Register, 1993).

In addition, feminist therapists address the power differential resulting from differences in gender, with variations in both status and physical strength being recognized as contributors to battering. Men, for example, are recognized as having more financial options, as receiving more emotional and social support for their efforts in the relationship, and as having more physical power in conflict situations. The impact of the difference in power on the perceptions of the battered woman, including her self-esteem, is also a focus of exploration and treatment (Goldner et al., 1990).

Finally, feminist therapists work toward expanding the options available to women. In recognizing that society limits the options of women, feminist therapists actively challenge the perception of these limitations. Social views that value women who are in relationships and who support their partners and families are explored. In this respect, many therapists utilize and refer to their own experiences as professional women in their collaboration with their clients when they explore the clients' experience and seek alternative solutions to their problems. In helping battered women increase their economic options, some therapists may validate the battered woman's experience with carefully formulated self-disclosures of their own struggle in a workplace economically controlled by men.

The Family as Focus

Feminist family therapists expand the views of feminist therapists and contribute significantly to the conceptualization of battered women by describing the context for individual functioning. A primary premise is that individuals are part of a greater family system and function as part of a greater whole. Family rules govern the individual's behavior, and individuals rarely, if ever, function independently of the influence of family expectations. Individual behavior, therefore, is viewed as not occurring independently, but in response to the patterns and covert rules of the family. Thus, a batterer has been described by some as a person who responds to cues given by his partner. Feminist family therapists suggest that this view holds the wife ultimately responsible for her husband's actions, including her own battering.

Feminist family therapists further maintain that society, in general, devalues the role of women in the family and tolerates the abuse of women by their male partners. Men are recognized as benefiting from their higher status and the unequal distribution of resources and rewards; equally important the family is recognized as perpetuating this lack of equality through devaluing the roles designated to women, particularly those of homemaker and mother. Violence against women within this context is regarded as the "most overt and effective means of social control" (Bograd, 1988: 14) because it keeps women in positions of lower status and under the direct control of men. Feminist family therapists challenge family systems therapists to expand their views of the family system to include the social context in which the family functions. Social rules govern the establishment of family rules and roles and, thereby, influence behavior patterns within the home. Standard descriptions of family violence by family therapists have also been challenged for obscuring the seriousness of the violence and relieving men of the responsibility for their actions. Discussions of "behavioral sequences" and "reciprocal interactions" detract from the clear understanding that individuals are ultimately responsible for their actions (Hansen, 1993). Such discussions are criticized as suggesting "co-responsibility" and ultimately "no responsibility" for the violence, thereby perpetuating the views that the victims' actions precipitated the abuse. Recent research indicates that, in fact, most activity on the part of the woman has little impact on stopping the actions of her partner once the violence has begun (Jacobson, 1993).

Battering and other forms of violence may, it is speculated, have become the social problems they are today because of a lack of institutional support against such behavior, including laws that provide legal protection to those accused of intimate violence. Protecting women from partner violence has been an uphill battle. While major changes in the legal system have taken place during the last two decades, protective (restraining) orders are not uniformly enforced. In many jurisdictions, as has been noted earlier, police are still reluctant to intervene in domestic matters—especially in cases which witnessing the act of violence must precede an arrest—while the level of protection afforded battered women is woefully inadequate to protect them from partners determined to inflict physical harm. Women are still more likely to be killed by their male partners than by anyone else (Browne, 1993).

American society takes violence so much for granted that neighbors are reluctant to intervene in domestic quarrels, physicians are unwilling to report injuries resulting from domestic altercations (Randall, 1990), clergy and family members are reluctant to support battered women who leave and, instead, encourage them to return to try yet again (Browne, 1987). Battered women receive little support for extricating themselves from the situation. This is clearly revealed by the high frequency with which the women blame themselves for the violence and return again and again to try yet again to make the relationship work. When a woman finally turns to a mental health professional, she is also likely to find little support. Examining police data on battered women, Goodstein and Page (1981) report that 65 percent of the women had received prior psychiatric care but did not return for a second visit. Given most therapists lack of appropriate assessment or interventions (Hansen, Harway, and Cervantes, 1991), the reluctance of battered women to return is not surprising. With the exception of feminist conceptualizations, most approaches to therapy have tended to pathologize the battered woman or to make her responsible for her predicament (Bograd, 1984; Caplan, 1991; Pittman, 1987).

The Clinical Practice

The clinical practice of working with spouse abuse provides therapists with the opportunity to integrate feminist therapeutic theory with standards of good clinical care. From this perspective, the primary therapeutic goal in working with battered women is to ensure the safety of the client. The first phase of treatment follows a model of crisis intervention and includes a thorough evaluation of immediate danger. Frequency and severity of abuse must be addressed at the time of the first contact because the client may not return for additional visits and her safety is of paramount concern. Several studies by Harway and Hansen (1993) indicate that even therapists who identify themselves as "feminist" often fail to address the immediate seriousness of the violence and may instead focus on the psychological concerns of the couple. This first phase of treatment also includes the development of a safety plan that incorporates such practical considerations as finances, legal assistance, and housing. These practical concerns require an expanded conceptualization of the role of therapist, one that goes beyond exploration of the psychological reality of the client to examine the practical reality and the provision of services within the expanded context of the client's environment. This practical approach to the assessment of seriousness and formulation of the safety plan is consistent with what has been described here as the "feminist therapy" and further validates the very real experiences of clients.

Therapists operating from a feminist perspective recognize that clients often seek help for their children before seeking help for themselves. Therefore, an evaluation of marital discord and violence is an appropriate component of the parents' interview when parents bring children to treatment who are experiencing emotional difficulties. Children who have witnessed abuse may experience symptoms of both withdrawal or aggression, and many of these children may have been abused themselves. Feminist therapists remain cognizant of the social context and recognize that women may feel greater responsibility for the safety of their children than they do for themselves. Thus, an evaluation and crisis intervention program that focuses on the safety of the children might be perceived as more feasible and acceptable to the victim of abuse. Also, clients may be more likely to return to therapy to aid in the adjustment of their children than to return to improve their own status.

Feminist therapists recognize that couples who are experiencing violence are not only unlikely to bring the violence to the attention of the therapist during the initial visit, but may not do so throughout therapy unless the therapist raises the question. Violence is often socially minimized by couples to the level of acceptability (e.g., "all couples fight"). The current social context dictates that men are likely to perceive the women as responsible for the functioning of the relationship. Therefore, men are likely to bring their partners to treatment with the expectation that the therapists will agree with them that their wives are at fault and the focus of the treatment will be to help the wife improve. Female partners in such abusive relationships are likely to perceive themselves as indeed responsible for the abuse they endure, but they are also likely to be afraid of further reprisal if they express their concerns about the violence. Assessment under such circumstances requires utmost sensitivity to these social and political realities. Although therapists cannot ensure the safety of their clients, such concerns are paramount in treatment. An evaluation of the severity and frequency of violence is appropriate for all couples who appear for treatment (Harway and Hansen, 1994). Such assessment is conducted during separate interviews with the clients to optimize the opportunity for the victims of abuse to describe the conflict without fear of retaliation. The assessment process includes crisis intervention and the confirmation of the clients' perceptions of social reality. As noted earlier, the economic reality is a very real concern in the formulation of alternatives to remaining in abusive relationships.

The evaluation of the batterer, too, is conducted within the social and political context. Batterers are most likely to be referred to treatment either by the legal system or by an abused spouse. They rarely seek help for themselves voluntarily. Because battering is recognized as including a range of behavior used to maintain control in the relationship (Harway and Hansen, 1994), treatment of batterers is most effective when they are included in systematic programs for men with similar problems or within groups specifically designed to address both the aggression and the need to exert such control. Feminist therapists recognize that psychotherapeutic interventions with batterers need to occur within the legal and social context and, therefore, should include natural and legal consequences for the acts of aggression.

Feminist therapy with battered women has several specific goals following the assessment and crisis intervention phase. First, battered women are viewed as victims of trauma; treatment, therefore, addresses the specific symptoms that have resulted from the traumatic experience. Helping the clients recognize the relationship between the events and their symptoms can assist them in reducing the perception of themselves as responsible (e.g., as "not handling things well" or "always having bad nerves").

As symptoms of panic, depression, and chronic hypervigilance decrease, clients can then focus on accessing the problem-solving skills they have used in other aspects of their lives. However, the immediate threat of abuse must be addressed and eliminated for any treatment to advance beyond the phase of crisis intervention. Battered women view themselves within the social–political context that often condemns them for what they have endured, a view often maintained by the abusive partner. Therapy helps such women recognize how these views and attitudes contribute to both their own sense of responsibility for their victimization, as well as their own self-condemnation. This phase of therapy helps empower the clients to view themselves as actively in charge of their lives and no longer victims.

Treatment of families with children have additional considerations. First and foremost, the events these children have witnessed need to be viewed within the context of other traumatic events. Because many of these children have witnessed their mothers being beaten, their sense of safety is likely to have been shattered and they are likely to be "trauma victims" themselves. To effectively treat these children, the symptoms of the trauma must be addressed. Subsequently, children often experience ambivalent feelings toward the abuser and toward the victim. Some studies have shown that children who witness the abuse of their mothers are more likely to be aggressive toward her than children who have not (Carlson, 1990). Children are also exposed to the views of the batterer who is likely to be directly and indirectly blaming the victim. Support for blaming the victim comes from the societal views that maintain that not only is the mother responsible for the emotional functioning in the family (particularly the responsibility of preventing her children from exposure to traumatic events), but that "parents aren't supposed to fight." Exposure to these events may result in feelings of anger by children toward the victim and sympathy toward the abuser. In addition, such children are less likely to have the opportunity to acquire alternative approaches to conflict and problem-solving skills, particularly between men and women. Thus, a primary focus of treatment is to address these ambivalent feelings, as well as to provide the opportunity for the acquisition of alternative approaches to conflict. The incorporation of the feminist perspective into the treatment of victims of spouse abuse, batterers, and their children can be useful in increasing the thoroughness of evaluation and the effectiveness of interventions.

Summary

Efforts on the part of feminist therapists to reduce the incidence of intimate violence and improve the plight of the battered woman are directed at multiple levels. At the social level, the value of women, the value of roles traditionally assigned to women, and opportunities for additional roles must increase. As Gelles and Straus (1989: 203) have written, "Our examination of family violence over the years has consistently found that socially structured inequality is a prime contributor to violence in the home." Increased sensitivity to the plight of victims of intimate violence is needed both legally and legislatively. Laws governing protection from abuse and prosecution of abusers must be continually reexamined and evaluated (Hart, 1993). The feminist perspective is grounded in the social and political context; currently our legal systems provide inadequate protection from abuse, and the consequences for abusers are neither substantial nor consistently administered (Hart, 1993). Improved opportunities for women to support themselves and their children economically when they leave the abuser must be developed. As noted previously, when victims of abuse reach the therapeutic environment, therapists often are unprepared to recognize and treat these presenting problems (Hansen, Harway, and Cervantes, 1991). Therapists need to increase their sensitivity to the incidence and intensity of violence in the client population. Sensitivity and respect for the victim, while providing treatment without pathologizing, is a major contribution of feminist therapy to the feminist perspective on intimate violence. Feminist family therapy adds the additional dimension of clarifying the focus of responsibility for the violent actions and, thereby, clarifying the direction of the interventions within the conceptual context of the family system. Family therapists have highlighted the need to recognize that all persons in the family experience the impact of the violence but do not necessarily share the responsibility for the acts.

Feminist therapists and feminist theorists have joined in their efforts to present a clear and contextually consistent conceptualization of intimate violence. Recommendations from the feminist perspective would include the continued exploration of the interaction between the social context and the interpersonal process of intimate violence. In understanding this interaction, society will be better prepared to establish interventions that are both effective and long-lasting.

PART IV

The Long Road Ahead

11

Confronting Intimate Violence

Looking toward the Twenty-First Century

ALBERT P. CARDARELLI

University of Massachusetts Boston

The stated goal of the present volume is to understand the nature and extent of violence and abuse among intimate partners regardless of their marital status or sexual preference. There are obvious reasons for this undertaking: the changing nature of the family and the growing numbers of intimate partners who have established alternative living arrangements over the last two decades, as well as newly emerging evidence that shows high levels of violence and abuse among dating and courtship couples and same-sex partners. Another reason for the undertaking is the paucity of empirical studies on patterns of abuse and violence along the continuum of interpersonal violence, especially that of intimate violence. The tendency to view these patterns as distinct categories of behavior with little in common has resulted in gaps in our knowledge regarding the varied forms of intimate violence; these gaps have been acknowledged throughout the chapters in the present volume.

In addressing these areas of concern, the contributors are in agreement that much more research is needed if the field of family and intimate violence is to establish integrated theories that take into account the differing types of violence found throughout intimate partnerships. Such research will also, it is argued, improve assessment of the risk of abuse and its relationship to other kinds of violence and, therefore, provide a more informed basis for protective interventions.

The Changing Nature of the Family and Intimate Partners

As Western culture continues to change, its institutions take on new meanings (Berger, 1995; Hunter, 1991; Etzioni, 1993). This is especially evident within the family where both structural and functional changes continue to take place (Bellah et al., 1985; Lasch, 1977; Dolgin, 1994; Skolnick, 1991; Swerdlow et al., 1989). Cultural and social changes continue to emerge and challenge the traditional cultural symbolic of the nuclear family. The two-parent household, male-centered and dependent on male decisions for family functioning, has been subject to political, economic, and social pressures. Women are entering the work force in unprecedented numbers; large numbers of children are supervised in day-care centers or left unattended at home; divorce rates continue to remain high, with many children living in families of only one biological parent; and increasing numbers of individuals regardless of their sexual preference choose to establish cohabiting relationships.

These changes should not, however, be taken as evidence of the decline of the American family (Popenoe, 1993), but rather as a sign of the diversity of intimate relationships that are part of the present culture (Shoni, 1993; Orthner, 1992; Marciano and Sussman, 1992; Hartinger, 1992). As these changes gain momentum, researchers must examine abuse and violence between intimate partners along the continuum of intimacy, rather than restrict their analyses to family structures centered on traditional spousal relationships.

Dating, Courtship, and Same-Sex Violence

The changes associated with the family and intimate partners are reflected in several of the issues examined by the writers of the present volume. Early research on family violence was mostly directed to married couples who were living together (Straus, 1978; Finkelhor and Yllö, 1983; Straus et al., 1980; Gelles, 1972). Few researchers addressed the possibility that violence and abuse may also have existed among those in dating and courtship relationships. Makepeace (chapter 2) notes, for example, that until the 1980s, little was known about the levels of violence among couples before marriage. In his review of the literature on courtship violence, Makepeace notes that such behavior has been found to exist even among young persons (age 12 to 14) in the pre-dating phases of the courtship process. Given that almost all youth will, at one time or another, participate in the courtship ritual, understanding the contribution of dating violence to the occurrence of violence in marriage and long-term intimate partnerships is critical to the establishment of effective protective interventions.

Even less attention has been paid to same-sex violence. As Renzetti (chapter 4) demonstrates, not only have there been few studies of abuse and violence among gay and lesbian partners, but the lack of representative samples has resulted in widely varying estimates of abusive behavior. Researchers, for example, know little about the kinds of violence that occur among same-sex couples in dating and courtship relationships as opposed to those couples who have long-term partnerships. In addition, as Renzetti notes, stress and tension associated with AIDS and the threat of "outing" further complicate attempts by researchers to understand the dynamics of same-sex violence. Furthermore, little is known about the informal sources of control for incidents of abuse and violence in the gay and lesbian communities. Few studies have addressed the unique problems that gay and lesbian victims encounter when they report abuse to law enforcement officials or seek assistance from shelters that are based on the premise that violence is a male activity directed against women (Witzer, 1993; Renzetti, forthcoming). Lastly, the general reluctance of many gay men and lesbians to acknowledge the existence of abuse and violence as serious issues has made it difficult for victims to get the help they need. As with violence among different-sex couples, batterers remain unaccountable for their behavior. Nevertheless, despite the paucity of studies, the evidence is clear that same-sex violence occurs. This means that researchers must not view intimate violence solely as an issue of spouse abuse, but as a problem that involves intimate partnerships in general. It is in the relationship, not marriage as such, that violence erupts.

Power, Intimacy, and Conflict Resolution

Although there has, by all accounts, been a massive increase in the number of empirical studies on family violence, knowledge of the patterns of violence along the continuum of interpersonal violence, especially that of violence between partners is fairly limited. Many of these studies, as the present volume has noted, deal mainly with correlates of intimate violence. There have been few attempts at developing integrated theoretical models capable of incorporating the patterns of abuse and violence that take place within the varied intimate partnerships discussed throughout this volume. As Miller and Wellford note (chapter 1), the development of effective strategies to respond to the existence of intimate violence will increasingly depend on the extent to which an understanding of this violence is informed by a comprehensive integrated model (Williams, 1992).

In addition, there have been few attempts to incorporate the major theoretical contributions from criminology and social psychology in the development of theoretical perspectives on intimate violence (Fagan and Wexler, 1987; Fagan, 1993; Baumgartner, 1993; Hotaling and Straus, 1989). First, in viewing intimate violence as one form of violence along the continuum of interpersonal violence, researchers will be better able to discern the differences and similarities among the varied patterns associated with stranger violence on the one end of the continuum and those of intimate violence at the other end. Second, in conceiving intimate violence as itself taking place along a continuum of intimacy (from dating to courtship to engagement to cohabitation to marriage and including ex-spouses), researchers can begin to document more conclusively the varied strategies of abuse and survival that occur within intimate partnerships, the factors associated with violence escalation and desistance, and the response of law enforcement and other social agencies to the violence itself. Such data should prove especially helpful in implementing effective responses by the criminal justice and social service systems (Tifft, 1993).

Based on the arguments and evidence presented throughout this volume, treatment strategies appropriate to marital partners who are victims of abuse and violence may be inadequate for those victimized in cohabitating relationships and may even be inappropriate for gay and lesbian victims with histories of abuse and violence. Intervention strategies directed to the particular patterns of intimate violence at each stage of intimacy are critical to the long-term reduction of intimate violence in American society.

Including Intimacy in the Intimate-Violence Equation

In an early analysis of the effects of asymmetric social relations within the family, Ball-Rokeach (1980) argued that because males generally occupy superordinate roles over females, they are more likely to use violence as a tactic for maintaining their positions of power. Conversely, the less acute the asymmetry of relations, the greater the likelihood that the parties will resort to nonviolent modes of conflict resolution (Ball-Rokeach, 1980). While Ball-Rokeach's model is important, in that it establishes a set of testable propositions, it fails to give due consideration to other factors that characterize the divergent types of family life and partnerships discussed throughout this volume. Without diminishing the role of power as a critical variable in understanding intimate violence, recent research indicates that partner relationships cannot be distinguished solely on the basis of power. Other elements, including intimacy and attachment to one's partner at different life stages are likely to influence the level of marital conflict in the relationship (Zietlow and Sillars, 1988; Prager, 1991).

To overcome the obstacles in establishing an integrated theoretical model that would explain violence and abuse among the varied categories of intimate partners, researchers must consider the relationship between the level of symmetry associated with the decision-making processes essential to the family or household, and the level of intimacy, namely, the degree of emotive commitment and mutual responsiveness between the partners themselves (Prager, 1991, 1989; Baxter and Dindia, 1990; Whiffen and Gotlib, 1989). This consideration must be directed to same-sex couples as well. As Renzetti (chapter 4) noted, the association between power and violence has been less strong among homosexual couples. While differences in intelligence and social class were positively related to severe forms of abuse, the degree of the victim's economic dependence on the batterer yielded contradictory findings. Furthermore, while batterers had a greater say in the decision-making process, it was not clear whether this arrangement existed before the onset of the battering or whether it emerged subsequent to the battering as a further means of control (Renzetti, 1992).

Though intimacy and commitment have not as yet been given the intense scrutiny by researchers that they deserve, they remain vital to the quality and stability of family life. The widespread growth of family therapists and marriage counselors and the willingness of so many couples to seek professional help in strengthening the quality of their relationships is testimony to the importance of intimacy and commitment. Even among dating and courtship couples, as Makepeace notes (chapter 2), the level of intimacy not only exerts a profound influence on the social, personal, and physical health of the partners, but its frustration may lead to aggressive behavior and violence.

By including intimacy in the intimate violence equation, writers of the present volume recognize the dynamic character of intimate partnerships. The fact that some relationships, for example, may be characterized by high levels of asymmetry in terms of power does not preclude the possibility of high levels of emotional commitment and dependence on the part of both partners. In these partnerships, it is hypothesized that violence is less likely to occur when conflict situations arise because the partners are able to achieve some compromise through a negotiated process that may or may not be fully democratic.

On the other hand, if there is a decline in the reciprocity of emotional dependence, challenges by the subordinate partner to the asymmetry of power may result in anger, threats, or physical aggression by the superordinate partner. In some instances, the parties may even displace their aggression to other convenient targets, such as the children (Ball-Rokeach, 1980). Figure 11.1 attempts to provide a general framework for determining some of the potential outcomes associated with the resolution of conflict in intimate partnerships.

In partnerships characterized by both symmetry of power and high reciprocity (i.e., mutual responsiveness), conflict is likely to be resolved through cooperative agreements arrived at through high levels of bi-directional communication. Conversely, in those relationships characterized by symmetry of power but with minimal levels of mutual responsiveness, conflict is likely to go unresolved. In the latter case, avoidance, anger, and dissent are possible outcomes.

Much work needs to be accomplished in order to determine the relationships between power, intimacy, and violence. The exclusion of any of these dimensions

FIGURE 11.1 Conflict Resolution Outcomes in Intimate Partnerships

		POWER	
		LOW SYMMETRY	HIGH SYMMETRY
INTIMACY	HIGH	Compromise Negotiated Agreements	Cooperative Agreements* Conciliation
	LOW	Anger Threats Displacement Hostile Imperatives Physical Aggression	Anger-Hostility Avoidance Dissent Quarrels

*High levels of bi-directional communication

lessens the chances of achieving an integrated theory of intimate violence that can incorporate the fragmented domains of inquiry that have dominated the field of family and intimate violence (Williams, 1992). Recent efforts at determining how differences between partners affect the nature of the relationships are headed in the right direction and should increase our understanding of how intimate partners establish nonviolent strategies when conflict situations arise (Wood et al., 1994; Prager, 1991; Pilkington and Richarson, 1988; Zietlow and Sillars, 1988).

Challenges and Prospects for Reducing Intimate Violence

Although significant advances have been made in the study of intimate violence, important areas of information vital to understanding and controlling its occurrence are still lacking. Some of these urgent areas are briefly discussed below.

Longitudinal Research on Intimate Violence

There are as yet no longitudinal studies of intimate violence that use representative samples or cohorts. Such studies would not only increase understanding of the dynamics associated with intimate violence, the effects of the violence on the victims, and the meanings attributed to the violence by the perpetrators, but they would help determine whether individuals who use violence in private intimate settings are likely to do so in the public realm and vice-versa (Fagan and Wexler, 1987; Fagan, Stewart, and Hansen, 1983; Kandel-Englander, 1992). Longitudinal studies would also enable researchers to examine the reasons why some offenders desist from interpersonal violence as they move through the life cycle (Williams, 1995; Zietlow and Sillars, 1988).

Typologies of Batterers

Intimate violence, like all forms of violence, may be a one-time event, an episodic activity, or a chronic pattern of behavior resistant to any formal or even informal sanctions as shown earlier in the chapters by Ptacek and Ferraro (chapters 6 and 7). Because any of these patterns can occur within the categories of intimate partnerships discussed throughout this volume, the development of offender typologies is critical to successful strategies of prevention and control. Arrest strategies, for example, as recent research has shown, do not have the same results for all offenders (Sherman and Smith, 1992; Dunford et al., 1990). Offenders who have a stake in conformity and who are better educated and employed are more likely to desist from further violence following arrest in contrast to those who are unemployed and have a criminal record (Fagan, 1984; Klein, 1994). Such typologies would provide a more precise picture of recidivist batterers and help to determine whether the persistence of abuse and violence is limited to specific relationships (e.g., marriage) or whether it is part of the batterer's repertoire of behavior regardless of the intimate relationships in which he finds himself. Johnson (1995) argues that two distinct forms of violence exist between intimate partners: couple violence and patriarchal terrorism. Couple violence is characterized by occasional outbursts of violence from either husbands or wives, while patriarchal terrorism involves systematic male violence.

Community Disorganization and Intimate Violence

Although criminologists have long been interested in the relationship between community and criminal behavior, there are few empirical studies in criminology concerned with the relationship between community and intimate violence (Fagan, 1993). Sampson, for example, (1986) noted that communities with high divorce rates may have a greater number of isolated persons, thereby, providing more vulnerable targets of victimization. In communities like these, strategies that address the connection between isolation and victimization are critical to the control of violence against women by either strangers or intimate partners. Furthermore, because of the spatial concentration of violence in neighborhoods with high rates of poverty, social isolation of families, which is known to increase the risk of spousal assault, is commonplace (Hotaling and Sugarman, 1990). The more pervasive social isolation becomes, the less likely strategies of control will be effective. In these communities, interpersonal violence involving strangers and acquaintances may become routine, leading many women to downplay the seriousness of violence in their own relationships. Since economic dependence is one of the main factors in keeping women from leaving their abusers, women living in poverty are especially vulnerable to persistent abuse and violence. Under these conditions, children will have a high risk of being exposed to violence either as victim or witness. This exposure can potentially increase the risk that violence will become part of the individual's life-style (Fagan and Browne, 1993; Durant et al., 1994; Carlson, 1990; Thornberry, 1994). Previous research has shown, for example, that through modeling, children learn that violence is an appropriate strategy to resolve conflict in intimate relationships (Straus et al., 1980; Kalmuss, 1984; O'Leary, 1988).

Although intimate violence exists across the economic spectrum, neighborhoods that are socially disorganized will require extraordinary efforts on the part of the police and other municipal and private agencies to prevent and control interpersonal violence, including that involving intimate partners. The growing acceptance of community policing in many cities gives researchers an opportunity to determine the relationship of community structure to the nature and extent of interpersonal violence and to establish the kinds of strategies that are logically related to the set of conditions associated with the violence itself. Such data will provide the police and social service agencies with an understanding of the complex interaction of variables associated with the intimate violence they are asked to prevent, reduce, or resolve.

Given that most people will continue to date, to live together, and to marry, incidents of intimate violence will continue to come to the attention of public authorities. The United States has one of the highest rates of violent crime among developed nations, the vast majority of which is perpetrated by men against men; this should not deter us from a serious examination of the values and beliefs that influence the widespread view that family and intimate violence is a less serious problem and therefore requires fewer resources and less attention. The prevention of intimate violence calls for long-term cultural and social changes aimed at devaluing violence in intimate relationships as an appropriate way of resolving conflict. While these cultural changes appear to be making small headway in the war against family and intimate violence, there is a continued need for improved protection for the victims of abuse and violence. There is, for example, much work to be accomplished in the ways in which the health service delivery system responds to the physical injuries caused by physical violence. Although intimate violence has been increasingly recognized as a major health risk to women, physicians seldom ask victims whether their injuries are the result of domestic violence (Fontanarosa, 1995).

While the criminal justice system in the United States has historically been viewed as the central institution responsible for providing a level of protection for all members of society it has, until recently, played only a minimal role in the prevention and control of intimate violence. The recent move toward mandatory arrest policies for domestic violence is a step in the right direction in spite of the mixed results (Sherman et al., 1992; Dunford et al., 1990; Berk et al., 1992; Pate and Hamilton, 1992; Klinger, 1995). Mandatory arrest makes people aware of the seriousness of intimate violence and highlights the fact that in all respects intimate violence is criminal behavior. Obviously, the relationships between arrest strategies, punishment, and persistent battering is critical to the social control of intimate violence.

A Concluding Note

As the end of the century approaches, increased attention continues to be given to the devastating effects associated with the high levels of family and intimate violence in the United States. As the earlier chapters have noted, a number of communities throughout the country have begun to develop comprehensive approaches to family and intimate violence, including shelters for battered women and children, early intervention and mandatory arrests, required treatment programs for batterers, and policies that make it more difficult for victims to dismiss charges once the case enters the criminal justice system (Hart, 1995). The recent passage of the Violence Against Women Act (Title IV of the Violent Control and Law Enforcement Act of 1994) and the creation of the Office of Domestic Violence in the Department of Justice are testimony to the continued persistence of women's advocacy groups to make people recognize that intimate violence is a serious national problem. In addition to the national recognition given to violence against women, the growing emphasis on human rights throughout the world, but especially in the West, demands that violence—even that within the private realm of intimate partnerships—be seen as a violation of these rights.

References

Acitelli, L. K., & Duck, S. W. (1987). Intimacy as the proverbial elephant. In D. Perlman & S. W. Duck (Eds.), *Intimate relationships* (pp. 297–308). Beverly Hills, CA: Sage.

Adams, D. (1988a). Stages of anti-sexist awareness and change for men who batter. In L. Dickstein & C. Nadelson (Eds.), *Family violence* (pp. 63–97). Washington, DC: Appi Press.

(1988b). Counseling men who batter: A profeminist analysis of five treatment models. In K. Yllö & M. Bograd (Eds.), *Feminist perspectives on wife abuse* (pp. 176–199). Newbury Park, CA: Sage.

Adams, D., & Penn, I. (1981). Men in groups: The socialization and resocialization of men who batter. Paper presented at the annual meeting of the American Orthopsychiatric Association.

Adams, G., Adams-Taylor, S., & Pittman, K. (1989). Adolescent pregnancy and parenthood: A review of the problem, solutions, and resources. *Family Relations, 38:* 223–230.

Adler, Z. (1987). *Rape on trial.* London: Routledge & Kegan Paul.

Aguirre, B. E. (1985). Why do they return? Abused wives in shelters. *Social Work, 30:* 350–354.

Akers, R. L. (1985). *Deviant behavior: A social learning approach.* Belmont, CA: Wadsworth.

Albelda, Randy, McCrate, Elaine, Melendez, Edwin, Lapidus, June, & the Center for Popular Economics. (1988). *Mink coats don't trickle down.* Boston: South End.

Alexander, P. C., Moore, S., & Alexander, E. R., III (1991). What is transmitted in the intergenerational transmission of violence? *Journal of Marriage and the Family, 53:* 657–668.

Allen, P. G. (1985). Violence and the American Indian woman. *Working together.* Seattle: Center for the Prevention of Sexual and Domestic Violence.

(1990). Violence and the American Indian woman. *The speaking profits us: Violence in the lives of women of color.* Seattle: SAFECO Insurance Company.

Allport, G. (1958). *The nature of prejudice.* New York: Doubleday.

Alsdurf, J. M. (1985). Wife abuse and the church: The response of pastors. *Response to the Victimization of Women and Children, 8*(1): 9–11.

Amsel, A. (1958). Role of frustrative non-reward in non-contiguous reward situation. *Psychological Bulletin, 55:* 102–119.

Arias, Ileana, & O'Leary, K. Daniel. (1984). Factors of moderating the intergenerational transmission of marital aggression. Paper presented at the 18th Annual Convention of the Association for the Advancement of Behavioral Therapy, Philadelphia, PA.

Arias, Ileana, Samios, Mary, & O'Leary, K. Daniel. (1987). Prevalence and correlates of physical aggression during courtship. *Journal of Interpersonal Violence, 2*(1): 82–90.

Asbury, J. (1987). African-American women in violent relationships: An exploration of cultural difference. In Robert L. Hampton (Ed.), *Violence in the black family: Correlates and consequences.* Lexington, MA: Lexington Books.

Asherah, K. L. (1990). The myth of mutual abuse. In P. Elliott (Ed.), *Confronting lesbian battering* (pp. 56–58). St. Paul: Minnesota Coalition for Battered Women.

Attorney General's Task Force on Violence. (1984). Washington, DC: U.S. Dept. of Justice.

Aukett, R., Richie, J., & Mill, K. (1988). Gender differences in friendship patterns. *Sex Roles, 19:* 57–66.

Avis, J. M. (1988). Deepening awareness: A private study guide to feminism and family therapy. *Psychotherapy and the Family, 3:* 15–46.

Bachman, R., & Saltzman, L. E. (1995). *Violence against women: Estimates from the redisigned survey.* Washington, DC: Bureau of Justice Statistics, U.S. Department of Justice.

Ball, Aimee Lee. (1994). The faces of abuse. *Harper's Bazaar* (November): 190–193, 216, 221.

Ball-Rokeach, S. J. (1980). Normative and deviant violence from a conflict perspective. *Social Problems, 28:* 45–62.

Bandura, A. (1973). *Aggression: A social learning analysis.* Englewood Cliffs, NJ: Prentice-Hall.

Bandura, A., Ross, D., & Ross, S. A. (1961). Transmission of aggression through imitation of aggressive models. *Journal of Abnormal and Social Psychology, 63:* 575–582.

Bannister, S. A. (1993). Battered women who kill their abusers: Their courtroom battles. In R. Muraskin & T. Alleman (Eds.), *It's a crime: Women and justice* (pp. 316–333). Englewood Cliffs, NJ: Regents/Prentice Hall.

Barak, G. (1985). *Beyond criminal justice reform: Feminist corrections and the movement against domestic violence.* Paper presented at the Academy of Criminal Justice Sciences, Las Vegas, NV.

Bard, M. (1971). The study and modification of intra-familial violence. In L. Singer (Ed.), *The control of aggression and violence* (pp. 149–164). New York: Academic Press.

Bard, M., & Sangrey, D. (1986). *The crime victim's book* (2nd ed.). New York: Brunner/Mazel.

Barnard, G. W., Vera, M., & Newman, G. (1982). Till death do us part: A study of spouse murder. *Bulletin of the American Academy of Psychiatry and Law, 10:* 271–280.

Barnes, G. E., Greenwood, L., & Sommer, R. S. (1991). Courtship violence in a Canadian sample of male college students. *Family Relations, 40:* 37–44.

Barnett, Ola W., & LaViolette, Alyce D. (1993). *It could happen to anyone: Why battered women stay.* Newbury Park, CA: Sage.

Bart, P. B., & Moran, E. G. (Eds.). (1993). *Violence against women: The bloody footprints.* Newbury Park, CA: Sage.

Baumgartner, M. P. (1993). Violent networks: The origins and management of domestic conflict. In R. B. Felson & J. T. Tedeschi (Eds.), *Aggression and violence: Social interactionist perspectives* (pp. 209–231). Washington, DC: American Psychological Association.

Baxter, L. A., & Dindia, K. (1990). Marital partners' perceptions of marital maintenance strategies. *Journal of Social and Personal Relationships, 7:* 187–208.

Beard, Christopher L., & Judd, Jacqueline J. (1992). Victims no more: Changes in domestic violence law. *Maryland Bar Journal, 25*(4): 29–32.

Bellah, R. N., Madsen, R., Sullivan, W. M., Swidler, A., & Tipton, S. M. (1985). *Habits of the heart: Individualism and commitment in American life.* Berkeley: University of California Press.

Belle, D. (1987). Gender differences in the social moderators of stress. In R. Barnett, L. Biener, & G. Baruch (Eds.), *Gender and stress* (pp. 121–143). New York: Free Press.

(1990). Poverty and women's mental health. *American Psychologist, 45:* 485–489.

Berger, B. M. (1995). *An Essay on Culture: Symbolic Structure and Social Structure.* Berkeley: University of California Press.

Berk, Richard A., Campbell, Alex, Klap, Ruth, & Western, Bruce. (1992). A Bayesian analysis of the Colorado Springs spouse abuse experiment. *Journal of Criminal Law and Criminology. 83*(1): 170–200.

Berk, R. A., Berk, S. F., Loseke, D. R., & Rauma, D. (1983). Mutual combat and other family violence myths. In D. Finkelhor, R. J. Gelles, G. T. Hotaling, & M. A. Straus (Eds.), *The dark side of families: Current family violence research.* Beverly Hills, CA: Sage.

Berk, R. A., Newton, P. J., & Berk, S. F. (1986). What a difference a day makes: An empirical study of the impact of shelters for battered women. *Journal of Marriage and the Family, 48:* 481–490.

Bernard, M. L., & Bernard, J. L. (1983). Violent intimacy: The family as a model for love relationships. *Family Relations, 32:* 283–286.

(1984). The abusive male seeking treatment: Jekyll and Hyde. *Family Relations, 33:* 543–548.

Bernardes, J. (1986). Multidimensional developmental pathways: A proposal to facilitate the conceptualization of family diversity. *Sociological Review, 34:* 590–610.

Bernstein, Susan E. (1993). Living under siege: Do stalking laws protect domestic violence victims? *Cardozo Law Review, 15:* 525–567.

Bersani, Carl A., Chen, Huey T., Pendleton, Brian F., & Denton, Robert. (1992). Personality traits of convicted male batterers. *Journal of Family Violence, 7*(2): 123–134.

Bettelheim, B. (1943). Individual and mass behavior in extreme situations. *Journal of Abnormal and Social Psychology, 38:* 417–452.

Biden, J. R., Jr. (1993). Violence against women: The congressional response. *American Psychologist, 48*(10): 1059–1061.

Bienen, L. (1983). Rape reform legislation in the United States: A look at some practical effects. *Victimology: An International Journal, 8*(1–2): 139–151.

Biller, H., & Borstelmann, L. (1967). Masculine development: An integrative review. *Merrill-Palmer Quarterly, 13:* 253–294.

Binney, V., Harkell, G., & Nixon, J. (1981). *Leaving violent men.* London: London Women's Aid Federation England.

Bird, G. W., Stith, S. M., & Schladale, J. (1991). Psychological resources, coping strategies, and negotiation styles as discriminators of violence in dating relationships. *Family Relations, 40:* 45–50.

Black, D. (1983). Crime as social control. *American Sociological Review, 48*(1): 34–45.

Blackman, Julie. (1989). *Intimate Violence: A Study of Injustice.* New York: Columbia University Press.

Blau, F. D. (1984). Occupational segregation and labor market discrimination. In B. Reskin (Ed.), *Sex segregation in the workplace: Trends, explanations, remedies* (pp. 117–143). Washington, DC: National Academy Press.

Bograd, M. (1984). Family systems approaches to wife battering: A feminist critique. *American Journal of Orthopsychiatry, 54:* 558–568.

(1988). Feminist perspectives on wife abuse: An introduction. In K. Yllö & M. Bograd (Eds.), *Feminist perspectives on wife abuse* (pp. 11–26). Newbury Park, CA: Sage.

Bologna, M. J., Waterman, C. K., & Dawson, L. J. (1987). Violence in gay male and lesbian relationships: Implications for practitioners and policy makers. Paper presented at the Third National Conference for Family Violence Researchers, Durham, NH.

Bowker, L. H. (1982). Battered women and the clergy: An evaluation. *Journal of Pastoral Care, 36:* 226–234.

——— (1983). *Beating wife-beating.* Lexington, MA: Lexington Books.

Bowker, L. H., & Maurer, L. (1985). The importance of sheltering in the lives of battered women. *Response to the victimization of women and children, 8:* 2–8.

Bowker, L. H., & Maurer, L. (1986). The effectiveness of counseling services utilized by battered women. *Women and Therapy, 5:* 65–82.

Braithwaite, J. (1981). The myth of social class and criminality reconsidered. *American Sociological Review, 46:* 36–57.

Brass, D. (1985). Men's and women's networks: A study of interaction patterns and influence in an organization. *Academy of Management Journal, 28:* 327–343.

Breines, G., & Gordon, L. (1983). The new scholarship on family violence. *Signs: Journal of Women in Culture and Society, 8:* 490–531.

Brisson, N. J. (1981). Battering husbands: A survey of abusive men. *Victimology, 6*(1–4): 338–344.

Broverman, I. K., Vogel, S. R., Broverman, D. M., Clarkson, F. E., & Rosenkrantz, P. S. (1972). Sex-role stereotypes: A current appraisal. *Journal of Social Issues, 26:* 59–78.

Brown, S., Goldman, M. S., Inn, A., & Anderson, L. R. (1980). Expectations of reinforcement from alcohol: Their domain and relation to drinking problems. *Journal of Consulting and Clinical Psychology, 48:* 419–426.

Browne, A. (1987). *When battered women kill.* New York: Macmillan/Free Press.

——— (1992). Violence against women: Relevance for medical practitioners. Council on Scientific Affairs, American Medical Association. *Journal of the American Medical Association, 267*(23): 3184–3189.

——— (1993). Violence against women by male partners: Prevalence, outcomes, and policy implications. *American Psychologist, 48:* 1077–1087.

Browne, A., & Williams, K. R. (1989). Exploring the effect of resource availability and the likelihood of female-perpetrated homicides. *Law and Society Review, 23:* 75–94.

——— (1993). Gender, intimacy, and lethal violence: Trends from 1976–1987. *Gender and Society, 7:* 78–98.

Brownmiller, S. (1975). *Against our will.* New York: Simon & Schuster.

Bryer, J. B., Nelson, B. A., Miller, J. B., & Krol, P. A. (1987). Childhood sexual and physical abuse as factors in adult psychiatric illness. *American Journal of Psychiatry, 144*(11): 1426–1430.

Buchanan, D. R., & Perry, P. A. (1985). Attitudes of police recruits towards domestic disturbances: An evaluation of family crisis intervention training. *Journal of Criminal Justice, 13:* 561–572.

Buikhuisen, W., Van Der Plas-Korenhoff, C., & Bontekoe, E. H. M. (1988). Alcohol and violence. In T. E. Moffit & S. A. Mednick (Eds.), *Biological contributions to crime causation* (pp. 261–276). Dordrecht, The Netherlands: Matinus Nijhoff.

Bumpass, L. L., Sweet, J. A., & Cherlin, A. (1991). The role of cohabitation in declining marriage rates. *Journal of Marriage and Family, 53:* 913–927.

Bunch, C., & Carillo, R. (1991). *Gender violence: A development and human rights issue.* New Brunswick, NJ: Center for Women's Global Leadership, Douglass College, Rutgers University.

Burch, B. (1987). Barriers to intimacy: Conflicts over power, dependency, and nurturing in lesbian relationships. In Boston Lesbian Psychologies Collective (Eds.), *Lesbian psychologies* (pp. 126–141). Urbana: University of Illinois Press.

Bureau of Justice Statistics. (1993). Highlights from 20 years of assistance. *Family violence: Interventions for the justice system.* Washington, DC: U.S. Department of Justice.

Bureau of Justice Statistics. (1994). *Violence against women,* NCJ-145325.

Burge, S. K. (1989). Violence against women as a health care issue. *Family Medicine,* September–October, 368–373.

Burgess, R. L., & Draper, P. (1989). The explanation of family violence: The role of biological, behavioral, and cultural selection. In Lloyd Ohlin & Michael Tonry (Eds.), *Family violence* (pp. 59–116). Chicago: University of Chicago Press.

Burke, P. J., Stets, J. E., & Pirog-Good, M. A. (1988). Gender identity, self esteem, and physical and sexual abuse in dating relationships. *Social Psychology Quarterly, 51:* 272–85.

Bush, Diane Mitsch. (1992). Women's movements and state policy reform aimed at domestic violence against women: A comparison of the consequences of movement mobilization in the U.S. and India. *Gender and Society, 6*(4): 587–608.

Butterfield, L. H., Friedlaender, Marc, & Kline, Mary-Jo. (Eds.). (1975). *The book of Abigial and John: Selected letters of the Adams family 1762–1784.* Cambridge: Harvard University Press.

Buzawa, E. S., & Buzawa, C. G. (1996). *Do arrests and restraining orders work?* Thousand Oaks, CA: Sage.

Buzawa, E. S., & Buzawa, C. G. (1990). *Domestic violence: The criminal justice response.* Newbury Park, CA: Sage.

(1992). *Domestic violence: The changing criminal justice response.* Westport, CT: Auburn House.

(1993). The impact of arrest on domestic assault. Special issue of the *American Behavioral Scientist, 36*(5).

Byrne, C., Arias, I., & O'Leary, D. K. (1992, November). Autonomy as a predictor of marital violence. Poster presented at the annual meeting of the Advancement of Behavior Therapy, Boston, MA.

Cahn, N. R., & Lerman, L. G. (1991). Prosecuting woman abuse. In M. Steinman (Ed.), *Woman battering: Policy responses* (pp. 95–112). Cincinnati, OH: Anderson Publishing Company.

Campbell, J. C. (1986). Nursing assessment for risk of homicide with battered women. *Advances in Nursing, 8*(4): 36–51.

Campbell, Jacquelyn C., Miller, Paul, & Cardwell, Mary M. (1994). Relationship status of battered women over time. *Journal of Family Violence, 9*(2): 99–111.

Cancian, F. M. (1985). Gender politics: Love and power in the private and public spheres. In A. S. Rossi (Ed.), *Gender and the life course* (pp. 253–264). New York: Aldine.

Caplan, P. J. (1991). How do they decide what is normal? The bizarre, but true, tale of the DSM process. *Canadian Psychology, 32:* 162–170.

Caplin, P. J., & Gakk-McCorquodale, I. (1985). Mother-blaming in major clinical journals. *American Journal of Orthopsychiatry, 55:* 345–353.

Cappell, Charles, & Heiner, Robert B. (1990). The intergenerational transmission of family aggression. *Journal of Family Violence, 5*(2): 135–152.

(1992, August). Intergenerational transmission of spousal aggression: Gender specific models of perpetration and target roles. Paper presented at the annual meeting of the American Sociological Association, Pittsburgh, PA.

Caringella-MacDonald, S. (1985). Sexual assault prosecution: An examination of model rape legislation in Michigan. In C. Schweber & C. Feinman (Eds.), *The aftermath of legally mandated change* (pp. 65–82). New York: Haworth Press.

(1988). Marxist-feminist interpretations of the aftermath of rape reforms. *Contemporary Crises, 12*(4): 125–144.

Carrillo, R. (1992). *Battered dreams: Violence against women as an obstacle to development.* New York: UNIFEM/United Nations Development Fund for Women.

Carlson, B. E. (1990). Adolescent observers of marital violence. *Journal of Family Violence, 5:* 285–299.

Carmody, D. C., & Williams, K. R. (1987). Wife assault and perceptions of sanctions. *Violence and Victims, 2*(1): 25–38.

Carp, E. Wayne (1991). Family history, family violence: A review essay. *Journal of Policy History, 3*(2): 203–223.

Carroll, J. (1980). A cultural-consistency theory of family violence in Mexican-American and Jewish ethnic groups. In M. A. Straus & G. T. Hotaling (Eds.), *The social causes of husband–wife violence* (pp. 68–81). Minneapolis: University of Minnesota Press.

Carter, David L. (1985). Hispanic perception of police performance: An empirical assessment. *Journal of Criminal Justice, 13*(6): 487–500.

Cate, C. A., Henton, J. M., Koval, J. F., Christopher, S., & Lloyd, S. (1982). Premarital abuse: A social psychological perspective. *Journal of Family Issues, 3:* 79–90.

Cazenave, N. A., & Straus, M. A. (1979). Race, class, network embeddedness and family violence: A search for potent support systems. *Journal of Comparative Family Studies, 10*(3): 281–300.

Ceasar, P. L. (1988). Exposure to violence in the families of origin among wife abusers and maritally non-violent men. *Violence and Victims, 3:* 49–36.

Chapman, J. R. (1990). Violence against women as a violation of human rights. *Social Justice, 17*(2): 54–70.

Charney, I. W. (1969). Marital love and hate, *Family Process, 8:* 1–24.

Chaudhuri, M., & Daly, K. (1992). Do restraining orders help? Battered women's experience with male violence and legal process. In E. S. Buzawa & C. G. Buzawa (Eds.), *Domestic violence: The changing criminal response* (pp. 227–252). Westport, CT: Auburn House.

Chesler, Phyllis. (1986). *Mothers on trial.* New York: McGraw-Hill.

Cochran, D. (1992). *Over 8500 domestic restraining orders filed since September in Massachusetts.* Boston: Office of the Commissioner of Probation.

Cohen, S. (1985). *Visions of social control.* Cambridge, England: Polity Press.

Cohn, E. G., & Sherman, L. S. (1987). Police policy on domestic violence, 1986: A national survey. Crime control reports, No. 5. Washington, DC: Crime Control Institute.

Coleman, D. H., & Straus, M. A., (1990). Marital power, conflict and violence in a nationally representative sample of American couples. In M. A. Straus & R. J. Gelles (Eds.), *Physical violence in American families: Risk factors and adaptions to violence in 8,145 families* (pp. 287–304). New Brunswick: Transaction Publishers.

Coleman, V. E. (1990). *Violence between lesbian couples: A between groups comparison.* Unpublished doctoral dissertation. University Microfilms International, 9109022.
(1992, August). Breaking the silence about lesbian battering: New directions in domestic violence. Paper presented at the annual meeting of the American Psychological Association, Washington, DC.

Coley, Soraya, Coley, M., & Beckett, Joyce O. (1988). Black battered women: A review of empirical literature. *Journal of Counseling and Development, 66:* 266–270.

Collins, R. (1971). A conflict theory of sexual stratification. *Social Problems, 19:* 3–20.

Comstock, Gary David. (1991). *Violence against lesbians and gay men.* New York: Columbia University Press.

Corcoran, M., Duncan, G. J., & Hill, M. S. (1984). The economic fortunes of women and children: Lessons from the panel study of income dynamics. *Signs: Journal of Women in Culture and Society, 10:* 232–248.

Coser, L. A. (1956). *The functions of social conflict.* Glencoe, IL: Free Press.

Counts, D. A., Brown, J. K., & Campbell, J. C. (Eds.). (1992). *Sanctions and sanctuary: Cultural perspectives on the beating of wives.* Boulder, CO: Westview Press.

Cronin, A. (1993, June 27). Two viewfinders, two pictures of gay America. *The New York Times.*

Davidson, B. P., & Jenkins, P. J. (1989). Class diversity in shelter life. *Social Work, 34*(6): 491–495.

Davidson, T. (1977). Wife beating: A recurring phenomenon throughout history. In M. Roy (Ed.), *Battered women: A psychosocial study of domestic violence.* New York: Nostrand Reinhold.

Davis, N. J. (1988). Battered women: Implications for social control. *Contemporary Crises, 12:* 345–372.

Davis, R. C., & Smith, B. (1995). Domestic violence reforms: Empty promises or fulfilled expectations? *Crime and Delinquency, 41:* 541–552.

Deal, J. E., & Wampler, K. S. (1986). Dating violence: the primacy of previous experience. *Journal of Social and Personal Relationships, 3:* 457–471.

Dean, C. W., & DeBruyn-Kops, M. (1982). *The crime and the consequences of rape.* Springfield, IL: Charles C. Thomas.

DeFrancis, V. (1963). *Child Abuse—Preview of a Nationwide Survey.* Denver: American Humane Association.

DeKeseredy, Walter S. (1988). *Woman abuse in dating relationships: The role of male peer support.* Toronto, Canada: Canadian Scholars' Press.

(1990). Male peer support and woman abuse: The current state of knowledge. *Sociological Focus, 23:* 129–139.

Dell, P. F. (1989). Violence and the systemic view: the problem of power. *Family Process, 28:* 1–14.

Demaris, A. (1990). The dynamics of generational transfer of courtship violence: A biracial exploration. *Journal of Marriage and the Family, 52:* 219–273.

Deming, M. B. (1983, March). *March rape case processing: Evaluation of legal reform.* Paper presented for the National Institute of Mental Health, Rockville, MD.

Deschner, J. (1984). *The hitting habit: Anger control for battering couples.* New York: Free Press.

Diamant, A. (1992, October 11). How the Quincy district court protects battered women. *The Boston Globe Magazine,* 14–15, 52–129.

Diamond, D. L., & Wilsnack, S. C. (1978). Alcohol abuse among lesbians: A descriptive study. *Journal of Homosexuality, 4:* 123–142.

Dobash, R. E., & Dobash, R. P. (1978). *The negotiation of daily life and the "provocation" of violence: A patriarchal concept in support of the wife beater.* Paper presented at the 9th World Congress of Sociology, Uppsala, Sweden.

(1979). *Violence against wives: A case against the patriarchy.* New York: Free Press.

(1984). The nature and antecedents of violent events. *British Journal of Criminology, 24*(3): 269–288.

(1992). *Women, violence, and social change.* London: Routledge.

Dobash, R. E., Dobash, R. P., & Cavanagh, K. (1985). The contact between battered women and social and medical agencies. In J. Pahl (Ed.), *Private violence and public policy: The needs of battered women and the response of the public services* (pp. 142–165). London: Routledge & Kegan Paul.

Dobash, Russell P., Dobash, R. Emerson, Wilson, Margo, & Daly, Martin. (1992). The myth of the symmetrical nature of domestic violence. *Social Problems, 39:* 71–91.

Dolgin, J. L. (1994). The family in transition from *Griswold* to *Eisenstadt* and beyond. *The Georgetown Law Journal 82:* 1519–1571.

Donato, K., & Bowker, L. (1984). Understanding the helpseeking behavior of battered women: A comparison of traditional service agencies and women's groups. *International Journal of Women's Studies, 7*(2): 99–109.

Donzelot, J. (1979). *The policing of families.* New York: Pantheon.

Dunford, Franklyn W. (1992). The measurement of recidivism in cases of spouse assault. *Journal of Criminal Law and Criminology, 83*(1): 120–136.

Dunford, F. W., Huizinga, D., & Elliott, D. S. (1990). The role of arrest in domestic assault: The Omaha police experiment. *Criminology, 28*(2): 183–206.

Duran, E., Guillory, B., & Tingley, P. *Domestic violence in Native American communities: The effects of intergenerational posttraumatic stress.* Unpublished manuscript.

Durant, R. H., Pedergast, R. A., & Cadenhead, C. (1994). Exposure to violence and victimization and fighting behavior. *Journal of Adolescent Health, 15:* 311–318.

Dutton, D. G. (1988a). *The domestic assault of women: psychological and criminal justice approaches.* Boston: Allyn and Bacon.

(1992a). *Empowering and healing the battered woman: A model for assessment and intervention.* New York: Springer.

(1992b). Assessment and treatment of PTSD among battered women. In D. Foy (Ed.), *Treating PTSD: Procedure for combat veterans, battered women, adult and child sexual assaults* (pp. 69–98). New York: Guilford Press.

(1994). Patriarchy and wife assault: The ecological fallacy. *Violence and Victims, 9:* 167–182.

(1995). *The domestic assault of women: Psychological and criminal justice perspectives* (rev. ed.). Vancouver: UBC Press.

Dutton, Donald, & Painter, Susan. (1981). Traumatic bonding: The development of emotional attachments in battered women and other relationships of intermittent abuse. *Victimology 6(1–4):* 139–155.

Eagly, A. (1983). Gender and social influence: A social psychological analysis. *American Psychologist, 38:* 971–981.

(1987). *Sex differences in social behavior: A social role interpretation.* Hillsdale, NJ: L. Erlbaum Associates.

Easteal, P., & Easteal, S. (1992). Attitudes and practices of doctors towards spouse assault victims: An Australian study. *Violence and Victims, 7(3):* 217–228.

Edleson, J. L. (1992). Domestic violence: The criminal justice response. *Violence Update, 3(6):* 10.

(1993). Advocacy services for battered women. *Violence Update, 4(4):* 1–2, 4, 10.

Edleson, Jeffrey L., Eisikovitz, Zvi C., & Peled, Einat. (1992). A model for analyzing societal responses to woman battering: Israel as a case in point. *International Social Work, 35:* 19–33.

Edleson, Jeffrey L., Eisikovitz, Zvi C., Guttman, Edna, & Sela-Amit, Michal. (1991). Cognitive and interpersonal factors in woman abuse. *Journal of Family Violence, 6(2):* 167–182.

Edleson, Jeffrey L., & Frank, Marilyn D. (1991). Rural interventions in woman battering: One state's strategies. *The Journal of Contemporary Human Services, 72(9):* 543–551.

Edleson, J. L., Miller, D. M., Stone, G. W., & Chapman, D. G. (1985). Group treatment for men who batter. *Social Work Research and Abstracts, 21:* 18–21.

Edleson, J. L., & Tolman, R. M. (1992). *Intervention for men who batter: An ecological approach.* Newbury Park, CA: Sage.

(1994). Group intervention strategies for men who batter. *Directions in Mental Health Counseling, 4(7):* 1–15.

Egley, L. C. (1982). Domestic abuse and deaf people: One community's approach. *Victimology, 7(1–4):* 24–34.

Eisenstein, Z. (1984). *Feminism and social equality.* New York: Monthly Review Press.

Eisikovitz, Zvi C., & Edleson, Jeffrey L. (1989). Intervening with men who batter: A critical review of the literature. *Social Service Review,* September, 384–414.

Elias, R. (1986). *The politics of victimization.* New York: Oxford University Press.

Elliott, D. (1989). The evaluation of criminal justice procedures in family violence crimes. In L. Ohlin & M. Jonry (Eds.), *Family violence.* Chicago: University of Chicago Press.

Elliott, D. S., & Ageton, S. S. (1980). Reconciling race and class differences in self-reported and official estimates of delinquency. *American Sociological Review, 45:* 95–110.

Elliott, P. (1990). Introduction. In P. Elliott

(Ed.), *Confronting lesbian battering.* St. Paul: Minnesota Coalition for Battered Women.

Ellis, D. (1992). Woman abuse among separated and divorced women: The relevance of social support. In E. C. Viano (Ed.), *Intimate violence: Interdisciplinary perspectives* (pp. 177–189). Washington, DC: Hemisphere.

Ellis, D., & DeKeseredy, W. S. (1989). Marital status and woman abuse: The DAD model. *International Journal of Sociology of the Family, 19:* 67–87.

Elmer, E. (1967). *Children in jeopardy: A study of abused minors and their families.* Pittsburgh: University of Pittsburgh Press.

Emerge. (n.d.). *Violent and controlling behavior toward children.* Checklist available from Emerge: A counseling and educational program for abusive men, 18 Hurley Street, Cambridge, MA 02141.

Eng, P. (1985). Aiding abused Asian women. *Wives Tales: A Newsletter About Ending Violence Against Women in the Home. 11*(1): 3.

Erikson, E. H. (1963). *Childhood and society.* New York: W.W. Norton.

Espin, O. M., & Gawelek, M. A. (1992). Women's diversity: Ethnicity, race, class, and gender in theories of feminist psychology. In L. S. Brown & M. Ballou (Eds.), *Personality and psychopathology: Feminist reappraisals.* New York: Guilford Press.

Estrich, S. (1987). *Real rape.* Cambridge, MA: Harvard University Press.

Etzioni, A. (1993). *The spirit of community: The reinvention of American society.* New York: Simon & Schuster.

Fagan, J. A. (1993). Social structure and spouse assault. In B. Forst (Ed.), *The socio-economics of crime and justice* (pp. 209–254). Armonk, NY: M. E. Sharpe, Inc.

Fagan, J. A., et al. (1984). *National family violence evaluation: Final report.* Washington, DC: Office of Juvenile Justice and Delinquency Prevention.

Fagan, J. A., & Browne, A. (1994). Violence between spouses and intimates: Physical aggression between men and women in relationships. In A. J. Reiss, Jr. & J. A. Roth (Eds.), *Understanding and controlling violence.* Washington, DC: National Academy Press.

(1993). Marital violence: Physical aggression between women and men in intimate relationships. In A. Reiss, Jr. & J. Roth (Eds.), *Understanding and Preventing Violence: Vol. 3. Social Influences.* Washington, DC: National Academy of Sciences.

Fagan, J. A., Friedman, S., & Lewis, V. S. (1984). *National family violence evaluation: Final report. Vol. 1, Analytic Findings.* San Francisco: URSA Institute.

Fagan, J. A., Stewart, D. K., & Hansen, K. V. (1983). Violent men or violent husbands: Background factors and situational correlates. In D. Finkelhor, et al. (Eds.), *The dark side of families: Current family violence research* (pp. 49–67). Beverly Hills, CA: Sage.

Fagan, J. A., & Wexler, S. (1987). Crime at home and crime in the streets: The relation between family and stranger violence. *Violence and Victims, 2:* 5–21.

Fain, C. F. (1981). Conjugal violence: Legal and psychosociological remedies. *Syracuse Law Review, 32*(2): 497–579.

Fairhurst, G. (1986). Male-female communication on the job: Literature review and commentary. In M. McLaughlin (Ed.), *Communication Yearbook 9* (pp. 83–116). Beverly Hills, CA: Sage Publications.

Faludi, Susan. (1991). *Backlash: The undeclared war against American women.* New York: Doubleday.

Farrington, David. Antisocial personality from childhood to adulthood. *The Psychologist, 4:* 389–94.

Faulk, M. (1977). Men who assault their wives. In M. Roy (Ed.), *Battered women: A psycho-sociological study of domestic violence.* New York: Van Nostrand Reinhold.

Faurre, L. C., & Maddock, J. M. (1994). Sexual meaning systems of engaged couples. *Family Relations, 43:* 53–60

Federal Bureau of Investigation. (1985). *Uniform crime reports: Crime in the United States.* Washington, DC: U.S. Government Printing Office.

Felten, E. (1991). A redefinition of the issue of rape. *Insight,* January 28, 50–53.

Ferraro, K. J. (1989a). The legal response to woman battering in the United States. In J. Hanmer, J. Radford, & E. Stanko (Eds.), *Women, policing and male violence* (pp. 155–184). London: Routledge.

(1989b). Policing woman battering. *Social Problems, 6*(1): 6174.

(1993). Cops, courts, and woman battering. In P. B. Bart & E. G. Moran (Eds.), *Violence against women.* Newbury Park, CA: Sage.

Ferraro, Kathleen, & Boychuk, Tascha. (1992). The court's response to interpersonal violence: A comparison of intimate and nonintimate assault. In E. S. Buzawa & C. G. Buzawa (Eds.), *Domestic violence: The changing criminal justice response* (pp. 209–226). Westport, CT: Auburn House.

Ferraro, Kathleen, & Johnson, John M. (1983). How women experience battering: The process of victimization, *Social Problems 30*(3): 325–339.

(1985). The new underground railroad. *Studies in Symbolic Interaction, 6:* 377–386.

Ferraro, Kathleen, & Pope, Lucille. (1993). Irreconcilable differences: Battered women, police, and the law. In N. Z. Hilton (Ed.), *Legal responses to wife assault* (pp. 96–123). Newbury Park, CA: Sage.

Field, H. S., & Bienen, L. B. (1980). *Jurors and rape: A study in psychology and law.* Lexington, MA: Lexington Books.

Fifield, L. (1975). On my way to nowhere: Alienated, isolated, drunk. Los Angeles: Gay Community Services Center.

Finkelhor, D., Gelles, R. J., Hotaling, G. T., &

Straus, M. (Eds.). (1983). *The dark side of families.* Beverly Hills, CA: Sage.

Finkelhor, D., & Yllö, K. (1985). *License to rape: Sexual abuse of wives.* New York: Holt, Rinehart, & Winston.

Finn, P. (1991). Civil protection orders: A flawed opportunity for intervention. In M. Steinman (Ed.), *Woman battering: Policy responses* (pp. 155–189). Cincinnati, OH: Anderson Publishing Co.

Fisher, M., & Stricker, G. (1982). *Intimacy.* New York: Plenum.

Flanzer, J. P. (1993). Alcohol and other drugs are key causal agents of violence. In R. J. Gelles & D. R. Loseke (Eds.), *Current controversies on family violence* (pp. 171–181). Newbury Park, CA: Sage.

Follingstad, D. R., Rutledge, L. L., McNeill-Harkins, K., & Polek, D. S. (1992). Factors related to physical violence in dating relationships. In E. Viano (Ed.), *Intimate violence* (pp. 121–135). Washington, DC: Hemisphere.

Follingstad, D. R., Wright, S., Lloyd, S., & Sebastian, J. A. (1991). Sex differences in motivations and effects in dating violence. *Family Relations, 40:* 51–57.

Follingstad, D. R., et al. (1991). Identification of patterns of wife abuse. *Journal of Interpersonal Violence, 6:* 187–204.

Fontanarosa, P. B. (1995). The unrelenting epidemic of violence in America: Truths and consequences. *JAMA, 273:* 1792–1793.

Ford, D. A. (1991). Preventing and provoking wife battery through criminal sanctions: A look at the risks. In D. K. Knudses & J. L. Miller (Eds.), *Abused and battered: Social and legal responses to family violence.* New York: Aldine DeGruyter.

Ford, D. A., & Regoli, M. J. (1993). The criminal prosecution of wife assaulters: Process, problems, and effects. In N. Z. Hilton (Ed.), *Legal responses to wife assault: Current trends and evaluation.* Newbury Park, CA: Sage, 127–164.

Ford, D. A., Reichard, R., Goldsmith S., & Regoli, M. J. (1996). Future directions for criminal justice policy on domestic violence. In E. S. Buzawa & C. G. Buzawa (Eds.), *Do arrests and restraining orders work?* (pp. 243–265). Thousand Oaks, CA: Sage.

Ford, D. Y. (1994). An exploration of perceptions of alternative family structures among university students. *Family Relations, 43:* 68–73.

Forsstrom-Cohn, B., & Rosenbaum, A. (1985). The effects of parental marital violence on young adults: An exploratory investigation. *Journal of Marriage and the Family, 47:* 467–472.

Fortune, M. (1981). *Family violence: A workshop manual for clergy and other service providers.* Rockville, MD: The National Clearinghouse on Domestic Violence.

Frankel, B. (1982). Intimacy and conjoint marital therapy. In M. Fisher & G. Stricker (Eds.), *Intimacy* (pp. 247–266). New York: Plenum.

Freedman, L. (1985). Wife assault. In C. Guberman & M. Wolfe (Eds.), *No safe place: Violence against women and children* (pp. 41–60). Toronto: The Women's Press.

Freeza, H., Padova, C. D., Pozzato, G., Terpin, M., Baraona, E., & Lieber, C. S. (1990). High blood alcohol levels in women: The role of decreased gastric alcohol dehydrogenase activity and first-pass metabolism. *The New England Journal of Medicine, 322:* 95–99.

Friedman, L. N., & Schulman, M. (1990). Domestic violence: The criminal justice response (pp 87–103). In A. J. Lurigio, W. G. Skogan, & R. C. Davis (Eds.), *Victims of crime: Problems, policies, and programs.* Newbury Park, CA: Sage.

Frieze, I. H. (1983). Investigating the causes and consequences of marital rape. *Signs, 8:* 532–552.

Frieze, I. H., Knoble, J. Washburn, C., & Zomnir, G. (1980). *Types of battered women.* Paper presented at the meeting of the Annual Research Conference of the Association for Women in Psychology. Santa Monica, CA.

Ganley, A. L. (1981). *Court-mandated counseling for men who batter: A three-day workshop for mental health professionals (participant's manual).* Center for Women Policy Studies, Washington, DC.

Ganong, L. H., Coleman, M., & Mapes, D. (1990). A meta-analytic review of family structure stereotypes. *Journal of Marriage and Family, 52:* 287–297.

Garbarino, J. (1977). The human ecology of child maltreatment. *Journal of Marriage and the Family, 39:* 721–736.

Garbarino, J., Schellenbach, C. J., Sebes, J., and Associates (1986). *Troubled youth, troubled families.* New York: Aldine de Gruyter.

Gayford, J. J. (1975). Wife battering: A preliminary survey of 100 cases. *British Medical Journal, 1:* 194–197.

Gelles, R. J. (1972). *The violent home: A study of physical aggression between husbands and wives.* Beverly Hills, CA: Sage.
(1980). Violence in the family: A review of research in the seventies. *Journal of Marriage and the Family, 42:* 873–885.
(1982). Applying research on family violence to clinical practice. *Journal of Marriage and Family, 44:* 9–20.
(1983). An exchange social theory. In D. Finkelhor, R. J. Gelles, G. T. Hotaling, & M. A. Straus (Eds), *The dark side of families: Current family violence research* (pp. 151–165). Beverly Hills, CA: Sage.
(1987). *Family violence* (2nd ed.), Newbury Park, CA: Sage Publications.
(1988, August). Violence and pregnancy: Are pregnant woman at greater risk of abuse? *Journal of Marriage and the Family,* 841–847.
(1993). Alcohol and other drugs are associated with violence—They are not its cause. In R. J. Gelles & D. R. Loseke (Eds.), *Current controversies on family violence* (pp. 182–196). Newbury Park, CA: Sage.

Gelles, R. J., & Cornell, C. (1990). *Intimate violence in families.* Newbury Park, CA: Sage.

Gelles, R. J., & Straus, M. A. (1979). Determinants of violence in the family: Toward a theoretical integration. In W. R. Burr, R. Hill, I. K. Nye, & I. L. Reiss (Eds). *Contemporary theories about the family.* New York: Free Press.

(1988) *Intimate violence: The causes and consequences of abuse in the American family.* New York: Simon & Schuster.

Gil, D. G. (1969). Physical abuse of children: Findings and implications of a nationwide survey. *Pediatrics, 44:* 857–864.

(1970). *Violence against children: Physical child abuse in the United States.* Cambridge, MA: Harvard University Press.

Gillespie, C. (1989). *Justifiable homicide: Battered women, self-defense, and the law.* Columbus: Ohio State University Press.

Gilligan, C. (1982). *In a different voice.* Cambridge: Harvard University Press.

Goldberg, W. G., & Tomlanovich, M. C. (1984). Domestic violence victims in the emergency department. *Journal of the American Medical Association, 251*(24): 3259–3264.

Goldner, V. (1985). Warning: Family therapy may be hazardous to your health. *Family Therapy Networker, 9*(6): 19–23.

(1990) Love and violence: Gender paradoxes in volatile attachments *Family Process, 29*(4): 343–364.

Gondolf, E. W. (1985). *Men who batter: An integrated approach for stopping wife abuse.* Holmes Beach, FL: Learning Publications.

(1987). Evaluating programs for men who batter: Problems and prospects. *Journal of Family Violence, 2:* 95–108.

(1988a). Research on men who batter: An overview, bibliography and resource guide. Bradenton, FL: Human Services Institute.

(1988b). Who are those guys? Toward a behavioral typology of batterers. *Violence and Victims, 3:* 187–203.

(1988c). *Battered women as survivors: An alternative to learned helplessness.* Lexington, MA: Lexington Books.

(1990). Battered women as survivors. Holmes Beach, FL: Learning Publications.

(1992). *Court response to "protection from abuse" petitions.* Unpublished paper available from the author at the Mid-Atlantic Addiction Training Institute, Indiana University of Pennsylvania, Indiana, PA 15705.

(1993). Treating the batterer. In M. Hansen & M. Harway (Eds.), *Battering and family therapy: A feminist perspective.* Newbury Park, CA: Sage.

Goode, W. J. (1969). Violence among intimates. In *Crimes of violence* Vol. 13. A Staff Report Submitted to the National Commission on the Causes and Prevention of Violence. Washington, DC: U.S. Government Printing Office.

(1971). Force and Violence in the Family. *Journal of Marriage and the Family, 33:* 624–636.

Goodman, E. (1989, May 23). Excuses, not penalties defense. *The Boston Globe,* 15.

Goodman, L. A., Koss, M. P., & Russo, N. F. (1993). Violence against women: Physical and mental health effects. *Applied and Preventive Psychology, 2:* 79–89.

Goodman, L. A., Koss, M. P., Fitzgerald, L. F., Russo, N. F., & Keita, G. P. (1993). Male violence against women: Current research and future directions. *American Psychologist, 48*(10): 1054–1058.

Goodstein, R. K., & Page, A. W. (1991). Battered wife syndrome: Overview of dynamics and treatment. *American Journal of Psychiatry, 139:* 1036–1044.

Goolkasian, G. A. (1986). *Confronting domestic violence: The role of criminal court judges.* Washington, DC: National Institute of Justice, U.S. Department of Justice.

(1987). *Confronting domestic violence: A guide for criminal justice agencies.* Washington, DC: Government Printing Office.

Gordon, L. (1988). *Heroes of their own lives: The politics and history of family vio-*

lence, Boston 1880–1960. New York: Viking.

Gordon, M. T., & Riger, S. (1989). *The female fear.* New York: The Free Press.

Grau, J., Fagan, J., & Wexler, S. (1985). Restraining orders for battered women: Issues of access and efficacy. *Women and Politics, 4*(3): 13–28.

Greenberg, L. F., & Johnson, S. M. (1986). Affect in marital therapy. *Journal of Marriage and Family Therapy, 12:* 1–10.

Gryl, F. E., Stith, S. M., & Bird, G. W. (1991). Close dating relationships among college students: Differences by use of violence and by gender. *Journal of Social and Personal Relationships, 8:* 243–264.

Guberman, C., & Wolfe, M. (Eds.). (1985). *No safe place: Violence against women and children.* Toronto: The Women's Press.

Gwartnery-Gibbs, P. A., Stockard, J., & Bohmer, S. (1987). Learning courtship aggression: The influence of parents, peers, and personal experiences. *Family Relations, 36:* 276–282.

Hagan, John, & Albonetti, Celeste. (1982). Race, class, and the perception of criminal injustice in America. *American Journal of Sociology, 88*(2): 329–355.

Hall-Apicella, V. (1983, August). Exploring attitudes of mental health professionals toward battered women. Paper presented at the annual meeting of the American Psychological Association. Anaheim, CA.

Hamberger, L. K., & Hastings, J. E. (1986). Personality correlates of men who abuse their partners: A cross validation study. *Journal of Family Violence, 1:* 323–341.
(1988). Characteristics of abusive men suggestive of personality disorders. *Hospital and Community Psychiatry, 39:* 763–770.
(1991). Personality correlates of men who batter and nonviolent men: Some continuities and discontinuities. *Journal of Family Violence, 6:* 131–148.

Hamberger, L. K., Saunders, D. G., & Hovey, M. (1992). The prevalence of domestic violence in community practice and rate of physician inquiry. *Family Medicine, 24*(4): 283–287.

Hamilton, J. A., & Jensvold M. (1992). Personality, psychopathology, and depression in women. In L. S. Brown & M. Ballou (Eds.), *Personality and psychopathology: Feminist reappraisals.* New York: Guilford Publications.

Hanks, S. E. (1992). Translating theory into practice: A conceptual framework for clinical assessment, differential diagnosis, and multi-modal treatment of maritally violent individuals, couples, and families. In E. Viano (Ed.), *Intimate violence* (pp. 157–176), Washington, DC: Hemisphere.

Hanmer, J., Radford, J., & Stanko, E. A. (Eds.). (1989). *Women, policing and male violence: International perspectives.* London: Routledge.

Hansen, M. (1993). Feminist and family therapy: A review of feminist critiques of approaches to family violence. In M. Hansen & M. Harway (Eds.), *Battering and family therapy: A feminist perspective.* Newbury Park, CA: Sage Publications.

Hansen, M., Harway, M., & Cervantes, N. (1991). Therapists' perceptions of severity in cases of family violence. *Violence and Victims, 6*(3): 225–235.

Hare-Mustin, R. T. (1978). A feminist approach to family therapy. *Family Process, 17:* 181–194

Harlow, C. W. (1991). *Female victims of violent crime.* Rockville, MD: U.S. Department of Justice.

Harlow, H., & Harlow, M. (1971). Psychopathology in monkeys. In H. D. Kimmel (Ed.), *Experimental psychopathology.* New York: Academic Press.

Harrell, A., Smith, B., & Newmark, L. (1993, May). *Court processing and the effects of restraining orders for domestic violence victims.* Washington, DC: The Urban Institute.

Hart, B. J. (1986). Lesbian battering: An examination. In K. Lobel (Ed.), *Naming the violence* (pp. 173–189). Seattle: Seal Press.
(1988). *Safety for women: Monitoring*

batterers' programs. Monograph available from the Pennsylvania Coalition Against Domestic Violence, 2505 North Front Street, Harrisburg, PA 17110–1111.

(1995). Coordinated community approaches to domestic violence. In *Violence against women research strategic planning workshop* (pp. 1–20). Washington, DC: National Institute of Justice.

Hartinger, B. (1992). Homesexual partners are changing America. In V. Wagner (Ed.), *The family in America: Opposing viewpoints* (pp. 55–62). San Diego: Greenhaven Press, Inc.,

Harvey, W. B. (1986). Homicide among young black adults: Life in the subculture of exasperation. In D. F. Hawkins (Ed.), *Homicide among black Americans* (pp. 153–171). Lanham, MD: University Press of America.

Harway, M. (1993). Battered women: Characteristics and causes. In M. Hansen & M. Harway (Eds.), *Battering and family therapy: A feminist perspective.* Newbury Park, CA: Sage Publications.

Harway, M., & Hansen, M. (1994). *Spouse abuse: Assessing and treating battered women, batterers, and their children.* Sarasota, FL: ProResource.

Hatty, S. E. (1989). Policing and violence in Australia. In J. Hanmer, J. Radford, & E. A. Stanko (Eds.), *Women, policing and male violence: International perspectives* (pp. 70–89). London: Routledge.

Hayes, C. D. (1987). *Risking the future: Adolescent sexuality, pregnancy, and childbearing, Vol. I.* Washington, DC: National Research Council.

Hearing on Violence Prevention Act, Formal Testimony. (1985). Harriet Tubman woman's shelter, presented by Kenyari Bellfield in U.S. Congress, House Subcommittee on Select Education of the Committee on Education and Labor, Domestic Violence: Hearing on H.R. 7297 and H.R. 8498, 95th Congress 2nd session.

Helfer, R. E., & Kempe, C. H. (Eds.). (1968). *The battered child.* Chicago: University of Chicago Press.

Helton, A. M. (1986). The pregnant battered woman. *Response to the Victimization of Women and Children, 9*(1): 22–23.

Helton, A., McFarlane, J., & Anderson, E. (1987a). Battered and pregnant: A prevalence study. *American Journal of Public Health, 77:* 1337–1339.

(1987b). Prevention of battering during pregnancy: Focus on behavioral change. *Public Health Nursing, 4:* 166–174.

Henton, J., Cate, R., Koval, J., Lloyd, S., & Christopher, S. (1983). Romance and violence in dating relations. *Journal of Family Issues, 4:* 467–482.

Herbert, M. D., & Mould, J. W. (1992). The advocacy role in public child welfare. *Child Welfare, 71*(2): 114–130.

(1992). *Trauma and recovery.* New York: Basic Books.

Herman, J., & Hirschman, L. (1993). Father-daughter incest. In P. B. Bart & E. G. Moran (Eds.), *Violence against women: The bloody footprints* (pp. 47–56). Newbury Park, CA: Sage.

Herzberger, S. (1983). Social cognition and the transmission of abuse. In D. Finkelhor, R. Gelles, G. Hotaling, & M. Straus (Eds.), *The dark side of families: Current family violence research* (pp. 317–329). Beverly Hills, CA: Sage.

Hilberman, E., & Munson, K. (1977–78). Sixty battered women. *Victimology: An International Journal,* Vol. 2, 460–470.

Hilbert, J., & Hilbert, H. (1984). Battered women leaving shelter: Which way do they go? *Journal of Applied Social Sciences, 8*(2): 292–297.

Hilton, N. Z. (Ed.). (1993). *Legal responses to wife assault.* Newbury Park, CA: Sage.

Hindelang, M. J. (1976). *An Analysis of Victimization Survey Results from the Eight Impact Cities.* Washington, DC: Department of Justice, Law Enforcement Assistance Administration.

Hindelang, M. J., Gottfredson, M. R., & Garofalo, J. (1978). *Victims of personal crime: An empirical foundation for a theory of personal victimization.* Cambridge, MA: Ballinger Publishing Company.

Hirschel, J. D., & Hutchison, I. W., III. (1992). Female spouse abuse and the police response: The Charlotte, North Carolina, experiment. *Journal of Criminal Law and Criminology, 83*(1): 73–119.

Hixson, R. F. (1987). *Privacy in a public society: Human rights in conflict.* New York: Oxford University Press.

Ho, C. K. (1990). An analysis of domestic violence in Asian-American communities: A multicultural approach to counseling. In L. S. Brown & M. P. P. Roots (Eds.), *Diversity and complexity in feminist therapy* (pp. 129–150). New York: Haworth Press.

Hobfoll, S. (1986). The ecology of stress and social support among women. In S. Hobfoll (Ed.), *Stress, social support, and women* (pp. 3–16). Washington, DC: Hemisphere Publishing Corp.

Hochschild, A. R. (1975). The sociology of feeling and emotion: Selected possibilities. In M. Millman & R. M. Kanter (Eds.), *Another voice: Feminist perspectives on social life and social science* (pp. 280–307). Garden City, NY: Anchor Books.

(1979). Emotion work, feeling rules, and social structure. *American Journal of Sociology, 85*(3): 551–575.

(1983). *The managed heart: Commercialization of human feeling.* Berkeley: University of California Press.

(1991). The economy of gratitude. In M. Hutter (Ed.), *The family experience: A reader in cultural diversity* (pp. 499–515). New York: Macmillan.

Hochschild, A. R., & Machung, A. (1989). *The second shift: Working parents and the revolution at home.* New York: Viking.

Hoff, Lee A. (1990). *Battered women as survivors.* London: Routledge.

Hogan, D. P. (1978). The variable order of events in the life course. *American Sociological Review, 43:* 573–586.

(1980). The transition to adulthood as a career contingency. *American Sociological Review, 45:* 261–276.

Holmstrom, L. L., & Burgess, A. W. (1978). *The victim of rape: Institutional reactions.* New York: Wiley.

Horne, F. (1993). The issue is rape. In R. Muraskin & T. Alleman (Eds.), *It's a crime: Women and justice* (pp. 305–315). Englewood Cliffs, NJ: Regents/Prentice Hall.

Horowitz, D. (1979). *States of mind: Analysis of change.* New York: Plenum.

Horton, A. L., Simonidis, K. M., & Simonidis, L. L. (1987). Legal remedies for spousal abuse: Victim characteristics, expectations, and satisfaction. *Journal of Family Violence, 2*(3): 265–279.

Hotaling, G. T., & Sugarman, D. B. (1986). An analysis of risk markers in husband to wife violence: The current state of knowledge. *Violence and Victims, 1:* 101–124.

(1990). A risk marker analysis of assaulted wives. *Journal of Family Violence, 5:* 1–13.

Hotaling, G. T., & Straus, M. with Lincoln, A. J. (1989). Intrafamily violence, and crime and violence outside the family. In L. Ohlin & M. Tonry (Eds.), *Family violence* (pp. 315–375). Chicago: The University of Chicago Press.

Hudson, W. W., & McIntosh, S. R. (1981). The assessment of spouse abuse: Two quantifiable dimensions. *Journal of Marriage and the Family, 43:* 873–884.

Hunter, J. D. (1991). *Culture wars: The struggle to define America.* New York: Basic Books.

Irvine, J. (1990). Lesbian battering: The search for shelter. In P. Elliott (Ed.), *Confronting lesbian battering* (pp. 25–30). St. Paul: Minnesota Coalition for Battered Women.

Island, David, & Letellier, Patrick. (1990). *Men who beat the men who love them: Battered gay men and domestic violence.* New York: Harrington Park Press.

Jacobson, N. S. (1993). *Domestic violence: What are the marriages like?* Paper presented at the annual convention of the American Psychological Association, Toronto, Canada.

Jaffe, P. G., Sudermann, M., Reitzel, D., & Killip, S. M. (1992). An evaluation of a secondary school primary prevention program on violence in intimate relationships. *Violence and Victims, 7*(2): 129–146.

Jaffe, P., Wolfe, D., Wilson, S., & Zak, L. (1986). Similarities in behavioral and social maladjustment among child victims and witnesses to family violence. *American Journal of Orthopsychiatry, 56:* 142–146.

Johnson, Ida M. (1992). Economic, situational, and psychological correlates of the decision-making process of battered women. *Families in Society, 73*(3): 168–176.

(1994). *Next time she'll be dead: Battering and how to stop it.* Boston: Beacon Press.

Johnson, M. P. (1995). Patriarchal terrorism and common couple violence: Two forms of violence against women. *Journal of Marriage and the Family, 57:* 283–294.

Johnson, N. (1985). Police, social work and medical responses to battered women. In N. Johnson (Ed.), *Marital violence* (pp. 109–123). London: Routledge and Kegan Paul.

Jones, E. F., Forrest, J. D., Goldman, N., Henshaw, S., Lincoln, R., Rosoff, J. I., Westoff, C. F., & Wulf, D. (1986). *Teenage pregnancy in industrialized countries.* New Haven, CT: Yale University Press.

Jurik, N., & Winn, R. (1990). Gender and homicide: A comparison of men and women who kill. *Violence and Victims. 5*(4): 227–242.

Kaci, J. H. (1990). Issues of the 1990s. *Response, 13*(1): 4.

Kahuna, V. (1990). Compounding the triple jeopardy: Battering in lesbians of color relationships. *Women and Therapy, 9:* 169–184.

Kalmuss, D. (1984). The intergenerational transmission of marital aggression. *Journal of Marriage and the Family, 46:* 11–19

Kalmuss, D. S., & Straus, M. A. (1982). Wife's marital dependency and wife abuse. *Journal of Marriage and the Family, 44:* 277–286.

(1983). Feminist, political, and economic determinants of wife abuse services. In D. Finkelhor, R. Gelles, G. Hotaling, & M. A. Straus (Eds.), *The dark side of families* (pp. 363–376). Beverly Hills, CA: Sage.

Kandel-Englander, E. (1992). Wife battering and violence outside the family. *Journal of Interpersonal Violence, 7:* 462–470.

Kaufman, P., Harrison, E., & Hyde, M. (1984). Distancing for intimacy in lesbian relationships. *Journal of Psychiatry, 53:* 419–421.

Kaufman Kantor, G., & Straus, M. (1987). The "drunken bum" theory of wife beating. *Social Problems, 34:* 213–230.

Kelly, C., Huston, T. L., & Cate, R. M. (1985). Premarital relationship correlates of the erosion of satisfaction in marriage. *Journal of Social and Personal Relationships, 2:* 167–178.

Kelly, E. E., & Warshafsky, L. (1987, July). *Partner abuse in gay male and lesbian couples.* Paper presented at the Third National Conference for Family Violence Researchers, Durham, NH.

Kelly, Liz. (1987). The continuum of sexual violence. In J. Hanmer & M. Maynard, (Eds.), *Women, violence and social control* (pp. 46–60). Atlantic Highlands, NJ: Humanities Press.

(1988a). How women define their experiences of violence. In K. Yllö & M. Bograd (Eds.), *Feminist perspectives on wife abuse* (pp. 114–132). Newbury Park, CA: Sage.

(1988b). *Surviving sexual violence.* Minneapolis: University of Minnesota Press.

Kempe, C. H., et al. (1962), The Battered Child Syndrone. *Journal of the American Medical Association, 181:* 17–24.

Kerber, L. (1991). Can a woman be an individual? The discourse of self-reliance. In R. O. Curry & L. B. Goodheart (Eds.), *American chameleon: Individualism in trans-national context* (pp. 151–166). Kent, OH: The Kent State University Press.

Kinports, K., & Fischer, K. (1993). Orders of protection in domestic violence cases: An empirical assessment of the impact of the reform statutes. *Texas Journal of Women and the Law,* 2(2): 163–386.

Klein, A. (1994). *Recidivism in a population of court-restrained batterers after two years.* Unpublished dissertation, Northeastern University.

Klingbeil, K. S., & Boyd, V. D. (1984). Emergency room intervention: Detection, assessment, and treatment. In A. R. Roberts (Ed.), *Battered women and the families* (pp. 7–32). New York: Springer.

Klinger, D. A. (1995). Policing spousal assault. *Journal of Research in Crime and Delinquency,* 32: 308–324.

Knitzer, J. E. (1976). Child advocacy: A perspective. *American Journal of Orthopsychiatry,* 46(2): 200–216.

Knudsen, D. D., & Miller, J. (Eds.). (1991). *Abused and battered: Social and legal responses to family violence.* New York: Aldine de Gruyter.

Koss, M. P. (1990). The women's mental health research agenda: Violence against women. *American Psychologist, 45:* 374–380.

——— (1993). Foreword. In M. Hansen & M. Harway (Eds.), *Battering and family therapy: A feminist perspective.* Newbury Park, CA: Sage Publications.

Koss, M. P., et al. (1995). *No safe haven: Male violence against women at home, at work and in the community.* Washington, DC: American Psychological Association.

Kramer, A. L. (1992a). Statement to the Massachusetts joint committee on the judiciary: Written testimony. Quincy, MA: Quincy District Court.

——— (1992b). Statement to the women's legislative caucus hearing on domestic violence, March 2: Oral testimony. Quincy, MA: Quincy District Court.

Krestan, J., & Bepko, C. S. (1980). The problem of fusion in lesbian relationships. *Family Process, 19:* 277–289.

Krupnick, J., & Horowitz, M. (1981). Stress response syndromes: Recurrent themes. *Archives of General Psychiatry, 38:* 428–435.

Kuhl, A. (1982). Community responses to battered women. *Victimology, 7*(1–4): 49–59.

Kurdek, L. A. (1991). The dissolution of gay and lesbian couples. *Journal of Social and Personal Relationships, 8:* 265–278.

Kurdek, L. A., & Schmitt, J. P. (1986). Relationship quality of partners in heterosexual married, heterosexual cohabiting, and gay and lesbian relationships. *Journal of Personality and Social Psychology, 6:* 1–9.

Kurtz, D. (1987). Responses to Battered Women: Resistance to Medicalization. *Social Problems, 34*(1): 501–513.

Kurz, Demie, & Stark, Evan. (1988). Not so benign neglect: The medical response to battering. In K. Yllö & M. Bograd (Eds.), *Feminist perspectives on wife abuse* (pp. 249–268). Newbury Park, CA: Sage.

LaBelle, L. (1979). Wife abuse: A sociological study of battered women and their mates. *Victimology, 4*(2): 258–267.

Lamanna, M. A., & Riedman, A. (1994). *Marriages and families.* Belmont, CA: Wadsworth.

Lane, K. E., & Gwartney-Gibbs, P. A. (1985). Violence in the context of dating and sex. *Journal of Family Issues, 6:* 45–59.

Langan, P. A., & Innes, C. A. (1986). *Preventing domestic violence against women.* Washington, DC: U.S. Department of Justice, Bureau of Justice Statistics.

Lasch, C. (1977). *Haven in a heartless world: The family besieged.* New York: Basic Books.

Leeder, E. (1988). Enmeshed in pain: Counseling the lesbian battering couple. *Women and Therapy, 7:* 81–99.

Lehnen, R. G., & Skogan, W. G. (1981). The national crime survey. In R. G. Lehnen & W. G. Skogan (Eds.), *Working papers: Vol. 1. Current and historical perspectives.*

Washington, DC: U.S. Department of Justice.

Lerman, L. (1981). Criminal prosecution of wife beaters. *Response to Violence in the Family, 4*(3): 1–19.

Lerman, L. G., (1986). Prosecution of wife beaters: Institutional obstacles and innovations. In M. Lystad (Ed.), *Violence in the Home: Inter-disciplinary Perspectives* (pp. 250–295). New York: Brunner/Mazel.

Lerman, L. G., Landis, L., & Gosozweig, S. (1983). State legislation on domestic violence. In J. J. Costa (Ed.), *Abuse of women: Legislation reporting and prevention* (pp. 39–57). Lexington, MA: Lexington Books.

Lerman, L., & Livingston, F. (1983). State legislation on domestic violence. *Response, 6:* 1–28.

Lester, D. (1980). A cross-culture study of wife abuse. *Aggressive Behavior, 6:* 361–364.

Levinger, G. (1966). Sources of marital dissatisfaction among applicants for divorce. *American Journal of Orthopsychiatry, 26:* 803–897.

Levitz-Jones, E. M., & Orlosky, J. L. (1985). Separation-individuation and intimacy capacity in college women. *Journal of Personality and Social Psychology, 49:* 156–169.

Levy, B. (1991). *Dating violence: Young women in danger.* Seattle, WA: Seal Press.

Lewis, R. A., Kozac, E. B., Milardo, R. M., & Grosnick, W. A. (1981). Commitment in same-sex love relationships. *Alternative Life styles, 4:* 22–42.

Lie, Gwar-Yong, & Gentlewarrier, Sabrina. (1991). Intimate violence in lesbian relationships: Discussion of survey findings and practice implications. *Journal of Social Service Research, 15:* 41–59.

Lie, G-Y., Schilit, R., Bush, J., Montagne, M., & Reyes, L. (1991). Lesbians in currently aggressive relationships: How frequently do they report aggressive past relationships? *Violence and Victims, 6:* 121–135.

Lifton, R. J. (1992). *Home from the war: Learning from Vietnam veterans.* Boston: Beacon Press.

Lindenbaum, J. P. (1985). The shattering of an illusion: The problem of competition in lesbian relationships. *Feminist Studies, 11:* 85–103.

Liss, M. B., & Stahly, G. B. (1993). Domestic violence and child custody. In M. Hansen & M. Harway (Eds.), *Battering and family therapy: A feminist perspective.* Newbury Park, CA: Sage.

Lloyd, S. A. (1991). The dark side of courtship: Violence and sexual exploitation. *Family Relations, 40:* 14–20.

Lloyd, S. A., Koval, J. E., & Cate, R. M. (1989). Conflict and violence in dating relationships. In M. A. Pirog-Good & J. E. Stets (Eds.), *Violence in dating relationships* (pp. 126–142). New York: Praeger.

Lockhart, Lettie L. (1984). A comparative analysis of the nature and extent of spouse abuse among black and white couples across different social classes. Unpublished dissertation. Florida State University School of Social Work.

———. (1985). Methodological issues in comparative racial analyses: The case of wife abuse. *Social Work Research and Abstracts, 21:* 35–41.

Lockhart, Lettie L., & White, B. (1989). Understanding marital violence in the black community. *Journal of Interpersonal Violence, 4:* 421–436.

Loeber, Rolf, & LeBlanc, Marc. (1990). Toward a developmental criminology. In Tonry & N. Morris (Eds.), *Crime and justice* (Vol. 12, pp. 375–475), Chicago: University of Chicago Press,

Loizos, P. (1978). Violence and the family: Some mediterranean examples. In J. P. Martin (Ed.), *Violence and the family.* (pp. 183–196). New York: Wiley.

Loseke, Donileen R., & Spencer E. Cahill. (1984). The social construction of deviance: experts on battered women. *Social Problems, 31:* 296–310.

Lott, B. (1981). *Becoming a woman: The socialization of gender.* Springfield, IL: C.C. Thomas.

———. (1990). The perils and promise of studying sexist discrimination in face-to face situations. In M. Paludi (Ed.), *Ivory power: Sexual harassment on campus* (pp. 53–66). Albany: State University of New York.

Loulan, J. (1987). *Lesbian passion.* San Francisco, CA: Spinsters/Aunt Lute.

Lynch, M. A. (1985). Child abuse before Kempe: An historical literature review. *Child Abuse and Neglect, 9:* 7–15.

MacAndrew, C., & Edgerton, R. B. (1969). *Drunken comportment: A social explanation.* Chicago: Aldine.

Maccoby, E. (1984). Gender as a social category. *Developmental Psychology, 24:* 755–765.

MacKinnon, C. A. (1982). Violence against women—A perspective. *Aegis* (33): 51–57.

Macklin, E. (1983). Nonmarital heterosexual cohabitation: An overview. In E. Macklin & R. Rubin (Eds.), *Contemporary families and alternative lifestyles.* (pp. 49–71). Beverly Hills, CA: Sage.

Maden, M. F., & Wrench, D. F. (1977). Significant findings in child abuse research. *Victimology, 2:* 196–224.

Maguigan, H. (1991). Battered women and self-defense: Myths and misconceptions in current reform proposals. *University of Pennsylvania Law Review, 140:* 379–486.

Mahoney, M. R. (1991). Legal images of battered women: Redefining the issue of separation. *Michigan Law Review, 1:* 43–49.

Maidment, S. (1985). Domestic violence and the law. In N. Johnson (Ed.), *Marital violence* (pp. 4–25). London: Routledge & Kegan Paul.

Makepeace, James. (1981). Courtship violence among college students. *Family Relations, 30:* 97–102.

(1983). Life events stress and courtship violence. *Family Relations, 32:* 101–109.

(1986). Gender differences in courtship violence victimization. *Family Relations, 35:* 383–88.

(1987). Social factor and victim offender differences in courtship violence. *Family Relations, 36:* 87–91.

(1988). The severity of courtship violence and the effectiveness of individual precautions. In G. T. Hotaling, D. Finkelhor, J. T. Kirkpatrick, & M. A. Straus (Eds.), *Family abuse and its consequences* (pp. 297–311). Beverly Hills, CA: Sage.

(1989). Dating, living together, and courtship violence. In M. A. Pirog-Good & J. E. Stets (Eds.), *Violence in Dating Relationships* (pp. 94–107). New York: Praeger.

Malone, J., Tyree, A., & O'Leary, K. D. (1989). Generalization and containment: Different effects of past aggression for wives and husbands. *Journal of Marriage and the Family, 51:* 687–697.

Mancini, M. M. (1978). The variable order of events in the life course. *American Sociological Review, 43:* 573–586.

(1984). Women's educational attainment and the timing of entry into parenthood. *American Sociological Review, 84:* 491–511.

Manley, N. J. (1982). Battered women: The victim's perceptions. Unpublished master's thesis, California State University, Sacramento.

Manzano, T. A. (1989, April). Domestic violence and chemical dependency: A dual–track program design (The Tulsa model). Paper presented at the Second National Working with Batterers Conference, Baltimore, MD.

Marano, Hara Estroff. (1993). Inside the heart of marital violence. *Psychology Today, 26(6):* 48, 89–91.

Marciano, T., & Sussman, M. B. (1992), The definition of family is expanding. In V. Wagner (Ed.), *The family in America: Opposing viewpoints* (pp. 40–46). San Diego: Greenhaven Press, Inc.

March, J. S. (1990). The nosology of posttraumatic stress disorder. *Journal of Anxiety Disorders, 4:* 61–82.

Margolies, L., Becker, M., & Jackson-Brewer, K. (1987). Internalized homophobia: Identifying and treating the oppressor within. In Boston Lesbian Psychologies Collective (Eds.), *Lesbian psychologies* (pp. 229–241). Urbana: University of Illinois Press.

Margolin, G. (1979). Cojoint marital therapy to enhance anger management and reduce spouse assault. *American Journal of Family Therapy, 7:* 13–24.

Marsh, Clifton E. (1993). Sexual assault and domestic violence in the African American community. *The Western Journal of Black Studies, 17*(3): 149–155.

Marsh, J. C., Geist, A., & Caplan, N. (1982). *Rape and the limits of law reform.* Boston: Auburn Publishing House.

Martin, D. (1976). *Battered wives.* San Francisco, CA: Glide Publications.

(1981). *Battered wives.* San Francisco, CA: Volcano Press, Inc.

Martin, S. E. (1989). The response of the clergy to spouse abuse in a suburban county. *Violence and Victims, 4*(3): 217, 225.

Massachusetts Caucus of Women Legislators. (1994). 1994 Victims of Family Violence. Report available from the Massachusetts Caucus of Women Legislators, Room 156, State House, Boston, MA 02133.

Massachusetts Coalition of Battered Women Service Groups. (1993). *A state of emergency exists for battered women and their children.* Massachusetts Coalition of Battered Women Service Groups, Boston.

Massachusetts Office for Victim Assistance. (1993, May). *A guide to domestic violence court advocacy in Massachusetts.* Massachusetts Office for Victim Assistance, Boston.

Massachusetts Trial Court. (1990). *A guide to public access to district court records.* Administrative Office of the District Court, Salem, MA.

(1993). *Interim annual report, 1992.* Office of the Chief Administrative Justice, Massachusetts Trial Court.

Maynard, M. (1985). The response of social workers to domestic violence. In J. Pahl (Ed.), *Private violence and public policy: The needs of battered women and the response of the public services* (pp.

125–141). London: Routledge and Kegan Paul.

McBride, J. (1995). *War, battering and other sports: The gulf between American men and women.* Atlantic Highlands, NJ: Humanities Press.

McDonald, P. L. (1989). Helping with the termination of an assaultive relationship. In B. Pressman, G. Cameron, & M. Rothery (Eds.), *Intervening with assaulted women: Current theory, research, and practice* (pp. 93–110). Atlantic Highlands, NJ: Lawrence Erlbaum Associates.

McFarlane, J., Anderson, E. T., & Helton, A. (1987). Response to battering during pregnancy: An educational program. *Response, 10*(2): 25–26.

McHugh, M. C. (1993). Studying battered women and batterers: Feminist perspectives on methodology. In M. Hansen & M. Harway (Eds.), *Battering and family therapy: A feminist perspective.* Newbury Park, CA: Sage Publications.

McLanahan, S., & J. Adams. (1987). Parenthood and psychological well-being. *Annual Review of Immunology, 5:* 237–257.

McLaughlin, S. C., Grady, W. R., Billy, J. O. G., Landale, N. S., & Winges, L. D. (1986). The effects of the sequencing of marriage and first birth during adolescence. *Family Planning Perspectives, 18:* 12–18.

McNeely, R. L., & Robinson-Simpson, G. (1987). The truth about domestic violence: A falsely framed issue. *Social Work, 32:* 485–490.

MCTFADA (Maricopa County Task Force Against Domestic Abuse) (1994). Why don't batterers leave? MCTFADA Newsletter, p. 5.

McWhirter, D. P., & Mattison, A. M. (1984). *The male couple: How relationships develop.* Englewood Cliffs, NJ: Prentice-Hall.

Meier, R. F., & Miethe, T. D. (1993). Understanding Theories of Criminal Victimization. In M. Tonry & N. Morris (Eds.),

Crime and justice: An annual review of research (pp. 459–499). Chicago: University of Chicago Press.

Mercy, J. A., & Saltzman, L. E. (1989). Fatal violence among spouses in the United States, 1975–1985. *American Journal of Public Health, 79:* 595–599.

Merry, S. (1981). *Urban danger.* Philadelphia: Temple University Press.

Messerschmidt, J. W. (1993). *Masculinities and crime: Critique and reconceptualization of theory.* Lanham, MD: Rowman and Littlefield.

Messner, Steven F. (1988). Research on cultural and socioeconomic factors in criminal violence. *Psychiatric Clinics of North America, 11:* 511 525.

Messner, Steven F., Krohn, M. D., & Liska, A. E. (1990). *Theoretical integration in the study of deviance and crime: Problems and prospects.* Albany: State University of New York Press.

Micklow, P. L. (1988). Domestic abuse: The pariah of the legal system. In V. B. Van Hasselt, R. L. Morrison, A. S. Bellack, & M. Hersen (Eds.), *Handbook of family violence* (pp. 407–434). New York: Plenum Press.

Miller, B. C., & Teaton, T. B. (1991). Age at first sexual intercourse and the timing of marriage and childbirth. *Journal of Marriage and Family, 53:* 719–732.

Miller, S. L. (1989). Unintended side effects of pro-arrest policies and their race and class implications for battered women: A cautionary note. *Criminal Justice Policy Review, 3:* 299–316.

——— (1993). Arrest policies for domestic violence and their implications for battered women. In R. Muraskin & T. Alleman, (Eds.), *It's a crime: Women and justice* (pp. 334–359). Englewood Cliffs, NJ: Regents/Prentice Hall.

Mintz, S., & Kellogg, S. (1988). *Domestic revolutions: A social history of American family life.* New York: Free Press.

Mitchell, R., & Hodson, C. (1983). Coping with domestic violence: Social support and psychological health among battered women. *American Journal of Community Psychology, 11:* 629–654.

Mitchell, W. E. (1992). Why Wape men don't beat their wives: Constraints toward domestic tranquility in a New Guinea society. In D. A. Counts, J. K. Brown, & J. C. Campbell (Eds.), *Sanctions and sanctuary: Cultural perspectives on the beating of wives.* (pp. 89–98). Boulder, CO: Westview Press.

Moffitt, Terrie. (1993). Adolescence-limited and life course persistent antisocial behavior: A developmental taxonomy. *Psychological Review, 100:* 674–701.

Moore, A. (1995). The effects of arrest, victim characteristics, and community context on misdemeanor domestic violence. Unpublished Ph.D. Dissertation, Department of Criminology, University of Maryland.

Moore, K. A. (1990). *Facts at a Glance: 1990.* Washington, DC: Child Trends.

Morash, M. (1986, June). Wife battering. *Criminal Justice Abstracts,* 252–271.

Morgenson, G. (1991, November 18). May I have the pleasure? *National Review, 53:* 36–46.

Moss, B. F., & Schwebel, A. I. (1993). Defining intimacy in romantic relationships. *Family Relations, 42:* 31–37.

Mugford, J., Mugford, S., & Esteal, P. W. (1989). Social justice, public perceptions, and spouse assault in Australia, *Social Justice, 3:* 103–123.

Myers, J. E. B., Tikosh, M. A., & Paxson, M. A. (1992). Domestic violence prevention statutes. *Violence Update, 3*(4–5): 5–9.

Nash, J. (1992). Factors related to infrequent domestic violence among the Nagovisi. In D. A. Counts, J. K. Brown, & J. C. Campbell (Eds.), *Sanctions and sanctuary: Cultural perspectives on the beating of wives* (pp. 99–110). Boulder, CO: Westview Press.

National Council of Juvenile and Family

Court Judges. (1992). *Family violence: State-of-the-art court programs.* National Council of Juvenile and Family Court Judges, Reno, NV.

National Research Council. (1993). *Understanding and Preventing Violence.* Washington, DC: National Academy of Sciences.

Nicoloff, L.K., & Stiglitz, E.A. (1987). Lesbian alcoholism: Etiology, treatment, and recovery. In Boston Lesbian Psychologies Collective (Eds.), *Lesbian psychologies* (pp. 283–293). Urbana: University of Illinois Press.

Norris, Lynn. (1994). Dangerously equal or equally dangerous? An analysis of women's violence against male intimate partners. Unpublished master's thesis, Arizona State University, Tempe.

NOW Legal Defense and Education Fund, & R. Cherow-O'Leary. (1987). *The state-by-state-guide to women's legal rights.* New York: McGraw-Hill.

Ochberg, F. M. (1980). Victims of terrorism. *Journal of Clinical Psychiatry, 41:* 73–74.

Ohlin, L., & Tonry, M. (Eds.) (1989). *Family violence.* Chicago: The University of Chicago Press.

Okun, L. (1986). *Woman abuse: Facts replacing myths.* Albany: State University of New York Press.

O'Leary, K. D. (1988). Physical aggression between spouses: A social learning perspective. In V. B. Van Hasselt, R. L. Morrison, A. S. Bellack, & M. Hersen (Eds.), *Handbook of family violence* (pp. 31–55). New York: Plenum.

(1993). Through a psychological lens: Personality traits, personality disorders, and levels of violence. In R. J. Gelles & D. R. Loseke (Eds.), *Current controversies on family violence* (pp. 7–30). Newbury Park, CA: Sage.

O'Leary, K. D., Barling, J., Arias, I., Rosenbaum, A., Malone, J., & Tyree, A. (1989). Prevalence and stability of physical aggression between spouses: A longitudinal analysis. *Journal of Consulting and Clinical Psychology, 57:* 263–268.

Orbuch, T. L., Veroff, J., & Holmberg, T. D. (1993). Becoming a married couple: The emergence of meaning in the first years of marriage. *Journal of Marriage and Family, 55:* 815–826.

Orlofsky, J. L. (1976). Intimacy status: Relationship to interpersonal perception. *Journal of Youth and Adolescence, 5:* 73–88.

Orlofsky, J. L., Marcia, J. E., & Lesser, I. M. (1973). Ego identity status and the intimacy versus isolation crisis of young adulthood. *Journal of Personality and Social Psychology, 27:* 211–219.

Orthner, D. K. (1992). The family is in transition. In V. Wagner (Ed.), *The family in America: Opposing viewpoints* (pp. 25–32). San Diego: Greenhaven Press, Inc.

Osthoff, S. (1992). Restoring justice: Clemency for battered women. *Response, 14*(2): 2–3.

Overby, A. (1971). Discrimination against minority groups. In L. Radzinowicz & M. E. Wolfgang (Eds.), *The criminal in the arms of the law.* New York: Basic Books.

Pagelow, M. D. (1981). *Woman-battering: Victims and their experiences.* Beverly Hills, CA: Sage.

(1984). *Family violence.* New York: Praeger.

(1990). Effects of domestic violence on children and their consequences for custody and visitation agreements. *Mediation Quarterly, 7*(4): 347–363.

Painter, S. L., & Dutton, D. (1985). Patterns of emotional bonding in battered women: Traumatic bonding. *International Journal of Women's Studies, 8:* 363–375.

Parke, R. D., & Collmer, C. W. (1975). Child abuse: An interdisciplinary analysis. In M. Hetherington (Ed.), *Review of child development research* (Vol. 5, pp. 1–102). Chicago: University of Chicago Press.

Parker, B., & Schumacher, D. (1979). The battered wife syndrome and violence in the nuclear family of origin: A controlled pilot study. *American Journal of Public Health, 67*(8): 760–763.

Parnas, R. I. (1967). The Police Response to the Domestic Disturbance. *Wisconsin Law Review, 4:* 914–960.

Parter, R. N., & Toth, A. M. (1990). Family, intimacy and homicide: A macro-social approach. *Violence and Victims, 5:* 195–210.

Pate, A. M., & Hamilton E. E. (1992). Formal and informal deterrents to domestic violence: The Dade County spouse assault experiment. *American Sociological Review, 57:* 691–697.

Paulson, M. T., & Blake, P. R. (1967). The abused, battered and maltreated child: A review. *Trauma, 9:* 1–136.

Paymar, M. (1993). *Violent no more: Helping men end domestic abuse.* Alameda, CA: Hunter House.

Pearlman, S. F. (1989). Distancing and connectedness: Impact on couple formation in lesbian relationships. *Women and Therapy, 8:* 77–88.

Pease, J. H., & Pease, W. H. (1990). *Ladies, women and wenches: Choice in constraint in antebellum Charleston and Boston.* Chapel Hill: The University of North Carolina Press.

Pence, E., & Paymar, M. (1986). *Power and control: Tactics of men who batter.* Minnesota Program Development, Inc., Duluth, MN.

Peplau, L. A., Cochran, S., Rook, K., & Padesky, C. (1978). Loving women: Attachment and autonomy in lesbian relationships. *Journal of Social Issues, 34:* 7–27.

Peterson, N. (1980). Social class, social learning, and wife abuse. *Social Service Review, 53:* 390–406

Petersen, R. (1980). Social class, social learning, and wife abuse. *Social Service Review, 54:* 390–406.

Pfohl, S. (1977). The discovery of child abuse. *Social Problems, 24:* 310 321.

Pilkington, C. J., & Richardson, D. R. (1988). Perceptions of risk in intimacy. *Journal of Social and Personal Relationships, 5:* 503–508.

Pillemer, K. (1985). The dangers of dependency: New findings on domestic violence against the elderly. *Social Problems, 33:* 146–158.

(1993). The abused offspring are dependent: Abuse is caused by the deviance and dependence of abusive caregivers. In R. J. Gelles & D. R. Loseke (Eds.), *Current controversies on family violence* (pp. 237–259). Newbury Park, CA: Sage.

Pirog-Good, M. A., & Stets, J. E. (1989). The help-seeking behavior of physically and sexually abused college students. In M. A. Pirog-Good & J. E. Stets (Eds.), *Violence in dating relationships* (pp. 108–125). New York: Praeger.

Pittman, F. (1987). *Treating families in transition.* New York: W.W. Norton.

Plass, M. S., & Gessner, J. C. (1983). Violence in courtship relations: A southern sample. *Free Inquiry in Creative Sociology, 11:* 198–202.

Pleck, E. (1983). Feminist responses to "crimes against women," 1868–1896. *Signs, 8*(3): 451–470.

(1987). *Domestic tyranny: The making of American social policy against family violence from colonial times to the present.* New York: Oxford University Press.

Pogrebin. (1974). Use of a psychiatric facility for parole evaluation justifiable. *International Journal of Offender, 18:* 270–274.

Polk, K. (1985). Rape reform and criminal justice processing. *Crime and Delinquency, 31:* 191–205.

Polsky, A. J. (1991). *The rise of the therapeutic state.* Princeton: Princeton University Press.

Popenoe, D. (1988). *Disturbing the nest: Family change and decline in modern societies.* New York: Aldine de Gruyter.

(1993). American family decline, 1960–1990: A review and appraisal. *Journal of Marriage and Family, 55:* 527–542.

Prager, K. J. (1991). Intimacy status and couple conflict resolution. *Journal of Social and Personal Relationships, 8:* 505–526.

(1989). Intimacy status and couple communication. *Journal of Social and Personal Relationships, 6:* 435–449.

Prescott, S., & Letko, C. (1977). Battered: A social psychological perspective. In M. M. Roy (Ed.), *Battered women: A psychosociological study of domestic violence.* New York: Von Nostrand Reinhold.

Ptacek, James. (1988). Why do men batter their wives? In Kersti Yllö & Michele Bograd (Eds.), *Feminist Perspectives on Wife Abuse* (Ch. 6, pp. 133–157). Newbury Park, CA: Sage.

Quarm, D., & Schwartz, M. D. (1985). Domestic violence in criminal court: An examination of new legislation in Ohio. In C. Schweber & C. Fieman (Eds.), *The aftermath of legally mandated change* (pp. 29–46). New York: Haworth.

Radford, Jill & Russell, Diana E. H. (1992). *Femicide.* New York: Twayne.

Randall, T. (1990). Domestic violence intervention calls for more than treating injuries. *Journal of the American Medical Association, 264*(8): 939–944.

Rasche, Christine E. (1988). Minority women and domestic violence: The unique dilemmas of battered women of color. *Journal of Contemporary Criminal Justice, 4:* 150–171.

Register, E. (1993). Feminism and recovering from battering: Working with the individual woman. In M. Hansen & M. Harway (Eds.), *Battering and Family therapy: A feminist perspective.* Newbury Park, CA : Sage Publications.

Reidy, R., & Von Korff, M. (1991). Is battered women's help seeking connected to the level of their abuse? *Public Health Reports, 106*(4): 360–364.

Reiss, Albert J., & Roth, J. (1993). *Understanding and preventing violence.* Washington, DC: National Academy of Science.

Renzetti, C. M. (1992). *Violent betrayal: Partner abuse in lesbian relationships.* Newbury Park, CA: Sage.
———. (forthcoming). The poverty of services for battered lesbians. *Journal of Gay and Lesbian Social Services.*

Riche, M. (1984). The systemic feminist. *Family Therapy Networker, 8:* 43–44.

Riddle, D. I., & Sang, B. (1978). Psychotherapy with lesbians. *Journal of Social Issues, 34:* 84–100.

Ridington, J. (1977–78). The transition process: A feminist environment as reconstitutive milieu. *Victimology: An International Journal, 2*(3–4): 563–575.

Riggs, D. S., & O'Leary, K. D. (1989). A theoretical model of courtship aggression. In M. A. Pirog-Good & J. E. Stets (Eds.), *Violence in dating relationships* (pp. 53–71). New York: Praeger.

Rindfuss, R. R., & VandenHeuvel, A. (1990). Cohabitation: Precursor to marriage or an alternative to being single? *Population and Development Review, 16:* 703–726.

Rivera, J. (1994). Domestic violence against Latinas by Latino males: An analysis of race, national origin and gender differentials. *Boston College Third World Law Journal, 14:* 231–257

Romero, Mary. (1985). A comparison between strategies used on prisoners of war and battered wives. *Sex Roles, 13:* 537–547.

Rosa, M. W. (1991). Adolescent pregnancy programs collection: An introduction. *Family Relations, 40:* 370–72.

Roscoe, B., & Benaske, N. (1985). Courtship violence experienced by abused wives: Similarities in patterns of abuse. *Family Relations, 34:* 419–424.

Rose, P., & Marshall, L. L. (1985). Gender differences: Effects of stress on expressed or received abuse. Paper presented at the 93rd Annual Convention of the American Psychological Association, Los Angeles, CA.

Rosen, K. H., & Stith, S. M. (1993). Intevention strategies for treating women in violent dating relationships. *Family Relations, 42:* 427–433

Rosenbaum, A. (1988). Methodological issues in marital violence research. *Journal of Family Violence, 3:* 91–104.

Rosenbaum, A., & O'Leary, K. D. (1981). Marital violence: Characteristics of abusive couples. *Journal of Consulting and Clinical Psychology, 49:* 63–71.

Rossi, P., Berk, R. A., & Edison, B. (1974). *The roots of urban discontent.* New York: Wiley.

Rounsaville, B. J. (1978–79). Theories in marital violence: Evidence from a study of battered women. *Victimology, 3*(1–2): 11–31.

Roy, Maria. (1977). *Battered women.* New York: Van Nostrand Reinhold.

Russell, D. E. H. (1982). *Rape in marriage.* New York: Macmillan.

(1990). *Rape in marriage* (rev. ed.). Bloomington: Indiana University Press.

Ryan, M. (1990). *Women in public: Between banners and ballots, 1825–1880.* Baltimore: The Johns Hopkins Press.

Sack, A. R., Keller, J. F., & Howard, R. D. (1982). Conflict tactics and violence in dating situations. *International Journal of Sociology of the Family, 12:* 89–100.

Saltzman, L. E. (1990). Battering during pregnancy: A role for physicians. *Atlanta Medicine, 64:* 45–48.

Saltzman, Linda E., Mercy, James A., Rosenberg, Mark L., Elsea, William R., Napper, George, Sikes, R. Keith, Waxweiler, Richard J., & the Collaborative Working Group for the Study of Family and Intimate Assaults in Atlanta. (1990). Magnitude and patterns of family and intimate assault in Atlanta, Georgia, 1984. *Violence and Victims, 5*(1): 3–17.

Sampson, R. J. (1986). Neighborhood family structure and the risk of personal victimization. In J. M. Byrne & R. J. Sampson (Eds.), *The social ecology of crime* (pp. 25–46). New York: Springer-Verlag.

Sanday, P. R. (1990). *Fraternity gang rape: Sex, brotherhood and privilege on campus.* New York: New York University Press.

Sandler, B. (1986). *The campus climate revisited: Chilly for women faculty, administrators, and graduate students.* Washington, DC: Project on the Status and Education of Women.

Saunders, D. G. (1988a). Other 'Truths' about domestic violence: A reply to McNeely and Robinson-Simpson. *Social Work.* March–April, 179.

(1988b). Wife abuse, husband abuse or mutual combat? In K. Yllö & M. Bograd (Eds.), *Feminist perspectives on wife abuse* (pp. 90–113). Newbury Park, CA: Sage.

(1992). A typology of men who batter: Three types derived from cluster analysis. *American Journal of Orthopsychiatry, 62*(2): 264–275.

Scanzoni, J., & Marsiglio, W. (1993). New action theory and contemporary families. *Journal of Family Issues, 1:* 105–132.

Schaefer, M. T., & Olson, E. H. (1981). Assessing intimacy: The PAIR inventory. *Journal of Marriage and Family Therapy, 7:* 47–60.

Schechter, Susan. (1982). *Women and male violence.* New York: Macmillan.

Schechter, S., & Gary, L. T. (1988). A framework for understanding and empowering battered women. In M. B. Straus (Ed.), *Abuse and victimization across the life span* (pp. 240–253). Baltimore: Johns Hopkins University Press.

Schilit, R., Lie, G., & Montagne, M. (1990). Substance use as a correlate of violence in intimate lesbian relationships. *Journal of Homosexuality, 19:* 51–65.

Schneider, Elizabeth. (1994). Legal reform efforts for battered women. Cited in MCTFADA Newsletter, p. 5.

Schoen, R., & Owens, D. J. (1992). A further look at first marriages and first unions. In S. J. South & S. E. Tolnay (Eds.), *The changing American family: Sociological and demographic perspectives* (pp. 109–117). Boulder, CO: Westview Press.

Schoen, R., & Weinick, R. (1993). Partner choice in marriages and cohabitations. *Journal of Marriage and Family, 55:* 408–414.

Schuler, M. (Ed.). (1992). *Freedom from violence: Women's strategies from around the world.* New York: OEF International/UNIFEM.

Schuller, Regina A., & Vidmar, Neil. (1992).

Battered woman syndrome evidence in the courtroom. *Law and Human Behavior, 16*(3): 273–291.

Schulman, M. (1979). A survey of spousal violence against women in Kentucky. Unpublished manuscript, Law Enforcement Administration, U.S. Department of Justice, Washington, DC.

Schultz, L. G. (1960). The wife assaulter. *Journal of Social Therapy, 6:* 103–112.

Schutte, N. S., Malouff, J. M., & Doyle, J. S. (1988). The relationship between characteristics of the victim, persuasive techniques of the batterer, and returning to a battering relationship. *Journal of Social Psychology, 128:* 605–610.

Schuyler, M. (1976). Battered wives: Emerging social problem. *Social Work, 21:* 488–491.

Schwartz, M. D. (1988a). Ain't got no class: Universal risk theories of battering. *Contemporary Crises, 12:* 373–392.

(1988b). Marital status and woman abuse theory. *Journal of Family Violence, 3:* 239–259.

(1990). Work status, resource equality, injury and wife battery: The National Crime Survey data. *Free Inquiry in Creative Sociology, 18*(1): 57–61.

Schwendinger, J. R., & Schwendinger, H. (1983). *Rape and inequality.* Newbury Park, CA: Sage.

Scott, J. P. (1963). The process of primary socialization in canine and human infants. *Monographs of the Society for Research in Child Development, 28*(1): 1–47.

Scully, D. (1990). *Understanding sexual violence: A study of convicted rapists.* Boston: Unwin Hyman.

Scyner, L. A., & McGregor, N. (1988). Women in second-stage housing: What happens after the crisis. *Canadian Journal of Community Mental Health, 7*(2): 129–135.

Sedlak, A. J. (1988). Prevention of wife abuse. In V. B. Van Hasselt, R. L. Morrison, A. S. Bellack, & M. Hersen (Eds.), *Handbook of family violence* (pp. 319–358). New York: Plenum Press.

Segovia-Ashley, Marta. (1978). Shelters—Short-term needs. In *Battered women: Issues of public policy* (pp. 98–108). Washington, DC: U.S. Commission on Civil Rights.

Shattuck, J. (1992, July). Organizing domestic violence offender services: Building coalitions. Paper presented at the National Lesbian and Gay Health Conference, Houston, TX.

Shepard, M. (1992). Predicting batterer recidivism five years after community intervention. *Journal of Family Violence, 7*(3): 167–178.

Shepard, Melanie F., & Campbell, James A. (1992). The abusive behavior inventory: A measure of psychological and physical abuse. *Journal of Interpersonal Violence, 7*(3): 291–305.

Shepard, M., & Pence, E. (1988). The effect of battering on the employment status of women. *Affilia, 3*(2): 55–61.

Sherman, L. W., & Berk, R. (1984). The specific deterrent effects of arrest for domestic assault. *American Sociological Review, 49:* 261–272.

Sherman, L. W., & Cotin, E. G. (1989). The impact of research on legal policy: The Minneapolis Domestic Violence Experiment. *Law and Society Review, 23:* 117–144.

Sherman, L. W., Schmidt, J. D., Rogan, D. P., Smith, D. A., Gartin, P. R., Cohn, E. G., Collins, D. J., & Bacich, A. R. (1992). The variable effects of arrest on criminal careers: The Milwaukee Domestic Violence Experiment. *The Journal of Criminal Law and Criminology 83*(1): 137–169.

Sherman, L. W., & Smith, D. (1992). Crime, punishment and stake in conformity: Legal and extralegal control of domestic violence. *American Sociological Review, 58*(3): 680–690.

Shields, N., & Hanneke, C. R. (1983). Battered wives' reactions to marital rape. In D. Finkelhor, R. J. Gelles, G. T. Hotaling, & M. A. Straus (Eds.), *The dark side of families* (pp. 131–148). Beverly Hills, CA: Sage.

Shoemaker, D. J., & Williams, J. S. (1987). The subculture of violence and ethnicity. *Journal of Criminal Justice, 15*(6): 461–472.

Silver, L. B. (1968). Child abuse syndrome: A review. *Medical Times, 96:* 803–818.

Skolnick, A., (1991). *Embattled paradise: The American family in an age of uncertainty.* New York: Basic Books.

Skurnik, J. (1983). Battering: An issue for women of color. *Off Our Backs, 13*(5): 8.

Smith, D. L., & Snow, R. (1978). Violent subcultures or subcultures of violence. *Southern Journal of Criminal Justice, 3:* 1–13.

Smith, Michael. (1991). Male peer support of wife abuse: An exploratory study. *Journal of Interpersonal Violence, 6*(4): 512–519.

Snyder, D. K., & Fruchtman, L. A. (1981). Differential patterns of wife abuse: A data based typology. *Journal of Consulting and Clinical Psychology, 49:* 878–885.

Sonkin, D. J. (1988). The male batterer: Clinical and research issues. *Violence and Victims, 3:* 65–79.

Sonkin, D. J., & Dutton, D. G. (Eds.). (1988). Special issue on wife assaulters. *Violence and Victims, 3*

Sonkin, D. J., Martin, D., & Walker, L. E. A. (Eds.). (1985). *The male batterer: A treatment approach.* New York: Springer.

Sohoni, N. K. (1993). The changing family and women's issues in the 1990s. *Feminist Issues,* Spring, 55–76.

Sorenson, S. B., & Telles, C. A. (1991). Self-reports of spousal violence in a Mexican-American and non-Hispanic White population. *Violence and Victims, 6:* 3–15.

Sorrells, J. M., Jr. (1977). Kids who kill. *Crime and Delinquency, 23*(3): 312–320.

Spiegel, J. P. (1980). Ethnopsychiatric dimensions in family violence. In M. R. Green (Ed.), *Violence and the family* (pp. 79–89). Boulder, CO: Westview Press.

Spohn, C., & Horney, J. (1992). *Rape law reform: A grassroots revolution and its impact.* New York: Plenum Press.

Stacey, J. (1993). Good riddance to the family: A response to David Popenoe. *Journal of Marriage and Family, 55:* 545–547.

Stacey, W. A., Hazlewood, L. R., & Shupe, A. (1994). *The violent couple.* Westport, CT: Praeger.

Stanko, E. A. (1985a). *Intimate intrusions: Women's experience of male violence.* London: Routledge & Kegan Paul.

(1985b). Legal protection: Some thoughts on legal intervention into male violence to women. Paper presented at the annual meeting of the American Society of Criminology, San Diego, CA.

Staples, R. (1976). Race and family violence: The internal colonialism perspective. In G. E. Lawrence & L. P. Brown (Eds.), *Crime and its impact on the black community.* Institute for Urban Affairs and Development Center. Washington, DC: Howard University.

Stark, E. (1990). Rethinking homicide: Violence, race, and the politics of gender. *International Journal of Health Services, 20*(1): 3–26.

Stark, E., & Flitcraft, A. (1985). Woman-battering, child abuse and social heredity: What is the relationship? In N. Johnson (Ed.), *Marital Violence. Sociological Review Monograph #31.* London: Routledge and Kegan Paul.

(1988). Violence among intimates: An epidemiological review. In V. B. Van Hasselt, R. L. Morrison, A. S. Bellack, & M. Hersen (Eds.), *Handbook of family violence* (pp. 293–317). New York: Plenum Press.

Stark, E., Flitcraft, A., Zuckerman, D., Grey, A., Robison, J., & Frazier, W. (1981). *Wife abuse in the medical setting: An introduction for health personnel.* (Monograph No. 7). Office of Domestic Violence, Washington, DC.

Steele, E., Mitchell, J., Graywolf, E., Belle, D., Chang, W., & Schuller, R. B. (1982). The human cost of discrimination. In D. Belle (Ed.), *Lives in stress: Women and depression* (pp. 109–119). Beverly Hills, CA: Sage.

Steinman, M. (1988). Anticipating rank and

file police reactions to arrest policies regarding spouse abuse. *Research Bulletin, 14*(3): 1–5.

(1991). Coordinated criminal justice interventions and recidivism among batterers. In M. Steinman (Ed.), *Women battering: Policy responses* (pp. 221–236). Cincinnati: Anderson.

Steinmetz, S. (1977). Wife-beating, husband beating: A comparison of the use of physical violence between spouses to resolve marital fights. In M. Roy (Ed.), *Battered women: A psychosociological study of domestic violence* (pp. 63–72). New York: Van Nostrand Reinhold.

(1978a). Violence between family members. *Violence and Family Review 1*(3): 1–16.

Steinmetz, S. K., & Straus, M. A. (1974). *Violence in the family.* New York: Dodd, Mead.

Stets, J. E. (1991a). Cohabiting and marital aggression: The role of social isolation. *Journal of Marriage and Family, 53:* 669–680.

(1991b). Psychological aggression in dating relationships: The role of interpersonal control. *Journal of Family Violence, 6:* 97–114.

Stets, J. E., & Henderson, D. A. (1991). Contextual factors surrounding conflict resolution while dating: Results from a national study. *Family Relations, 40:* 29–36.

Stets, J. E., & Pirog-Good, M. A. (1987). Violence in dating relationships. *Social Psychology Quarterly, 52:* 225–233.

Stets, J. E., & Straus, M. A. (1989). The marriage license as a hitting license: A comparison of assaults in dating, cohabiting, and married couples. *Journal of Family Violence, 4:* 161–180.

(1990). Gender differences in reporting of marital violence and its medical and psychological consequences. In M. A. Straus & R. J. Gelles (Eds.), *Physical violence in American families: Risk factors and adaption to violence in 8,145 families*

(pp. 151–165). New Brunswick, NJ: Transaction Publishers.

Stith, Sandra, Jester, Stephanie B., & Bird, Gloria W. (1992). A typology of college students who use violence in their dating relationships. *Journal of College Student Development, 33:* 411–421.

Stith, Sandra, & Rosen, Kitt. (1990). Overview of domestic violence. In S. Stith, M. K. Williams, & K. Rosen (Eds.), *Violence hits home.* New York: Springer.

Stout, Karen D. (1991). A continuum of male controls and violence against women: A teaching model. *Journal of Social Work Education, 27*(3): 305–319.

Straus, M. A. (1974). Cultural and social organizational influences on violence between family members. In R. Prince & D. Barrier (Eds.), *Configurations: Biological and cultural factors in sexuality and family life* (pp. 53–69). Lexington, MA: D.C. Heath.

(1979). Measuring intrafamily conflict and violence: The conflict tactics (CT) scales. *Journal of Marriage and the Family, 41:* 75–88.

(1986). Medical care costs of intrafamily assault and homicide. *Bulletin of the New York Academy of Medicine, 62:* 556–561.

(1990a). The conflict tactics scales and its critics: An evaluation and new data on validity and reliability. In M. A. Straus & R. J. Gelles (Eds.), *Physical violence in families: Risk factors and adaption to violence in 8,145 families* (pp. 49–73). New Brunswick, NJ: Transaction Publishers.

(1990b). The national family violence surveys. In M. A. Straus & R. J. Gelles (Eds.), *Physical violence in American families: Risk factors and adaption to violence in 8,145 families* (pp. 3–16). New Brunswick, NJ: Transaction Publishers.

(1993). Physical assault by wives: A major social problem. In R. J. Gelles & D. R. Loseke (Eds.), *Current controversies on family violence* (pp. 67–87). Newbury Park, CA: Sage.

Straus, M. A., & Gelles, R. (1986). Societal

change and change in family violence from 1975 to 1985 as revealed by two national surveys. *Journal of Marriage and the Family, 48:* 465–79.

(1988). *Intimate violence.* New York: Simon and Schuster.

(1990). How violent are American families? Estimates from the National Family Violence Resurvey and other studies. In M. A. Straus & R. J. Gelles (Eds.), *Physical violence in American families* (pp. 95–132). New Brunswick, NJ: Transaction Publishers.

Straus, M. A., Gelles, R. J., & Steinmetz, S. K. (1980). *Behind closed doors: Violence in the American family.* New York: Anchor Press/Doubleday.

Straus, M. A., & Smith, C. (1990). Violence in Hispanic families in the United States: Incidence, rates and structural interpretations. In M. A. Straus & R. J. Gelles (Eds.), *Physical violence in American families: Risk factors and adaptations to violence in 8,145 families.* New Brunswick, NJ: Transaction Publishers.

Stubbing, E. (1990). Police who think family homicide is preventable are pointing the way. *Response, 13*(1): 8.

Strube, M. J., & Barbour, L. S. (1983). The decision to leave an abusive relationship: Economic dependence and psychological commitment. *Journal of Marriage and the Family, 45:* 785–793.

Strube, M. J., & Barbour, L. S. (1984). Factors related to the decision to leave an abusive relationship. *Journal of Marriage and the Family, 45:* 837.

Sugarman, D. B., & Hotaling, G. T. (1989). Dating violence: Prevalence, context, and risk markers. In M. A. Pirog-Good & J. E. Stets (Eds.), *Violence in dating relationships* (pp. 3–32). New York: Praeger.

Sullivan, C. M. (1991). The provision of advocacy services to women leaving abusive partners: An exploratory study. *Journal of Interpersonal Violence, 6*(1): 45–54.

Sullivan, C. M., Basta, J., Tan, C., & Davidson, W. S., II. (1992). After the crisis: A needs assessment of women leaving a domestic violence shelter. *Violence and Victims, 7*(3): 267–275.

Sullivan, C. M., Tan, C., Basta, J., Rumptz, M., & Davidson, W. S., II. (1992). An advocacy intervention program for women with abusive partners: Initial evaluation. *American Journal of Community Psychology, 20*(3): 309–332.

Sullivan, C. M., Campbell, R., Angelique, H., Eby, K. K., & Davidson, W. S. (1994). An advocacy intervention program for women with abusive partners: Six month followup. *American Journal of Community Psychology, 22*(2).

Sullivan, H. S. (1953). *The interpersonal theory of psychiatry.* New York: W.W. Norton.

Swerdlow, A., Bridenthral, R., Kelly, J., & Vine, P. (1989). *Families in flux.* New York: The Feminist Press at the City University of New York.

Syers, M., & Edleson, J. L. (1992). The combined effects of coordinated criminal justice intervention in woman abuse. *Journal of Interpersonal Violence, 7*(4): 490–502.

Symonds, M. (1978). The psychodynamics of violence-prone marriages. *American Journal of Psychoanalysis, 38*(3): 213–222.

(1979). Violence against women: The myth of masochism. *American Journal of Psychotherapy, 33:* 161–173.

Tannen, D. (1990). *You just don't understand: Women and men in conversation.* New York: Ballantine.

Taub, N. (1983). Adult domestic violence: The law's response. *Victimology: An International Journal, 8*(1–2): 152–171.

Telch, C. F., & Lindquist, C. U. (1984). Violent versus nonviolent couples: A comparison of patterns. *Psychotherapy, 21:* 242–248.

Teske, R. H. C., Jr., & Parker, M. L. (1983). Spouse abuse in Texas: A study of women's attitudes and experiences. Huntsville, TX: Survey Research Program, Criminal Justice Center, Sam Houston State University.

Thompson, C. (1989). Breaking through walls

of isolation: A model for churches in helping victims of violence. *Pastoral Psychology, 38:* 35–38.

Thornberry, T. P. (1994). Violent families and youth violence. U.S. Department of Justice. Office of Juvenile Justice and Delinquency Prevention (Fact Sheet, No. 21).

Tifft, L. L. (1993). *Battering of women: The failure of intervention and the case for prevention.* Boulder, CO: Westview Press.

Toby, Jackson. (1957). Social disorganization and stake in conformity: Complementary factors in the predatory behavior of hoodlums. *Journal of Criminal Law, Criminology, and Police Science, 48:* 12–17.

——— (1974). Violence and the masculine ideal: Some qualitative data. In S. Steinmetz & M. A. Straus (Eds.), *Violence in the family* (pp. 58–65). New York: Harper and Row.

Toch, H. (1992). *Violent men: An inquiry into the psychology of violence.* Washington, DC: The American Psychological Association.

Tolman, Richard M. (1989). The development of a measure of psychological maltreatment of women by their male partners. *Violence and Victims, 4*(3): 159–177.

Tolman, R. M., & Bhosley, G. (1991). The outcome of participation in a shelter-sponsored program for men who batter. In D. D. Knudsen & J. L. Miller (Eds.), *Abused and battered: Social and legal responses to family violence* (pp. 113–122). New York: Aldine DeGruyter.

Tong, R. (1984). *Women, sex, and the law.* Totowa, NJ: Rowman and Allenheld Publishers.

Torres, S. (1991). A comparison of wife abuse between two cultures: Perception, attitudes, nature, and extent [Special issue]. *Issues in Mental Health Nursing: Psychiatric Nursing for the 90's: New concepts, new therapies, 12:* 113–131.

Totman, J. (1978). *The murderers: A psychosocial study of criminal homicide.* San Francisco: R & E Research Associates.

United Nations. (1989). *Violence against women in the family.* New York: United Nations.

U.S. Bureau of the Census. (1989). *Statistical abstract of the United States* (109th ed.). Washington, DC: U.S. Government Printing Office.

U.S. Commission on Civil Rights. (1982). *Under the rule of thumb: Battered women and the administration of justice.* Washington, DC: U.S. Government Printing Office.

U.S. Commission on Civil Rights. (1982). *Under the rule of thumb.* Washington, DC: U.S. Government Printing Office.

U.S. Department of Justice. (1983). *Report to the nation on crime and justice: The data.* Washington, DC: U.S. Department of Justice.

U. S. Department of Justice, Bureau of Justice Statistics. (1990). *Criminal Victimization in the United States.* Washington, DC: U.S. Government Printing Office.

University of Pennsylvania Law Review. (1968). *Police discretion and the judgment that a crime has been committed: Rape in Philadelphia, 117:* 277–322.

Vargo, S. (1987). The effects of women's socialization on lesbian couples. In Lesbian Psychologies Collective (Eds.), *Lesbian psychologies* (pp. 161–174). Urbana: University of Illinois Press.

Vaselle-Augenstein, R., & Ehrlich, A. (1992). Male batterers: Evidence for psychopathology. In E. C. Viano (Ed.), *Intimate violence* (pp. 139–154). Washington, DC: Hemisphere.

Viano, E. C. (Ed.). (1992). *Intimate violence: Interdisciplinary perspectives.* Washington, DC: Hemisphere.

Vinton, L. (1992). Battered women's shelters and older women: The Florida experience. *Journal of Family Violence, 7*(1): 63–72.

Walby, S. (1989). Theorizing patriarchy. *Sociology, 23*(2): 213–234.

——— (1990). *Theorizing patriarchy.* Oxford: Basil Blackwell.

Walker, G. A. (1990). *Family violence and the women's movement: The conceptual politics of struggle.* Toronto: University of Toronto Press.

Walker, L. E. (1978). Battered women and learned helplessness. *Victimology, 2:* 525–534.

——— (1979). *The battered woman.* New York: Harper and Row.

——— (1983). Victimology and the psychological perspectives of battered women. *Victimology, 8*(1–2): 82–104.

——— (1984). *The battered woman syndrome.* New York: Springer.

——— (1989). *Terrifying love.* New York: Harper Perennial.

Waller, W. (1937). The rating and dating complex. *American Sociological Review, 2:* 727–734.

Walther, D. J. (1986). Wife abuse prevention: Effects of information on attitudes of high school boys. *Journal of Primary Prevention, 7*(2): 84–89.

Waring, E. M. (1988). *Enhancing marital interaction through facilitating cognitive self-disclosure.* New York: Brunner/Mazel.

Warshaw, C. (1993). Limitations of the medical model in the care of battered women. In P. B. Bart & E. G. Moran (Eds.), *Violence against women: The bloody footprints* (pp. 134–146). CA: Sage.

Washburn, C., & Frieze, I. H. (1981). Methodological issues in studying battered women. Paper presented at the First National Conference for Family Violence Researchers, University of New Hampshire, Durham, NH.

Wauchope, B. (1988). Help-seeking decisions of battered women: A test of learned helplessness and two stress theories. Paper presented at Eastern Sociological Society, Durham, New Hampshire.

Weathers, B. (1980). Alcoholism and the lesbian community. In N. Gottlieb (Ed.), *Alternative services for women* (pp. 158–169). New York: Columbia University Press.

Weiner, J. P., & Boss, P. (1985). Exploring gender bias against women: Ethic for marriage and family therapy. *Counseling and Values, 30:* 9–23

Weiss, J. (1989). Family violence research methodology and design. In L. Ohlin & M. Tonry (Eds.), *Family violence, crime and justice: A review of research* (Vol. 11, pp. 117–162). Chicago: University of Chicago Press.

Weiss, R. S. (1979). A new marital form: The marriage of uncertain duration. In H. Gans, et al. (Eds.), *On the making of Americans: Essays in honor of David Reisman* (pp. 221–233). Philadelphia: University of Pennsylvania Press.

Wesson, Mimi. (1994). Digging up the roots of violence. *Women's Review of Books, 11*(6): 1, 3.

Wheeler, D. (1985). The fear of feminism in family therapy: The risk of making waves. *Family Therapy Networker, 9*(6): 53–55.

Whiffen, V. E., & Gotlib, I. H. (1989). Stress and coping in maritally distressed and nondistressed couples. *Journal of Social and Personal Relationships, 6:* 327–344.

Whitbourne, S. K., & Weinstock, C. (1979). *Adult Development: The differentiation of experience.* New York: Holt, Rinehart & Winston.

White, Evelyn C. (1985). *Chain chain change: For black women dealing with physical and emotional abuse.* Seattle, WA: Seal Press.

Whitehurst, Robert N. (1974). Violence in husband-wife interaction. In S. Steinmetz & M. A. Straus (Eds.), *Violence in the family* (pp. 75–81). New York: Harper and Row.

Williams, K. R. (1992). Social sources of marital violence and deterrence: Testing an integrated theory of assaults between partners. *Journal of Marriage and the Family, 54:* 620–629.

Williams, Kirk R., & Hawkins, Richard (1992). Wife assault, costs of arrest, and the deterrence process. *Journal of Research in Crime and Delinquency, 29*(3): 292–310.

Williams, L. (1981). Violence against women. *Black Scholar, 12*(1): 18–24.

Wilson, G. T., & Lawson, D. M. (1976). Expectancies, alcohol, and sexual arousal in male social drinkers. *Journal of Abnormal Psychology, 85:* 587–594.

Wilson, M. I., & Daly, M. (1992). Who kills whom in spouse killings? On the exceptional sex ratio of spousal homicides in the United States. *Criminology, 30*(2): 189–215.

Winick, C. (1968). *The new people: Desexualization in American life.* New York: Pegasus.

Witzer, E. (1993). Seeing the invisible victims: Domestic violence in lesbian relationships—A guide for judges and others in the legal community. Unpublished manuscript.

Wolfgang, Marvin, Sellin, T., & Figlio, R. (1972). *Delinquency in a birth cohort.* Chicago: University of Chicago Press,

Wood, Gale Goldberg, & Middleman, Ruth R. (1992). Groups to empower battered women. *AFFILIA, 7*(4): 82–95.

Wood, J. T., et al., (1994). Dialectic of difference: A thematic analysis of intimates' meanings for differences. In K. Carter & M. Presnell (Eds.), *Interpretive approaches to interpersonal communication* (pp. 115–136). Albany, NY: State University of New York Press.

Wyatt, G. E. (1992). The sociocultural context of African American and White American women's rape. *Journal of Social Issues, 48:* 77–92.

Yates, D. L. (1985). Correlates of attitudes towards the police: A comparison of black and white citizens in Austin, Texas. Unpublished dissertation. University of Texas at Austin. Ann Arbor, MI: University Microfilms International.

Yllö, Kersti. (1988). Political and methodological debates in wife abuse research. In K. Yllö & M. Bograd (Eds.), *Feminist perspectives on wife abuse.* Newbury Park, CA: Sage.

(1993). Through a feminist lens: Gender, power, and violence. In R. J. Gelles & D. R. Loseke (Eds.), *Current controversies on family violence* (pp. 47–62). Newbury Park, CA: Sage.

Yllö, K., & Bograd, M. (1988). *Feminist perspectives on wife abuse.* Newbury Park, CA: Sage Publications.

Yllö, K., & Straus, M. A. (1981). Interpersonal violence among married and cohabiting couples. *Family Relations, 30:* 339–347.

Zalba, S. R. (1966). The abused child: I, a survey of the problem. *Social Work, 11:* 3–16.

Zambrano, M. M. (1985). *Mejor sola que mal acompanada.* Seattle, WA: Seal Press.

Zawitz, M. W. (1994). *Violence between intimates.* Washington, DC: Bureau of Justice Statistics, U. S. Department of Justice.

Zietlow, P. H., & Sillars, A. L. (1988). Life-stage differences in communication during marital conflicts. *Journal of Social and Personal Relationships V,* 223–245.

Zimbardo, P. G., Haney, C., & Banks, W. C. (1973, April 8). A Pirandellian prison: The mind is a formidable jailer. *New York Times Magazine,* pp. 38–60.

Zorza, J. (1992). The criminal law of misdemeanor domestic violence, 1970–1900. *Journal of Criminal Law and Criminology, 83*(1): 46–72.

CASES CITED

Eisenstadt v. *Baird,* 405 U.S. 438 (1972).

Griswold v. *Connecticut,* 381 U.S. 479 (1965).

Roe v. *Wade,* 410 U.S. 113 (1973).

Thurman v. *Torrington,* 595 F. Supp. 1521 (D. Conn.) (1984).

Index

Landis, L., 146, 147, 149, 150, 152
Lane, K. E., 31, 37, 41
Langan, P. A., 6, 52, 145
Language, gender-biased, 170
Lapidus, J., 139
Lasch, C., 5, 6, 179
LaViolette, A. D., 93, 124, 127, 155
Learned behavior, intimate violence as, 23–24, 40, 80–81
Learned helplessness, 41, 128
Leaving abusive relationship, 133–35, 138
  attempts to deny women's efforts at, 112–15
  barriers to, 14, 102–3, 134–35, 155
LeBlanc, M., 26
Leeder, E., 72
Legal actions
  in harm-reduction approach, 99–100
  retaliation and coercion related to, 117–19
  women's evaluations of, 67–68
Legal assistance to victims of abuse, 99, 138–39
Legal sanctions, deterrent effects of, 95
Legislative initiatives, 8, 104–5, 148–49, 163
Lehnen, R. G., 133, 155
Lerman, L. G., 9, 105, 146, 147, 149, 150, 151, 152, 163
Lesbian couples. See Same-sex partners, violence
  and abuse among
Lester, D., 154
Letellier, P., 6, 18, 72–76, 79, 87, 88
Lethal outcomes. See Homicide
Letko, C., 21
Levinger, G., 91
Levitz-Jones, E. M., 3
Lewis, R. A., 85, 86
Lewis, V. S., 95
Lie, G-Y., 71, 74, 75, 79, 80
Lieber, C. S., 78n
Life experiences, courtship violence and, 43
Life-style exposure approach, 94
Lifton, R. J., 115
Lincoln, R., 32
Lindenbaum, J. P., 85
Lindquist, C. U., 39
Lion, 22
Liss, M. B., 170
Livingston, F., 163
Lloyd, S., 6, 9, 31, 32, 36, 40, 41, 42
Lockhart, L. L., 20, 21, 55
Loeber, R., 26
Loizos, P., 20
Longitudinal research on intimate violence, 183
Loseke, D. R., 21, 124, 132
Lott, B., 168
Louganis, Greg, 6
Loulan, J., 6, 71
Loving contrition, period of, 62–63
Low-income housing, need for, 139
Lynch, M. A., 5

MacAndrew, C., 78
McBride, J., 103

Maccoby, E., 168
McCrate, E., 139
McDonald, P. L., 163
McFarlane, J., 53, 161
McGregor, N., 159
McHugh, M. C., 166
McIntosh, S. R., 21
Macklin, E., 41
McLanahan, S., 44
McLaughlin, S. C., 44
McNeely, R. L., 74
McWhirter, D. P., 3
Maddock, J. M., 35, 38
Maden, M. F., 91
Madsen, R., 44, 179
Maguigan, H., 53, 64
Mahoney, M. R., 67, 105, 112–13, 115, 122, 155
Maidment, S., 151, 152
Makepeace, J., 6, 12, 30, 31, 33–37, 39, 40, 41, 43, 150, 179, 182
Malone, J., 40, 46
Malouff, J. M., 155, 159
Mancini, M. M., 44
Mandatory arrest policies, 130, 149, 152, 185
Manley, N. J., 127
Manzano, T. A., 78
Mapes, D., 44
Marano, H. E., 124, 126
Marciano, T., 179
Marden, 25
Margolies, L., 86
Margolin, G., 23
Marital anticipation, violence and, 34–35
Marital rape, 50, 52, 60–61, 149, 151, 152
Marital violence, 6–7, 12–13, 48–69
  continuum of, 56–65
    early warning signs, 57–59
    lethal violence, 64–65
    onset of violence, 56–57
    patterns of violence over time, 61–63
    sexual violence, 60–61
    verbal abuse and threats, 59–60
  incidence, prevalence and severity of, 48–55
    assaults during pregnancy, 52–53
    lethal outcomes, 53–54
    mutual violence, 50 51
    physical assault, 48–50
    physical outcomes, 51–52
    sexual assault, 50, 52, 65
    special risk factors, 54–55
  wife abuse as misdemeanor, 6–7
  women's movement and public awareness of, 7
  women's responses to assaults, 65–68
Marriage, cohabitation compared to, 36–37
Marsh, J. C., 151
Marshall, L. L., 6
Marsiglio, W., 44
Martin, D., 25, 48, 57, 93, 115, 139, 144, 146, 147, 148
Martin, S. E., 158, 164
Mate selection, 44